Collectibles for the
Kitchen,
Bath
& Beyond

A Pictorial Guide

by Ellen Bercovici, Bobbie Zucker Bryson and Deborah Gillham

Published by

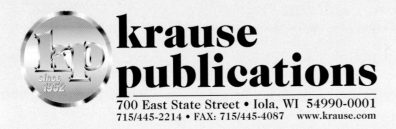

**krause
publications**

700 East State Street • Iola, WI 54990-0001
715/445-2214 • FAX: 715/445-4087   www.krause.com

Please call or write for our free catalog of publications. Our toll-free number to place an order or obtain a free catalog is 800-258-0929 or please use our regular business telephone 715-445-2214.

Library of Congress Catalog Number: 2001091078
ISBN: 0-87349-278-1

❖ Dedication

We dedicate this book to Alan Bryson, and our friends and families who we treasure even more than our collections.

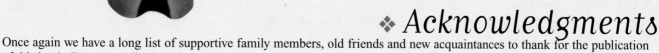

❖ Acknowledgments

Once again we have a long list of supportive family members, old friends and new acquaintances to thank for the publication of this book. Every contribution, from the smallest snippet of information to the endless supply of photos and invaluable knowledge, is greatly appreciated. Our deepest gratitude to these kind folks who allowed us into their homes, their heads and their hearts:

Ralph and Diane Bass; Hank Belasco; Morty and Marilyn Berman; Kerri Brooks; Mary Ann Bustraan; Kathy Cable, Creative Director, and Carol Anne Frantum, Artist/Designer, Miller Studio, Inc.; Patricia and Sterling Carberry; Betty Franks; Rachel Glasser, Gift & Dec Magazine; Maddy Gordon; Vonnie M. Green; Peggy and Kurt Grunert; Helene Guarnaccia; Ken and Sondra Krueger; Maria Lampert of the British Patent Office; Marc and Shona Lorrin; Jerry and Jeannie Marcus; Cindy Meadow; Belkis Perez and John Dobbins, N4M Design; Joyce Rickard; Sally Schulze; John and Alison Sturgul Collection; Sigmund Wohl; Suit Wong; and Susan Zappa.

We also acknowledge the supporters of our first book, and the generous individuals whose contributions can be seen throughout these pages:

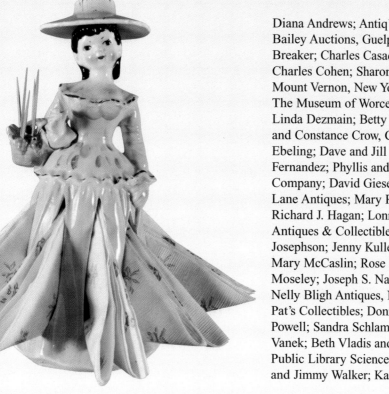

Diana Andrews; Antiq's and Things; Michele Bady; Dan Bailey Auctions, Guelph, Ontario, Canada; Lois M. Breaker; Charles Casad; Linda Church; Debbie Coe; Charles Cohen; Sharon Cohen and Rodney Lee of the Mount Vernon, New York Public Library; Wendy Cook of The Museum of Worcester Porcelain, Worcester, England; Linda Dezmain; Betty Dial; John Dougherty; Steve Dowell and Constance Crow, Crow's Nest Antiques; Brent and Jude Ebeling; Dave and Jill Emigh; Sandy Feinhold; Joann Fernandez; Phyllis and Shelley Galinkin, Bulldog Glass Company; David Giese; Harold and Sheryl Glenn, Memory Lane Antiques; Mary R. Grace; Ann Greco; Sam Gresham; Richard J. Hagan; Lonnie Haley; Minda Hamann; Johnsons' Antiques & Collectibles, Mitchell, SD; Herb and Farryl Josephson; Jenny Kuller; Sally Lapin; Don MacDonald; Mary McCaslin; Rose Marie Melda; Steven Middaugh; Jo Moseley; Joseph S. Natale and Diana L. Jamison-Natale; Nelly Bligh Antiques, Newcastle, Australia; Pat Nelson, Pat's Collectibles; Donna Nickell; Julie Peterson; Jim Powell; Sandra Schlaman; Susan Scott; Ellen Supnick; Judy Vanek; Beth Vladis and the entire Staff of the New York Public Library Science, Industry & Business Library; Carol and Jimmy Walker; Kathy and Tony Zadjura; Laura Zucker.

❖ TABLE OF CONTENTS

❖ Introduction

More than six years have passed since we first conceived the idea of a volume showcasing our favorite collections. We had certain goals: lots of great photos, factual information and prices that reflected true market values; in other words, a book written for collectors by collectors.

Non-collectors frequently ask the question, "So what's your book about?" Many have never heard of a napkin doll, some are too young to remember laundry sprinkler bottles or stringholders, and the majority have never used a pie bird. After thinking about this for a while, we've come up with the perfect description: Our book is a compilation of funky items that are for the most part "functionally obsolete." Once indispensable in the home, their roles have been replaced by more modern conveniences.

Since we submitted our first book there have been fluctuations in market values and the discovery of additional historical facts. But here's the most exciting news of all … we've found more napkin dolls, laundry sprinkler bottles, blade banks, pie birds, whimsical cups and baby feeder dishes, stringholders and egg timers just screaming to be shared with the collecting community. In order to broaden your scope of these items, we've swapped out many of the photos in KBBI with new pictures that will show you color variations and different views. Be sure to re-read all the photo captions— that's where we've added lots of additional details and of course, the current values.

You'll notice that we've also revamped the "Beyond" chapter with wider coverage on some popular items that fit in nicely with the main chapters in the book.

So, again we're delighted to present not only our prized possessions, but also those of numerous people around the world who, like us, continue to delight in shopping, sharing and the excitement of the find. If you think we were out-of-control before ... well, we'll let you be the judge about this second edition!

Happy collecting,

Ellen   Bobbie   Deborah

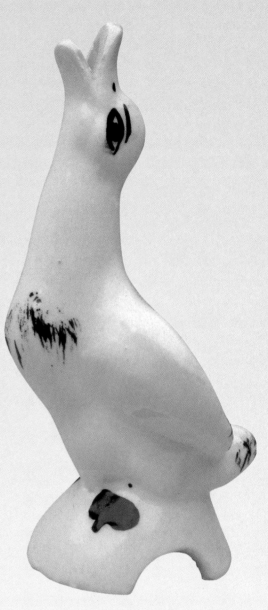

❖ Chapter Numbering and Identification System

The letter/number identification system introduced in Collectibles for the Kitchen, Bath and Beyond was so well received that we're continuing to use it here. It's been exciting to hear collectors speaking "our language" when describing a stringholder as an SH-130, or to read an auction description that references blade bank BB-314. In case you're not familiar with this system, it's been organized by subject matter into sub-categories. For example, all egg timers appear with an ET prefix, toothbrush holders with a TBH prefix. The prefix is followed by a number denoting the item's classification (e.g., in the case of the stringholders, 100s for birds, 200s for cats and so on). Unless otherwise noted, items in photos are numbered left to right.

No one is perfect and that includes us! In a few instances we've discovered material substantiating that an item was featured in the wrong section, so we've moved it to its correct classification. These changes are indicated within   wreaths. For example, ND-127 was misidentified as a handmade napkin doll, when in reality she is a commercial piece now listed as ND-314 in the American and Miscellaneous category of the first chapter. When we found a variation of an existing item, instead of assigning a new number, we've renumbered with an "A" and "B" classification.

❖ *Displaying Your Collections*

An accumulation is clutter, but a collection divine … at least that's the credo we live by! Even the smallest of collections can threaten to turn an otherwise orderly home into a chaotic house of horrors if some thought isn't given to how they will be displayed. In our first book we shared photos of how we show off our own collections. Now, here's how some of our friends showcase their special treasures.

From the collection of Peggy and Kurt Grunert

From the collection of Vonnie Green

From the collection of Morty Berman

*From the collection of
Jerry and Jeannie Marcus*

From the collection of Jim Powell

*From the collection of
Brent and Judy Ebeling*

❖ Pricing

Although we've heard people swear by the values in our book, it is important to remember that the prices quoted are offered as guidelines only. We continue to list average retail values, which are determined by polling collectors and dealers in different parts of the country and by factoring in prices quoted in the "For Sale" section of trade periodicals. In Book I we did not consider online prices in assigning values. We'd be negligent if we didn't address the market fluctuations in the last few years specifically caused by online auctions. Like it or not, Internet buying is here to stay. So we've also added online pricing to the mix in determining values. That's why you'll notice some big price ranges in certain chapters; this is particularly true with the laundry sprinkler bottles.

While some of the chapter values have changed dramatically since our first book, others have seemed to stagnate. As we collectors all know, today's top-selling collectible can be tomorrow's shelf sitter. And if, at the time of publication, an item in this book is not the hottest thing out there, that could change by the time you read this paragraph.

These values reflect retail prices of items in mint or near mint condition. Any sort of damage—chips, cracks and other surface blemishes generally decrease a piece's value and desirability. From time to time you'll see notations about the condition of a collectible's cold paint. This refers to the common practice of first firing a ceramic piece, then applying a topcoat of paint. As the years progress, this process can cause the paint to peel. Some people are not bothered by this all-too-often condition; others deduct anywhere from ten to thirty percent of the item's worth.

Values sometimes vary from one region to another, as does the rarity of a piece. In the end, a collector's desire to own a certain item and "what the market will bear" usually dictates the final price.

❖ Reproductions and New Issues

We've added this commentary to our second book because of the controversy surrounding the increasing number of reproductions and new issues facing collectors.

We define reproductions as copies of old pieces made to look exactly like the original. In some cases these pieces are marked accordingly, but more often than not, they have no identifiable markings to distinguish their age and origin or the maker's name and date. Some of these copies are so good that even the experienced, knowledgeable collector has trouble separating the old from the new. These reproductions are usually made for the sole purpose of charging a price that would be realized for a vintage piece. The collecting community frowns upon this practice.

Conversely, new issues are usually similar to the old with minor shape, style or size variations. In many cases a particular design is completely new. These are sold as legitimate collector items and are clearly marked with date and/or manufacturer information. We like these items and applaud the talented craftspeople who produce and are responsible for them.

Throughout these pages we've attempted to educate the collector about known reproductions and share any information we've learned to help make the distinction between old and new. At this time, pie birds and stringholders are the two categories hardest hit. And now napkin dolls have fallen prey to this craze. As the other items become more popular, don't be surprised to see additional reproductions on the market.

❖ Back Talk

One of the greatest benefits of writing a collectibles book has been making new friends. We've also added to our collections and helped others find that one piece "they couldn't live without." When we asked people to contact us with information about their collections and for feedback on the book, we were delighted with the response. That's right, we want back talk! If you're electronically connected, we can be reached as follows: Ellen: bercovici@erols.com; Bobbie: napkindoll@aol.com; Debbie: dgillham@erols.com. If you prefer to use snail mail, we can be reached in care of the publisher, Krause Publications, 700 E. State Street, Iola, Wisconsin 54990-0001. Sorry, but due to the volume of mail we receive, only letters including a large, self-addressed stamped envelope can be answered.

❖ About the Authors

When Ellen Bercovici added reamers as one of her collections, she never dreamed she would meet two other people as passionate about antiquing. Already hooked on pie birds, stringholders, brass hands, vintage sand toys, and Halloween and Black memorabilia, she found that she couldn't live without sprinkler bottles and figural egg timers! Now more than seventy-five sprinklers, one hundred and sixty-five egg timers and several years later, Ellen's charming Maryland home is a showcase for her various collections, as well as the quality Royal Copenhagen figurines prized by husband Marty. Ellen takes every opportunity to accompany her husband on business trips so she can haunt the shops from coast to coast.

The solitary napkin doll that sits on the kitchen counter in Bobbie Zucker Bryson's home is never lonely … this lady that started it all now has relatives (one hundred and thirty-five to be exact) occupying various rooms throughout her Victorian Cape Cod-style home in the New York City suburbs. Over the past few years she and collecting conspirator, husband Alan, have grown their stringholder collection to over a hundred, along with the ever expanding displays of reamers, ribbon dolls, figural tea balls, plant waterers, depression glass and kitchenware, Uncle Sam collectibles and miscellaneous bric-a-brac. When she's not engineering a new opportunity to promote the Collectibles for the Kitchen, Bath and Beyond book, she continues to write freelance articles in such publications as The Antique Trader, and for various online Web sites. She has also expanded her professional interests by moving into the exciting world of e-commerce for a major catalog company and online retailer.

Ten years after relocating to the East coast, Deborah Gillham has decided that her next move may not be quite as easy. That's because her once modest collections of whimsical children's cups and baby feeder dishes have swelled into triple digits. And that razor blade bank that was simply added as a decorative powder room accessory now vies for space with more than seventy-five others in a variety of shapes and sizes. Along the way egg separators came to stay, and soon the kitchen also included a few stringholders and more than five hundred reamers, joining her already impressive collections of Hall Pastel Tulip dinnerware and over four hundred toothbrush holders. Deborah is a relationship manager with a prominent financial company.

Now when they are together, Bobbie, Ellen and Deborah spend as much time talking about and promoting their book as they do shopping. It seems everywhere they go, someone has a story to tell about that napkin doll that got away, or a blade bank that isn't listed in the book. That still leaves plenty of time, however, to uncover new treasures for each other's collections and maybe to start thinking about the next special object that could lead to a future obsession!

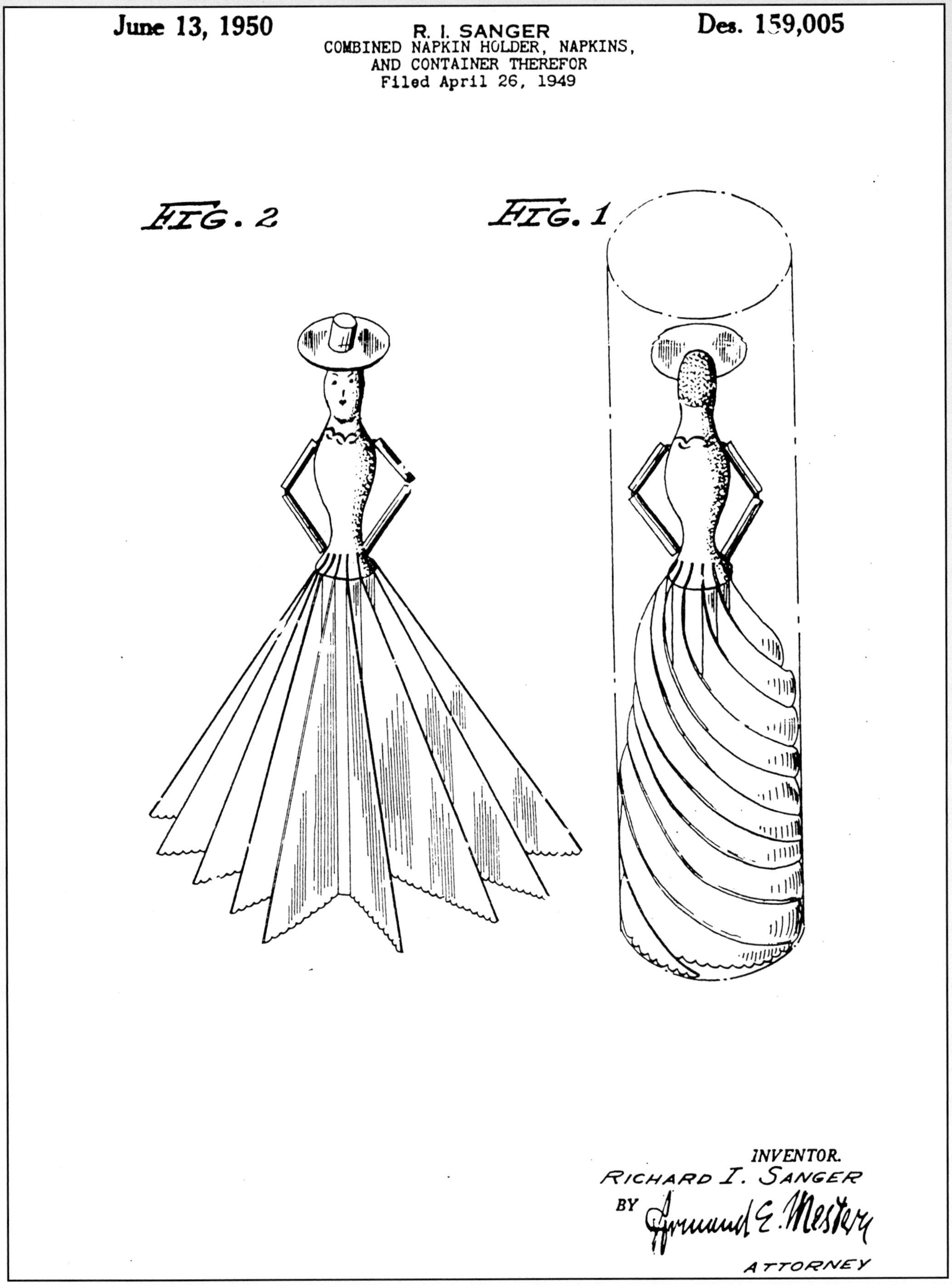
June 13, 1950
R. I. SANGER
COMBINED NAPKIN HOLDER, NAPKINS, AND CONTAINER THEREFOR
Filed April 26, 1949
Des. 159,005
FIG. 2
FIG. 1
INVENTOR.
RICHARD I. SANGER
BY
ATTORNEY

Original 1950 Design Patent for ND-401.

Napkin Dolls

During the period immediately following World War II, popular household accessories were colorful, decorative and functional. Imported novelty items like figural salt and pepper shakers, lady head vases and kiddie toothbrush holders lined the shelves of variety and department stores. And if you were a housewife during the late 1940s through the 1950s, chances are a napkin doll sat on your kitchen counter or resided in a corner cabinet waiting to take her place on the next party buffet.

The first time we saw a ceramic woman with slits in the skirt, we were puzzled about her purpose. And we were not the only ones scratching our heads about this once obscure collectible. Wooden models have been misidentified as miniature dress forms and cardholders, while the wire bottom lady chef (ND-505) bore the descriptive tag "unusual wine bottle topper." The various names they're known by—napkin ladies/dolls/girls and figural napkin holders—also add to the confusion.

Today, napkin dolls have regained their position in the kitchen as well as in the display shelves in collectors' homes. Why have they become such a hot commodity? Maybe it's the individualistic charm of the handmade ladies; Holland Mold, Byron Molds and Jamar-Mallory Studios were among the top producers of molds for the craft classes so popular in the 1950s. Or is it the funky appeal of the jewel-studded Japanese figures with their expressively painted faces, imported by companies such as Kreiss and Company, Artmark, Lipper and Mann, and Betsons? Collectors of California pottery have taken a shine to the lovely ladies by California Originals/Heirlooms of Tomorrow … and the renowned German manufacturer Goebel is responsible for some beauties made of ceramic, wood, and wire that are coveted by Goebel, half-doll, and napkin lady collectors.

When we wrote our first book we were fairly certain that we had exhausted the napkin doll market. How wrong we were! This chapter features more than fifty new pieces spread across the different categories. We've not only added more photos, but also replaced some of those from the first edition of *Collectibles for the Kitchen, Bath and Beyond* with fresh, new pictures in different colors.

You'll also want to pay close attention to the photo captions. We've uncovered some interesting facts that are helping us to better identify manufacturing dates and origins. Just look at the new details we've listed in the wire-bottom section—we now know that ND-507, formerly identified as foreign, is definitely German (check out the copy of the original patent). Many of the wire-bottoms like ND-503 are now showing up with "Davar Original Japan" stickers, and a number of Japanese look-alikes for Goebel's hula girl (ND-501) have surfaced. Neither Goebel nor any of the other sources we've talked to can explain the similarity in design.

Some of the new information has prompted us to move pieces from one classification to another. For example, the discovery of our bartender (formerly ND-312) with a "Viking-Hand Made in Japan" sticker meant he would now reside with the other Japanese models; he's been renumbered as ND-235. Imagine our amazement when the twin to our surprised little girl holding a basket (formerly ND-127) was featured in a recent online auction both in yellow and pink. Since every detail was exact, we've realized that she's probably not handmade, and for now she's been re-classified as ND-313.

The dreaded "R" word (Reproduction) has finally caught up with napkin dolls. When we first saw a red ND-206 with fur, we assumed someone repainted her and applied the trim. Alarm bells started ringing when the same lady appeared in yellow and another in dark green, both with a "Crabby Onion" label. This label is also showing up on other items, leading us to believe that someone is specializing in the reproduction of period collectibles. One piece actually sold in an online auction for $85! *Buyers beware*! How can you tell the difference between the old and new? The Kreiss ladies are usually stamped with the company name, have a more refined painted finish with flowers on the bodice. There are also a number of new-issue napkin dolls being inexpensively sold in mail order catalogs—ND-318 and ND-319 are two examples. Both of these pieces are incised "Made Exclusively For Lillian Vernon." Unfortunately, some of the others are not marked and selling online for ridiculous prices. They're all actually neat additions to a collection and make great gifts, but not if you're paying the price for a vintage item!

The quest for new napkin dolls and new information continues. Keep your eyes open at garage sales, antique shows and online auctions … the next discovery could be yours.

❖ "Hand-maidens" Napkin Dolls

ND-100: "Rosie," Holland Mold (H-132), 10-7/8", was first manufactured in 1950. $60-75. ND-101: The more uncommon "Small Rosie," (H-827), is 7-1/2". $65-85. The original price for undecorated figurines was $11.40 per dozen.

These were all recently cast from an original Holland Mold (ND-101). We've encouraged the talented ceramicist to sign and date each one to avoid confusion with the older dolls. $20-30.

ND-103A: Holland Mold's "Daisy" model No. 514, first manufactured in 1958, 7-1/4". $75-95.

ND-102: This 8-1/2" Holland Mold has napkin slits in back only. $75-95.

ND-103B: According to Holland Mold, the braids were crafted separately and then attached. $75-100.

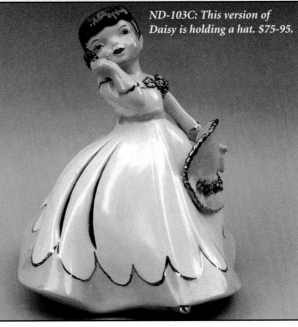

ND-103C: This version of Daisy is holding a hat. $75-95.

ND-104: This sweet 6-1/2" miss holding a heart is marked "Brockmann" on the bottom and has slits in the back only. Also found in pink. $65-85.

ND-105: We believe this unmarked 9-3/4" doll is another version of "Rosie." The turkey holds toothpicks. "Go-with" salt and pepper shakers, 3-3/8", complete the set. Set: $100-135; Napkin doll only: $75-95; Shakers only: $25-35.

ND-107: This petite Holland Mold (H-730) is only 5". $65-85.

ND-106: "Rebecca" (H-265), 10-1/2", debuted in 1950 and was discontinued in the early 1960s. According to Holland Mold she was not designed as a napkin doll and is most often found without the slits. $150-195.

ND-108: Holland Mold's "Dottie"(H-446) is ca. 1955, 6-1/2". $75-95.

ND-109: 9" "Christine," Mallory Ceramic Studios-Jamar, was not designed as a napkin doll. Flowers encircling her waist and shoulders are exquisite. $135-150.

ND-111: These dolls, 8-1/2", are often marked "copyright Byron Molds." $65-85.

Left: ND-112: She's marked "Cal. Cer. Mold. Co.," 12-1/2". $65-85.
Right: ND-113: This ceramics class project resembles the California Originals napkin doll ND-302, 11-1/2". $60-70.

ND-110: This 12" mold is marked Willoughby Studio, Betty Jane, with a copyright mark. The brown trim appears to be applied separately and the handle mimics an image of her pouring the pitcher. $100-125.

ND-114: Eva's Napkins is incised "60 C.O. 56." She is an S-Quire Mold (California), 10-3/4". $95-125.

ND-115: "Marybelle," 9-3/4", is mold P71 and was pictured in a 1950s catalog from The House of Ceramics, Memphis, Tenn. The unfinished figurines sold for $10.80 per dozen. $150-195.

ND-116A /116B/116C: The unmarked ladies on the left and right are 9-1/2", and the one in the center, 9". The model on the left has slits in the back for napkins and holes in front for toothpicks. The one on the right has holes in her hat for toothpicks. $95-110.

ND-116D: This doll is often found holding a tray for toothpicks, 8-1/2". $95-110.

ND-117: Due to variances in the mold, these leggy ladies range from 9" to 9-3/4". $125-150.

ND-118: The ceramist who decorated this 9" doll applied beautiful pink roses. $75-95.
ND-119: These 9" ladies appear to be offering guests cream and sugar. Also found holding a ceramic basket. $125-140.

ND-120A: Atlantic Mold lady, 11", is found with different hairdos, always holding a lily. $65-75.

ND-120B/C

ND-121: This 6-3/4" Holland Mold lady holds a rib-boned-hat behind her back. $95-115.

ND-122: Colonial blue girl, 7-3/4", with slits in back only. $75-95.

ND-123: This lovely lady is decorated with gold trim and three-dimensional flowers, 11-1/2". $130-155.

ND-124: A statuesque 10", she balances a toothpick tray on her head. $75-95.

ND-125: She has a beautiful luster finish with gold trim that continues to the large bow in back, 7-1/2". $75-85.

ND-126: Unusual doll handcrafted in the California pottery style. The napkin slits are in the rear of her skirt. 12-1/2". $125-150.

ND-128: Miss Mexico is 9" tall. $100-115.

ND-129: Dressed for a winter outing, she was found in a second-hand store, 11". $80-95.

ND-127 reclassified as ND-313

ND-130: Broad slits in this 10" country gal will easily hold cloth napkins. $75-95.

ND-131: "Frances," 11-1/2", is marked "Edith King Originals, 1953." $75-95.

ND-132: "Tina," by Mallory Ceramic Studio, 9-1/2". $75-85.

ND-134: Handmade version of the California Originals Spanish dancer, 17". Because of their unique quality they sometimes command higher prices than the commercial models. $130-150.

ND-133 reclassified as ND-314

ND-135/136/137: These examples of new napkin dolls were made in the late 1990s. $25-40.

ND-138: New "Lady Jane" by Mallory Ceramic Studio is holding a fan, 9-3/4". $35-45. A slightly taller 10" vintage piece was found marked "Jam Calif © '61." $55-65.

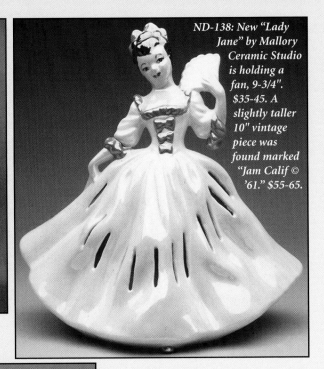

ND-139: This one-of-a-kind gift to a friend is marked "Arecibo, Puerto Rico, 1990," 12-1/2". $35-50.

Left: ND-140: Candlestick columns seem to support her on either side, 10". $115-135.

ND-141: This 10-3/4" beauty is signed and dated by her maker, "Goldie Stranky." $90-110.

ND-142: The beautiful roses on her dress are carried on to the pitcher, unmarked, 11". $95-115.

ND-143: The napkin slits surround the ruffled dress on this sweet little girl, 8". $75-95.

ND-146: The flowers on her dress are beautiful. She's signed by the talented artist, "Helen Lewis, 1959," 9-1/2". $95-135.

Right: ND-145: This demure miss looks like she was made from corn husks, 9-1/2". There are slits in the front only. $50-60.

ND-147: The 9" diameter of this doll's base makes her unusual, 12". $85-110.

ND-148: This Alberta Molds lady is marked "Alberta, '49," 10". $75-95.

Below: ND-144: The jagged slits on this woman give new meaning to the phrase "rough cut." The bottom is marked, "To Ginny, 1982, Sue Ferguson," 9-3/4". $75-85.

ND-149: Like ND-113, this homemade lady resembles the ND-302 California Originals doll, 12". $70-90.

ND-150: Only 25 sets were made of this 2-1/2" mini napkin doll by talented ceramist Sandy Srp. The shakers are 1-1/4". Set: $100.

ND-154 This young woman, with slits in the back of her skirt, has a mysterious quality about her, 6-1/4". $50-65.

ND-153: We thought this lady was very different, 10-1/2". $55-65.

ND-151: Lovely blonde holding an umbrella with slits on the reverse side only, 7-1/2". $60-75.

ND-152: This pink lady, 11", only holds a few napkins in the back of her dress. $40-50.

ND-200: Umbrella lady with bell, 9", and matching 4" salt and pepper shakers. This pink set is harder to find than the green. Set: $115-140. Napkin doll only: $70-85. Shakers only: $25-40.

ND-201: "Marie Antoinette," 9", with companion 4" shakers. The original sticker reads, "Original Dee Bee Co., Imports, Hand Painted Japan." Set: $115-140. Napkin doll only: $70-85; shakers only: $25-35.

ND-202/203: Fan masks a candleholder, marked Kreiss & Co., 10-1/2" and 8-3/4". Also found in yellow. $75-95.

ND-204: Kreiss & Co. 10-1/4" napkin doll trimmed in fur, carrying a muff. Also found in green, pink and blue. She's pictured here with her Kreiss male companion. Notice the toothpick holes in his bouquet. Set: $165; Napkin doll only: 95-110; Companion only: $35-50.

ND-205: The hat on this 9" doll hides a candleholder. $60-75.

ND-206: "Jennifer" napkin doll, 9-3/4", with 4-3/4" salt and pepper shakers, marked Kreiss & Co. The shakers, which have fragile necks that break easily, represent 50 percent of value. The tray has toothpick holes. A green set was discovered in the original box. The top lid read: "DISPLAY CANDLE AND NAPKINS INCLUDED; GLASS HANDLE WITH CARE. From Sears, Roebuck & Co., 4640 Roosevelt Blvd., Phila. 32 Pa. Rev. 7-21-48." The two labels on the sides said: "PASSED JIS S-3002 J.P.I.A." and "Kreiss Jennifer Napkin Holder, Salt and Pepper Set in Green with 1 Package of 8, 14" yellow napkins." The Sears Roebuck archives have no record of this item ever selling through the catalog, which leads us to believe that it may have only been available in the retail stores. Also found in blue. Set: $125-150. Napkin doll only: $65-75. Shakers only: $40-50.

ND-207: Napkin ladies with fruit baskets, 8-3/4". Original box, which still bears the "S. Klein on the Square," a New York department store, label, with the companion shakers was a real find. Instead of the usual inked Kreiss and Company mark, this doll has a Lipper and Mann foil sticker. Set: $125-150. Napkin doll only: $50-65. Shakers only: $20-25. (Add $35-45 for box.)

ND-210: Gold bow on hat, 8-1/2", marked Kreiss & Company. $60-75.
ND-211: "Colonial Dame" with foil "Betson" label and ink-stamped "Betson Hand Painted," 9". Also found in yellow, green and pink. $75-90.

ND-208/209A: Expressive eyes with gold trim, 9-1/4" and 9", ink-marked Japan; also found unglazed. $75-85.

ND-209B: Notice the difference in her dress, 9". $75-85.

18026 NAPKIN HOLDER
2 Assorted
1/3 dz. Min., 9½" High   15.00 dz.

Above: 1966 Lugene's Wholesale Souvenir and Gift Catalog, Branson, MO.

ND-212: Jewel-studded Kreiss & Co. dolls, 10-3/4", holding a poodle. Candleholder is masked by hat. Also in yellow and blue. $100-125.

ND-213: She's similar to ND-214, except the bird is lying flat against her chest. $75-95.
ND-214: Luster-finish ladies, 10-1/2" with a bird perched on extended hand. The tray on her head holds toothpicks. $75-95.

ND-217/216/215: Holt Howard's Sunbonnet Miss, 5", was sold with rice paper napkins. These little ladies make an attractive display together. $125-150.

ND-218/219/221/222: These lovely "pink ladies" all have Japan ink-stamped on the bottom: 8-1/2", 8-1/2", 9-1/4". $65-85. ND-222: Peasant woman, 9-1/4", is found in many colors. $60-75.

Right: 1958 Holt Howard Catalog.

5037 Sunbonnet Miss
5" high $1.25
What a party perker! Comes complete with eight lovely rice paper napkins. Miss is pink, blue or yellow. Be sure to order matching candles. 4 ea. color to 1 doz. min. Ind. box.

ND-223: She carries a wonderful ceramic fruit basket that has holes for toothpicks, 10-1/2". Also found in yellow. $100-135.

ND-220: This difficult-to-find doll extends a toothpick tray, 9-3/4". $75-95.

ND-224: Jolly Santa, 6-3/4", with slits in rear. Marked "Japan," with a "Sage Store" label. $95-150.

ND-225: Unmarked 6" "St. Nick" with toothpick holes in his hat, has a 1950s look. He's wearing a "Napco Japan" silver label. $75-85.

ND-226: *Oriental woman, 10-1/4", carries salt and pepper shakers on her hips. Her hat conceals a candleholder and there are holes below her waist and back for toothpicks. The paper label on the bottom says, "Hachiya Brothers, No. 81435, Made in Japan." $125-150.*

ND-227: *When napkins are inserted into this angel's shoulders they form wings, 5-3/8". Also found in pink. $100-115.*

ND-228: *Enesco "Genie At Your Service," 8". The lantern holds toothpicks. Set: $150-175; Napkin doll only: $100-135; Shakers only: $35-50.*

ND-229: *Oriental lady, 9-1/4", holds a fan. She is signed "Betsons Hand Painted," and has a Japan sticker. $95-125.*

ND-230: *In 1998, this unusual 9-1/2" doll was featured in a Formica countertop ad. The tag line on the ad read: "Counters to match anything that could end up on the kitchen counter." $75-95.*

ND-231: *Candleholders sit behind the floppy brims of these Kreiss & Co. 10" ladies. The pink girl still has the F.W. Woolworth $1.98 price sticker. $65-85.*

NAPKIN DOLL CENTERPIECE

⑦ This frivolous young lady in her pastel party clothes, will hold a candle atop her head and lend her billowy slotted skirt for use as a holder for paper napkins. Charming centerpiece that you'll surround with flowers and use as an ornament, too. **(2½ lbs.) H2602 9½″ Doll . . . . . . $2.98** '

1957 Helen Gallagher Foster House Spring & Summer Gifts for Casual Living catalog, Peoria, IL.

ND-232: Wide brimmed hats are topped by candleholders, 10-7/8″. The green bottom is ink-stamped "© Kreiss & Company, 1957," and the blue is marked "Betsons Hand Painted." $60-75.

ND-233: This 8-1/2″ smaller version has the jeweled-eyes and facial features so typical of Kreiss napkin ladies. $45-65.

ND-234: Rare Kreiss & Company angel, 11″, has a candleholder in her halo. $90-110.

ND-235: Bartender/waiter, 8-3/4″, with tray to hold candle. The foil sticker says, "Viking Handmade, Made In Japan." Set: $125-150. Napkin doll only: $85-100. Shakers only: $20-25. (Formerly ND-312.)

ND-236: Black rooster with yellow and red trim, 10-1/4″. The 6-1/4″ companion shakers have a "Made In Japan" paper label. Set: $55-65; Napkin doll only: $35-45; Shakers only: $10-15. (Formerly ND-309.)

ND-300: *Spanish dancers are found in many colors and three sizes: 8-3/4", 13" and 15". Commercial ones are marked on bottom, "#460, California Originals USA." $85-150.*

ND-301A: *This lady often has the California Originals foil label, 13-3/4". Found in many color combinations. $65-85.*

ND-301B: *This unusual black version of ND-301A is slightly taller, 14". $75-95.*

ND-302: *One of the most common napkin dolls, this 13" California Originals is found trimmed in a variety of colors. $75-95.*
ND-303: *This rare example is similar to ND-302, but she has her hands clasped in front of her dress, 13". $95-125.*

ND-304: *A California Originals look-a-like, she is completely underglazed, 12-3/4". $75-95.*

CANDLELIGHT napkin holder girl makes unusual centerpiece. Retails for $9. Heirlooms of Tomorrow, Inc., 3601 Aviation Blvd., Manhattan Beach, Calif.

Above: The Gift & Art Buyer, July 1953. This trade magazine reflects wholesale prices.

Left: ND-305A/B: Marcia of California napkin doll, with molded apron and bowl on head, has an iridescent finish, 13". Also found with a pink luster finish. ND-305B is much more difficult to find and is valued about 20 percent higher. $95-150.

D-96 NAPKIN DOLL – Hands on Hips
13½" tall
D-97 NAPKIN DOLL – Hands up
13½" tall
COLORS: Pink, Blue, Yellow

Above: 1958 Marcia of California catalog.

ND-306: On example of this 9-1/4" deco-look-ing lady recently surfaced with a "Chas. Brown & Sons, San Francisco," paper label. $65-85.

ND-307: Doll, 10-3/4", extends a round tooth-pick tray. $75-85.
ND-308: Although similar in appearance to ND-307, the tray is oblong and attached at her waist, 10-3/4". $75-85.

ND-309 reclassified as ND-236

ND-310: Little ladies with large compartments, rather than individual slits, 7-7/8", marked "3475" on bottom. $75-95.

ND-312 reclassified as ND-235

ND-313: Surprised little girl holding basket, 6-1/2". The napkin slits are in the back of her skirt. $90-110. (Formerly ND-127.)

ND-314: The only chalkware dolls we've ever seen, 13". $95-125. (Formerly ND-133.)

ND-311: Napkins insert into rooster's tail and the eggs are salt and pepper shakers, 5-1/4". $35-45.

ND-315: Half-doll "Suzette," 10", has a plastic base; she sold for $3.00 each/$5.50 for two complete with napkins. The Halldon Company absorbed the fourteen cents it took to mail her. $125-150.

Cocktail Napkin Hostess In Beautiful Hand Painted China

Newest creation in a figurine that holds 14 cocktail napkins for your guests. Her name is Suzette. She's a proud beauty, hand painted on China, and is cute and practical. The colored napkins complete her attractiveness by forming a stunning pleated ballerina skirt. A conversation piece that will cause many compliments. She stands 10 inches high and has a plastic base for firm footing. Price complete with napkins only $3.00, or 2 for $5.50, postpaid. Too new yet to be had in stores. Order direct on our money back guarantee. Sorry, no C.O.D.'s.

HALLDON COMPANY, STUDIO 4
1011 Kane Concourse, Surfside 41, Florida

Above: House and Garden, November, 1957.

Right: The original box insert explains how to use, other uses for this "Napkin Hostess," and how to order additional dolls. Stamped on the side it says, "We have had so many requests for additional napkins of the same design, if you too like them we shall be glad to send you 5 complete sets of 70 napkins for one dollar post paid."

```
NAPKIN HOSTESS-------DIRECTIONS FOR USE
                PATENT PENDING

PUT RUBBER TUBING OVER KNOB ON TOP OF PLASTIC
STAND. (SHOULD THIS BE HARD TO DO, DIP KNOB
AND RUBBER TUBING IN WATER.)

FOLD PAPER NAPKIN VERY GENTLY INTO THE SHAPE
OF A TRIANGLE.  PLEASE DO NOT MAKE A CREASE
IN THE NAPKIN.

INSERT THE TIP OF THE TRIANGULAR SHAPED NAP-
KIN ABOUT HALF AN INCH INTO THE PLASTIC SLIDE.
START AT THE BOTTOM AND PUSH GENTLY UPWARDS.

WHEN ALL NAPKINS HAVE BEEN INSERTED, GENTLY
PUSH THE CHINA TOP DOWN OVER THE RUBBER TUB-
ING UNTIL THE NAPKIN TIPS ARE COVERED.

THE NAPKINS CAN BE ADJUSTED AND RE-FLUFFED,
SIMPLY BY INSERTING ONE OR TWO FINGERS INTO
THE PLEATS.  WHEN FINISHED THE NAPKINS SHOULD
LOOK LIKE A BEAUTIFUL, FLUFFY SKIRT.
----------------------------------------------

OTHER USES FOR THE NAPKIN HOSTESS

AS A PLAY DOLL FOR LITTLE GIRLS IT IS UNSUR-
PASSED. THEY JUST LOVE TO DRESS AND UNDRESS
IT. YOUNG LADIES LIKE TO PRACTICE SETTING
AN ATTRACTICE TABLE. WITH DIFFERENT AND INEX-
SPENSIVE PAPER NAPKINS THEY CAN MAKE ALMOST
UNLIMITED COLOR COMBINATIONS. IT APPEALS TO
THEIR VIVID IMAGINATIONS.

IF NOT AT YOUR DEALER, PLEASE USE THIS COUPON.
THE HALLDON COMPANY,
1011 KANE CONCOURSE, SURFSIDE 41, FLORIDA

ENCLOSED IS $ 3.00( OR $ 5.50 FOR TWO ) FOR
NAPKIN HOSTESS, INCLUDING FREE SET OF NAPKINS.
WE PAY THE POSTAGE.

NAME :_____

ADDRESS :_____
```

ND-316: Collectors call this fabulous full-figured girl "Heidi." She appears to be standing on a mountain, 15". $125-150.

ND-317: The top half of the "Sweetie" resembles a plastic doll, 11". She's also been found as a brunette. One owner found the original 1959 store receipt for $1.49. $40-60.

INSTRUCTIONS

Insert short or long stem into base and doll body.

To Dress Me . . .
Use 9½ x 9½ inch cocktail napkin with short stem, 12½ x 12½ inch luncheon napkin with long stem.

WE SUGGEST USING SCALLOPED EDGED NAPKIN

Fold napkin into triangle, do not crease, insert into slots to waistline, this forms my skirt.

Use Christmas, Birthday, Shower, Wedding, or any other desired napkin, then I will be ready for any occasion.

Ribbon may be changed by using that which adheres to itself when moistened.

Sweetie NAPKIN DOLL

ND-318: This 9" lady is ca. 1998. The bottom is marked "Made Exclusively for Lillian Vernon," and is sold in their catalog and online store for $9.98.
ND-319: Featured in their 2000 holiday catalog, this new issue Lillian Vernon angel was priced at $9.98. She's also incised, "Made Exclusively for Lillian Vernon."

ND-320: "Can Can" serviette holder is British made, 4". $95-135.

CAN CAN
NOVELTY
Serviette Holder
BRITISH MADE

❖ Wooden Napkin Dolls

ND-400: This 8" doll has moveable arms and "strawberry" toothpick-holder hat. $60-75.

ND-401: Servy-Etta, a Woodnote product, is marked USD Pat. No. 159,005. Found in a variety of colors. $35-45. (Add $25-35 for box and instructions.)

Napkin Lady

As she greets guests, she's a dignified napkin holder, shaped as a doll, wearing a ballerina skirt. But she's soon a strip tease queen. Her dress is a skirt made of alternating colored paper napkins in the 12 slots. One by one, guests strip her. Colorful, hand painted wood, 11" high. Ideal table decoration. Complete with assorted colored napkins.
H 1427 . . . . $1.95

1951 Bancrofts Gifts Catalog, Chicago, IL.

ND-402A: Complete with original box, unusual Swedish model, 11-1/2", has a musical base and included three packages of decorative napkins. $40-50. (Add $35-45 for box, napkins and instructions.)
ND-402B/402C: Although similar in appearance, these 10" Swedish wooden ladies (Patent No. 11381) have minor decorative differences, usually in the waist or hat. Name of Swedish geographic regions are painted on the base. $25-35.

Right: The Gift & Art Buyer, February, 1952 This trade magazine reflects wholesale prices.

New! SWEDISH IMPORTS FOR Christmas Selling

These rare but inexpensive Scandinavian imports, artistically caricature Christmas humor. The active little fairy tale people, as well as the napkin and candlestick holder are colorfully hand decorated and finished.

For complete descriptions and price list, write to:

TORA HOLM *Scandinavian Imports* • 118 East 28th St., New York 16.

NAPKIN DOLL is a lady from Sweden who's an artful stripteaser that could give Gypsy Rose Lee lessons. She's made of natural wood and her colorful skirt consists of 14 paper napkins with provincial patterns. They slip into slits, are easy to remove, easy to replace. 10" doll with 25 napkins, $1.98 ppd. Bit O' Sweden Imports, Box H, Brookfield, N.Y.

Above: House Beautiful, *December 1955.*

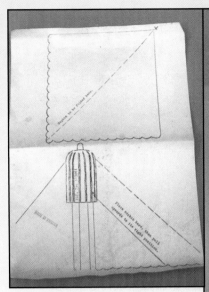

Left: Original box insert with instructions for folding napkins.

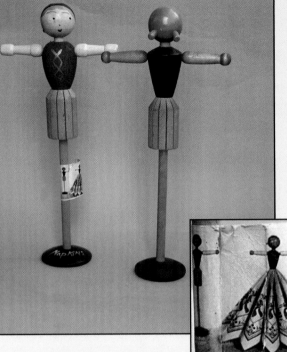

ND-403A: These Japanese napkin dolls are often incorrectly identified as coaster holders or miniature dressmaker forms, 11-1/4". $30-40.

ND-403B: Unusual black model. $60-75.

ND-404: The hat on this wooden lady is notched in the back, 11". $30-40.

ND-405: At 12-1/4", she's the largest wooden napkin doll we've found. $40-50.

ND-406: The paper label on this 6" brown napkin lady reads, "Ave 13 Nov 743, A. Sinfonia, Tel 2350 Petropolis." Doll is marked with the number "385." $65-85.

ND-407: This 6-3/4" lady has a fuller skirt than ND-406. One example had this label: "BONATTO & CIA. LTDA.- Arlelalos de Madeira Rua 21 de Abril, 272- Curillba, Parana 82- Ind. Braslleeria." $65-85.

ND-408: Doll, 6-3/8", has a much shorter body. $65-85.

ND-409: Wooden lady with pointy hat, 7". $60-75.

ND-410: Although the body is a different shape, the face and hat on this 6-3/4" doll is the same as ND-409. $60-75.

ND-414: Notice the detail on this 10-1/4" lady's hands. Also found in red. $40-50.

ND-415: This napkin doll was found at a flea market in Finland, 10-1/4". $40-50.

ND-411: The arms resemble ND-409 and ND-410 but the face and body are much fuller, 7-1/2". $60-75.

ND-412: This doll appears to be from the same family as ND-406 to ND-408, 7-1/2". $65-85.

ND-413: We've dubbed this lady "Mary Poppins." Despite her worn condition, she's really an unusual piece, 7". $50-65.

ND-416A/416B: We're delighted to show you this wonderful napkin doll from Finland, 10-1/4". Although the body is the same on both, notice the differences in the size of the face and hat. $40-50.

NAPKIN LADY. As she greets guests, she's a dignified doll wearing a bouffant skirt. But she soon becomes an ingenious strip-tease queen. Dress her in a skirt made of paper napkins—either 12 luncheon size or 24 cocktail size—and one by one guests strip her. Made in Finland of hand-painted wood, 10½" high, she's $2 without napkins, ppd. No c.o.d.'s. Smillans House, 5424 N. Lawler Ave., Chicago 30, Ill.

House Beautiful, October 1949.

ND-417: This wooden chef was found with the original seed packet motif napkins, 12-3/4". $60-75.

ND-418: When napkins are inserted into the rear of our "Dodo" bird, they form a tail, 7". $25-35.

ND-419: At first glance this wooden model appeared to be like the typical Swedish napkin doll. Look again—this 11-1/4" piece has a larger, flatter face and a thicker body. $35-45.

❖ Wire Bottom Napkin Dolls

ND-500: *This wonderful Goebel doll, shown in her original box with napkins, is coveted by both napkin and half-doll collectors. Mold NA 35, produced by W. Goebel Porzellanfabrik between 1950-1957, was modeled by master sculptor Gerhard Skrobek from a design by Mrs. Erna Reinhert (aka "Nasha"). She bears the TMK2 trademark and is marked "Goebel, W. Germany," 8-1/2". $195-225. (Add $25-45 for original box, napkins and instructions.) Napkins are held in place by wires attached to a wood base. Sticker on base reads, "DBGM angemeldet"(German Federal Utility Model).*

ND-501: *Native Goebel doll was produced between 1957-1964. It displays the TMK3 trademark and is marked "Goebel, W. Germany," 9-1/2". $195-225. Look-alikes marked "Japan" have recently surfaced. $135-150.*

ND-502: *Lovely Goebel half-doll from the Pearl Lovell collection in England. She is mold number X97, modeled by Gerhard Skrobek in 1957, 8-1/4". $225-250.*

German instructions: "Please watch. Carefully fold the napkin like the sample on top. Proceed to push the pointy part from the bottom up through the top."

ND-503: *This beauty carries a basket of fruit with toothpick holes, 7-1/2". It has a "Davar Originals Japan" sticker. $95-110.*

ND-504: *Unusual 9" baker with wire bottom is marked "2026." Tray of rolls has holes for toothpicks. $95-110.*

ND-507: *This all-metal deco beauty, 8-7/8", is marked "E Kosta DBGM 1744970;" ca. 1957. $115-135.*

ND-505: *Lady chef carries a pie in one hand and loaf of bread in the other. Both have toothpick holes, 7". $95-110.*

ND-506: *Our 7" Santa Claus was a real find. He's holding a gift in one hand and a stocking with toothpick holes in the other. $150-175.*

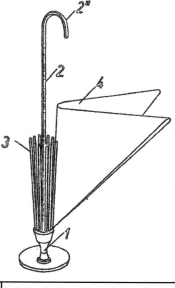

Original 1957 German Patent for ND-507.

ND-508: Colorful 9" umbrella is foreign. Napkins slip into wire rings at the base. $15-35.

ND-509: This Canadian napkin umbrella was found with the original napkins and box, 9-1/2". $30-40.

PORTE SERVIETTES

NAPKIN HOLDER

ND-513: Ceramic half-doll milk-maid, 6", has a "Davar Originals" sticker. $95-110.

ND-510: The wires in their tails hold napkins, 4-3/8". Removable heads on these Lefton birds are salt and pepper shakers. $25-35.

ND-511: Ceramic chicken with wire tail, 7", has a gold foil label "Our Own Imports Japan." $15-25.
ND-512: This ceramic chicken with wire tail is marked "T.C., U.S.A.," 6-1/4", and matching shakers, 3-1/2". Set: $30-40; Napkin doll only: $15-25; Shakers only: $5-10.

ND-514: The wire bottom on this lovely lady is much heavier than the others, 8". $135-175.

These three ladies, who share many characteristics with the Goebel dolls, appear to be part of a series. According to Goebel's records, their company did not make them.

ND-515: Mexican lady with original box, marked "Napkin Holder, No. 405," 9". $150-185. (Add $10-15 for original box.)

ND-516: This little Dutch girl was found with original napkins in a box of junk, 9-1/4". $150-185.

ND-517: The original box with this Holland Miss notes that she is "Napkin Holder No. 406," 9-1/2". $150-185. (Add $10-15 for original box.)

ND-518: This unique black metal napkin doll, 8", is wearing a felt bikini top. She was found in an Australian flea market; however, since she is unmarked, her exact origins remain a mystery. $150-175.

ND-519: When napkins are inserted into this wiry form the skirt really flares, 8-1/2". $135-175.

❖ Wannabes

Some people believe that if it has holes, slits or wires, and will hold napkins, it must be a napkin doll. Wrong! We've surveyed a number of collectors and they all agree … there is no such thing as a "napkin doll for two." That misleading tag was affixed to a ceramic lady planter in a Pennsylvania mall. Here are some other examples of objects being mislabeled as napkin dolls.

Holt Howard letter caddy.

There is a great deal of debate over this Santa's real purpose. Although many of us have this smiling fellow in our collection, we think he may have been designed to hold holiday greeting cards.

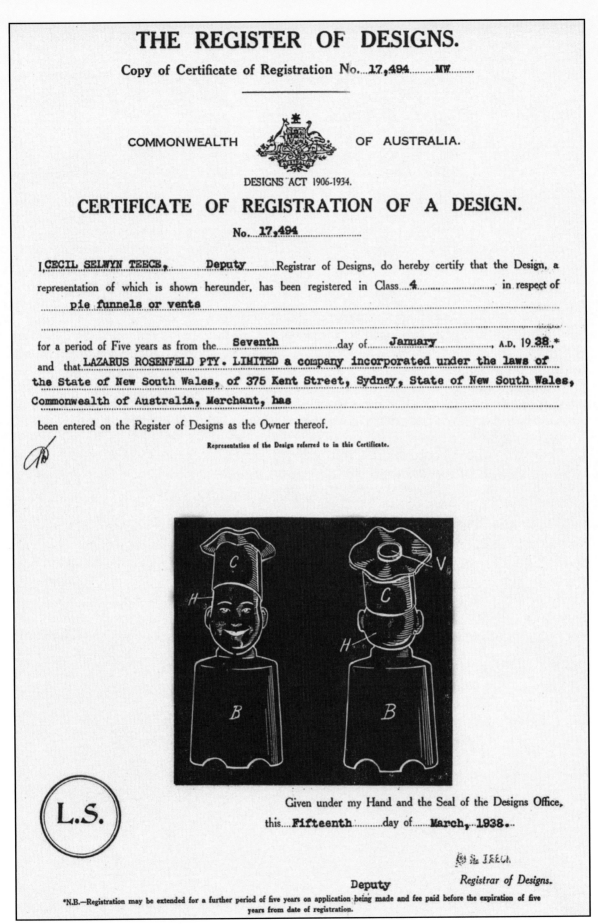

THE REGISTER OF DESIGNS.

Copy of Certificate of Registration No....17,494........MW........

COMMONWEALTH   OF AUSTRALIA.

DESIGNS ACT 1906-1934.

CERTIFICATE OF REGISTRATION OF A DESIGN.

No...17,494....

I, CECIL SELWYN TEECE,   Deputy   Registrar of Designs, do hereby certify that the Design, a representation of which is shown hereunder, has been registered in Class....4...................., in respect of ....pie funnels or vents

....

for a period of Five years as from the.......Seventh...............day of.......January............., A.D. 19.38.*
and that LAZARUS ROSENFELD PTY. LIMITED a company incorporated under the laws of the State of New South Wales, of 375 Kent Street, Sydney, State of New South Wales, Commonwealth of Australia, Merchant, has

been entered on the Register of Designs as the Owner thereof.

Representation of the Design referred to in this Certificate.

Given under my Hand and the Seal of the Designs Office, this....Fifteenth..........day of......March, 1938..

L.S.

Deputy   Registrar of Designs.

*N.B.—Registration may be extended for a further period of five years on application being made and fee paid before the expiration of five years from date of registration.

Original Registered Design for PB-136A

36 Pie Birds

Pie Birds

According to a 1933 patent for a pie ventilator, "The principal object of the invention is the provision of an article … which entirely eliminates the possibility of the juices of the pie rising to the top of the upper crust during the baking operation." Whether you call them pie birds, vents, steamers, or funnels, these unique objects all have the same purpose—to allow enough steam to escape, thus ensuring a dry top crust.

We have the ingenuity of the English to thank for this simple yet functional invention. As you will note from the early 1900s patents included in this chapter, the designs for these turn-of-the-century, funnel-shaped examples were quite plain. It took a few years to recognize how much more desirable the pie vent would be if it were decorative as well. Today vintage figural pie birds in the shapes of chefs, elephants, birds and a variety of other unique forms are the pieces so desirable to collectors.

Although style varies, the distinguishing feature of these hollow objects is the arches at the base to allow steam to enter, with an opening in the top for steam to escape. Although most are ceramic, glazed inside and out, there are a few exceptions; see the glass PB-316 from Scotland on page 54. Although the earliest birds were black and white, more colorful designs soon became popular.

Pie birds didn't really catch on in the United States until the 1930s, but once they did, the market was humming with examples manufactured by the leading pottery companies and distributed by the major importers of the era. Unfortunately many of these older American-made pieces were unmarked and their true origins were lost with the demise of the glass and ceramics industry in this country. That's why we get so excited when an original catalog, label or magazine advertisement can shed light on a vintage model's age and manufacturer.

This chapter probably has more content revisions than any other in the book. Our thanks go to the many knowledgeable collectors who were kind enough to correct our misconceptions and fill in the missing blanks on dates, manufacturers and other pertinent details. We suggest you study each caption carefully to see what's changed from the first edition of *Collectibles for the Kitchen, Bath and Beyond*. We've also added some new photos that are sure to set your collecting juices flowing. And of course, there's always new material surfacing … so if you have even the smallest bit of information on anything in the book, we'd love to hear from you.

There are a large number of new edition pie birds, both from the United States and England, that can be welcome additions to anyone's collection. However, in our book we are mainly focusing on the earlier pie birds that are getting increasingly difficult to find. While most of the new pie birds are marked accordingly, there are some that are not signed and have been altered to look "used."

Our advice to collectors is to know the dealers from whom you are buying, and be sure they stand behind their merchandise. We tend to shy away from endorsements like "Well, I bought it as old," or "It looks old to me," which usually means even the seller won't (or can't) attest to its being the real McCoy. In the end, allow us to repeat: *Buyers beware!*

We hope that when you've finished reading this chapter there will be more than four and twenty pie birds in your collection.

❖ English & Australian Pie Birds

The English invented these handy devices, and they continue to be the source of many "new issue" and reproduction pie birds.

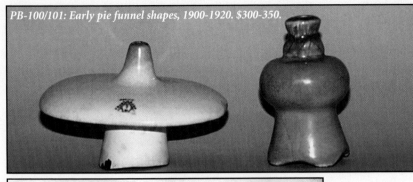

PB-100/101: Early pie funnel shapes, 1900-1920. $300-350.

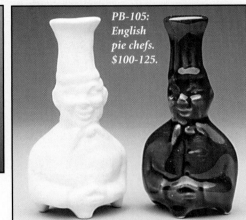

PB-105: English pie chefs. $100-125.

Grimwades Hygenic Table and Kitchenware catalog.

The "Hygienic" Table & Kitchen Ware, White.

PB-102/103/104: English shopkeepers often used ceramic pie vents as advertising vehicles, 1910-1930. $100-150. PB-104 is designed by Leonard Lumdsden Grimwade.

PB-106/107/108/109/110: Variety of advertising pie vents from England and Australia: (left to right) $75-120, $150, $150-200 (marked "The Gourmet Crust Holder and Vent, Challis' Patent," on top of base also called the "pie lifter"), $50, $100-150.

PB-111: Unusual pie vent, "The Bleriot Pie Divider," 1910-1920. Patented April 7, 1910 by Leonard Lumsden for Grimwades of the Waltlands, Wolstanton, Saffordshire. $500+.

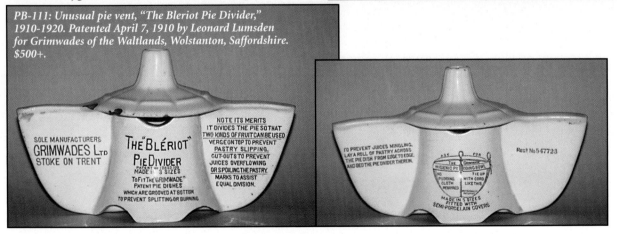

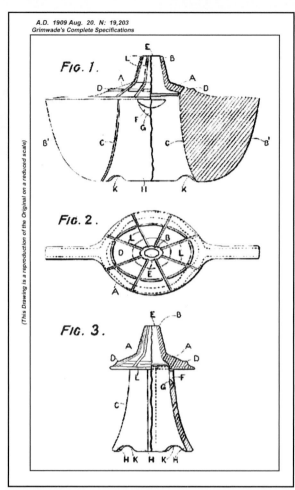

A.D. 1909 Aug. 20. N: 19,203
Grimwade's Complete Specifications

(This Drawing is a reproduction of the Original on a reduced scale)

FIG. 1.

FIG. 2.

FIG. 3.

Original 1909 Patent for PB-111.

PB-112/113/114: Most common English pie birds were painted black. PB-112/114: $30-40. PB-113: This particular example is marked "Midwinter." Designed by Clarice Cliff, she registered this bird in 1936. In 1950 this same bird was also marked with the "Newport Pottery Co., England" until the company was sold to Midwinter Pottery in 1964. Some models are marked "RD 809138." $50-60.

PB-115A: Dark gray elephant. $75-100.

PB-115B: Similar white elephant is embossed "England" on the back of the base. $50

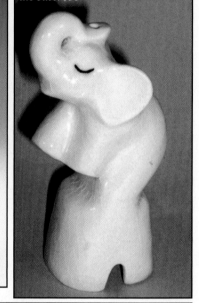

PB-116: Creiciau Pottery, Wales, U.K., produced these two dragons, designed in 1968 and manufactured until 1982. Even though these are "newer" vents they are very desirable and costly. $250.

CYMRU
WELSH
PIE DRAGON
WALES

PB-117: This unusual two-headed black and yellow blackbird was manufactured by Barn Pottery, Devon, England. $100-150. Beware: this pie bird is being reproduced.

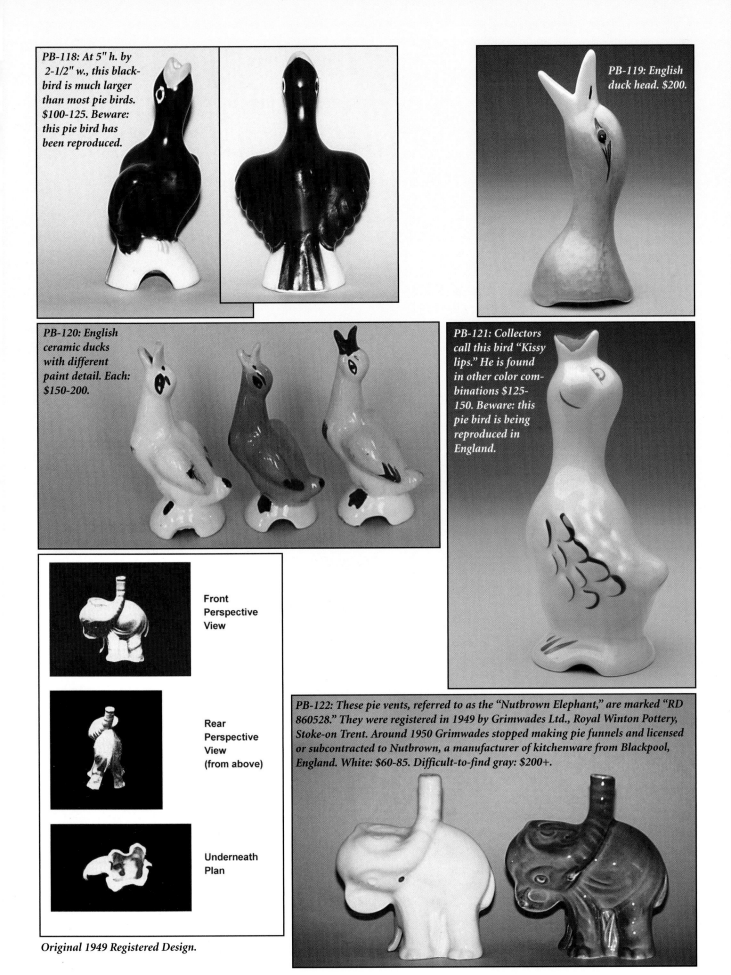

PB-118: At 5" h. by 2-1/2" w., this black-bird is much larger than most pie birds. $100-125. Beware: this pie bird has been reproduced.

PB-119: English duck head. $200.

PB-120: English ceramic ducks with different paint detail. Each: $150-200.

PB-121: Collectors call this bird "Kissy lips." He is found in other color combinations $125-150. Beware: this pie bird is being reproduced in England.

Front Perspective View

Rear Perspective View (from above)

Underneath Plan

PB-122: These pie vents, referred to as the "Nutbrown Elephant," are marked "RD 860528." They were registered in 1949 by Grimwades Ltd., Royal Winton Pottery, Stoke-on Trent. Around 1950 Grimwades stopped making pie funnels and licensed or subcontracted to Nutbrown, a manufacturer of kitchenware from Blackpool, England. White: $60-85. Difficult-to-find gray: $200+.

Original 1949 Registered Design.

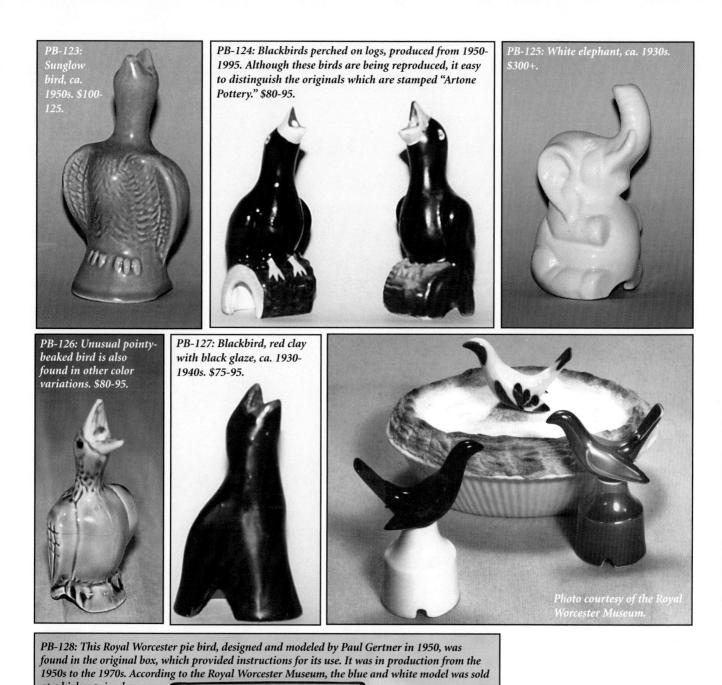

PB-123: Sunglow bird, ca. 1950s. $100-125.

PB-124: Blackbirds perched on logs, produced from 1950-1995. Although these birds are being reproduced, it easy to distinguish the originals which are stamped "Artone Pottery." $80-95.

PB-125: White elephant, ca. 1930s. $300+.

PB-126: Unusual pointy-beaked bird is also found in other color variations. $80-95.

PB-127: Blackbird, red clay with black glaze, ca. 1930-1940s. $75-95.

Photo courtesy of the Royal Worcester Museum.

PB-128: This Royal Worcester pie bird, designed and modeled by Paul Gertner in 1950, was found in the original box, which provided instructions for its use. It was in production from the 1950s to the 1970s. According to the Royal Worcester Museum, the blue and white model was sold at a higher price; however in today's collectibles market the brown is more desirable. Although the base of this bird is usually found in white, the Royal Museum of Worcester Porcelain explained that the base was also manufactured in gold, silver and copper in the late 1960s. Since these colors were very expensive to produce, they were discontinued after a very short run. Brown: $150+. Blue and White $90-110. Black: $65-75. Gold/Silver/Copper base: $250+. (Add $20 for box.)

Royal Worcester Pie Bird

PB-129: Blackbird, clay with black and yellow glaze, ca. 1960-1970s. $75-100.

PB-130: These homemade baby chicks, less than 2", were designed for a child's pie, ca. 1990-91. Each: $40-50. Beware: these are now being produced by two different makers.

PB-131: Tiny blackbird for a child's pie, 2-3/4". See PB-151 for size comparison. $95-125.

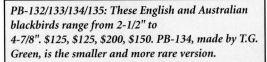

PB-132/133/134/135: These English and Australian blackbirds range from 2-1/2" to 4-7/8". $125, $125, $200, $150. PB-134, made by T.G. Green, is the smaller and more rare version.

PB-136A: Australian Servex Chef, 4-5/8", is marked inside "Servex Oven China, Bohemia, Guaranteed Heatproof, RD 17494 Aust., RD 4098 N.Z."
PB-136B: Chef with the buttons is marked "SERVEX Oven Table China, HOLLAND, Guaranteed Heatproof" inside the bottom. Either version: $100-150.

PB-137/138: These chefs resemble the American "Benny the Baker." The smaller of the two holds measuring spoons instead of a pie crimper. $150.

PB-139: Australian blackbird in a pie, 4". $300+.

PB-140: Rosebud funnel. $150-175.

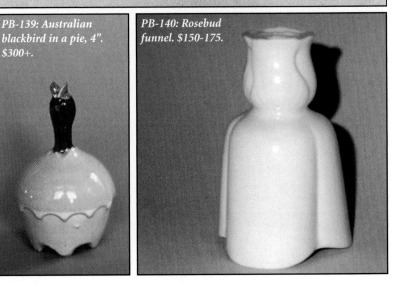

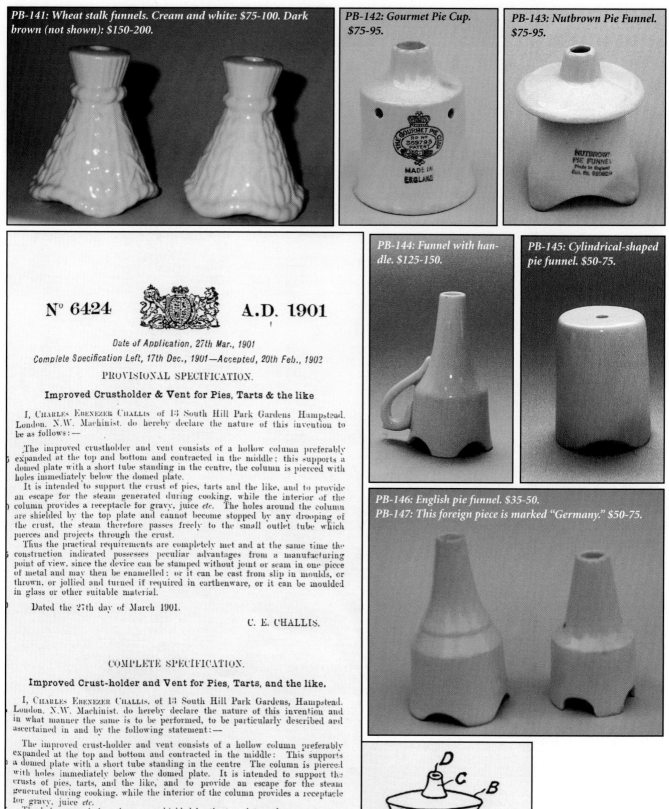

PB-141: Wheat stalk funnels. Cream and white: $75-100. Dark brown (not shown): $150-200.

PB-142: Gourmet Pie Cup. $75-95.

PB-143: Nutbrown Pie Funnel. $75-95.

PB-144: Funnel with handle. $125-150.

PB-145: Cylindrical-shaped pie funnel. $50-75.

PB-146: English pie funnel. $35-50.
PB-147: This foreign piece is marked "Germany." $50-75.

Nº 6424   A.D. 1901

Date of Application, 27th Mar., 1901

Complete Specification Left, 17th Dec., 1901—Accepted, 20th Feb., 1902

PROVISIONAL SPECIFICATION.

Improved Crustholder & Vent for Pies, Tarts & the like

I, CHARLES EBENEZER CHALLIS of 13 South Hill Park Gardens Hampstead. London. N.W. Machinist. do hereby declare the nature of this invention to be as follows:—

The improved crustholder and vent consists of a hollow column preferably expanded at the top and bottom and contracted in the middle; this supports a domed plate with a short tube standing in the centre, the column is pierced with holes immediately below the domed plate.

It is intended to support the crust of pies, tarts and the like, and to provide an escape for the steam generated during cooking, while the interior of the column provides a receptacle for gravy, juice *etc*. The holes around the column are shielded by the top plate and cannot become stopped by any drooping of the crust, the steam therefore passes freely to the small outlet tube which pierces and projects through the crust.

Thus the practical requirements are completely met and at the same time the construction indicated possesses peculiar advantages from a manufacturing point of view. since the device can be stamped without joint or seam in one piece of metal and may then be enamelled: or it can be cast from slip in moulds, or thrown, or jollied and turned if required in earthenware, or it can be moulded in glass or other suitable material.

Dated the 27th day of March 1901.

C. E. CHALLIS.

COMPLETE SPECIFICATION.

Improved Crust-holder and Vent for Pies, Tarts, and the like.

I, CHARLES EBENEZER CHALLIS, of 13 South Hill Park Gardens, Hampstead. London. N.W. Machinist. do hereby declare the nature of this invention and in what manner the same is to be performed, to be particularly described and ascertained in and by the following statement:—

The improved crust-holder and vent consists of a hollow column preferably expanded at the top and bottom and contracted in the middle: This supports a domed plate with a short tube standing in the centre The column is pierced with holes immediately below the domed plate. It is intended to support the crusts of pies, tarts, and the like, and to provide an escape for the steam generated during cooking. while the interior of the column provides a receptacle for gravy, juice *etc*.

The holes around the column are shielded by the top plate and cannot become stopped by any drooping of the crust, the steam therefore passes freely to the small outlet tube which pierces and projects through the crust.

Thus the practical requirements are completely met, and at the same time

[*Price 8d.*]

Original 1901 Gourmet Pie Cup Patent.

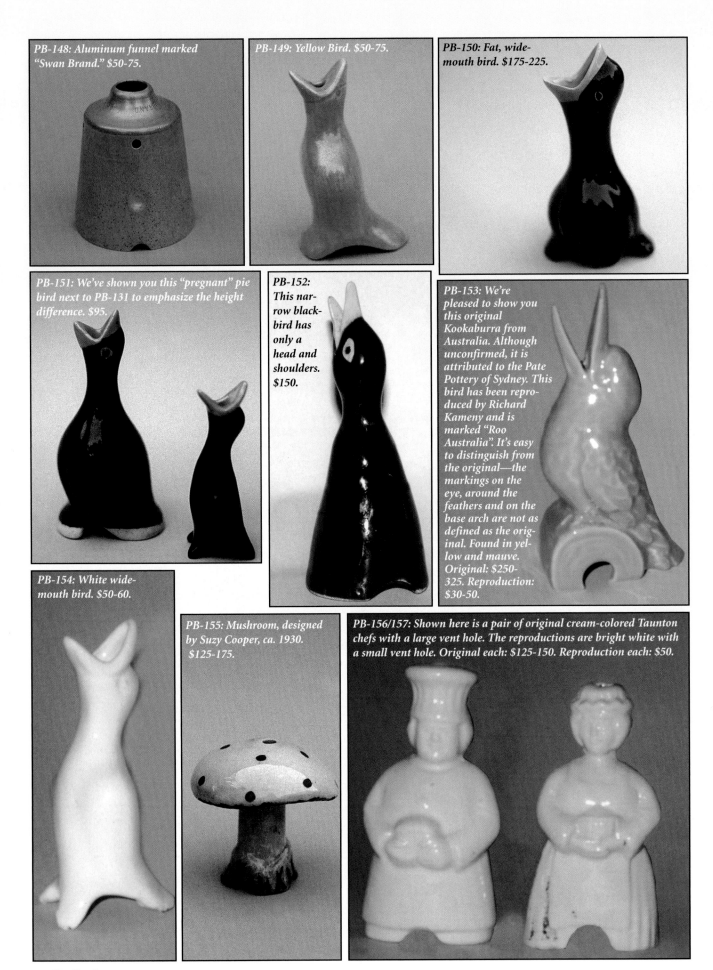

PB-148: Aluminum funnel marked "Swan Brand." $50-75.

PB-149: Yellow Bird. $50-75.

PB-150: Fat, wide-mouth bird. $175-225.

PB-151: We've shown you this "pregnant" pie bird next to PB-131 to emphasize the height difference. $95.

PB-152: This narrow blackbird has only a head and shoulders. $150.

PB-153: We're pleased to show you this original Kookaburra from Australia. Although unconfirmed, it is attributed to the Pate Pottery of Sydney. This bird has been reproduced by Richard Kameny and is marked "Roo Australia". It's easy to distinguish from the original—the markings on the eye, around the feathers and on the base arch are not as defined as the original. Found in yellow and mauve. Original: $250-325. Reproduction: $30-50.

PB-154: White wide-mouth bird. $50-60.

PB-155: Mushroom, designed by Suzy Cooper, ca. 1930. $125-175.

PB-156/157: Shown here is a pair of original cream-colored Taunton chefs with a large vent hole. The reproductions are bright white with a small vent hole. Original each: $125-150. Reproduction each: $50.

PB-158: Pie bird collectors refer to this Australian piece as "Dopey" or "Clown." Notice he has a body instead of a vent-shaped base. $300+.

PB-159: Although we featured this Dopey in KBBI as an American example, we've since learned that he is Australian and was not made for Disney. Regardless, he is still highly desirable to both pie bird and Disney collectors. $750+. Beware: he's being reproduced and marked "Hand Maid." (Formerly PB-227).

PB-160: Fred the Flour Grader pie funnel, by Spillers, the manufacturer of Homepride flour, is available in 3-1/2", 4", and 4-1/2". He was originally introduced in 1978; a model with large round black eyes that touch the hat was produced in the 1990s. You can also tell the difference by running your finger over the eyes and mouth. The 1978 model has a slight indentation. Original: $75-100. New issue: $50-75.

PB-161: English Audrelia pie funnel. $300-350.

Right: This original flour sack shows how Fred was marketed as a premium.

Most American birds date to the early 1940s and are quite desirable in the collecting market.

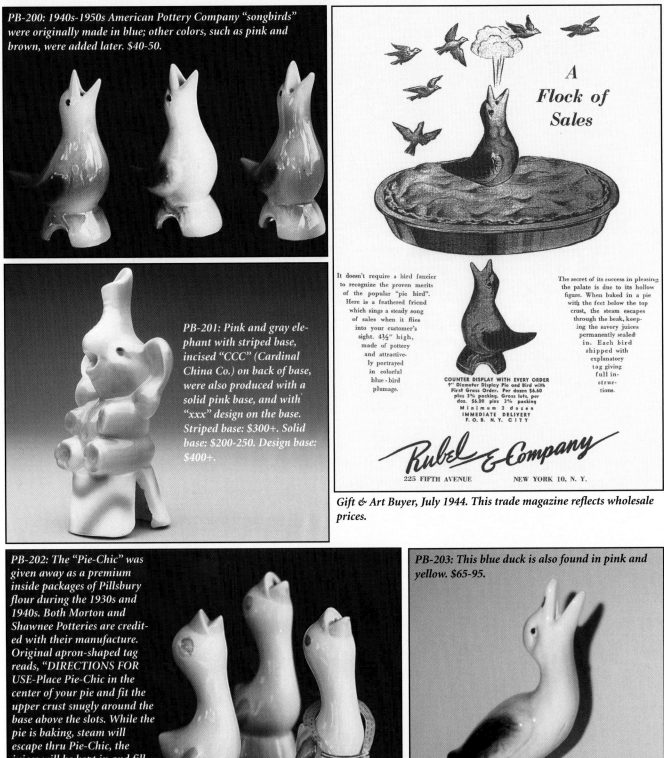

PB-200: *1940s-1950s American Pottery Company "songbirds" were originally made in blue; other colors, such as pink and brown, were added later. $40-50.*

PB-201: *Pink and gray elephant with striped base, incised "CCC" (Cardinal China Co.) on back of base, were also produced with a solid pink base, and with "xxx" design on the base. Striped base: $300+. Solid base: $200-250. Design base: $400+.*

A
Flock of Sales

It doesn't require a bird fancier to recognize the proven merits of the popular "pie bird". Here is a feathered friend which sings a steady song of sales when it flies into your customer's sight. 4½" high, made of pottery and attractively portrayed in colorful blue-bird plumage.

The secret of its success in pleasing the palate is due to its hollow figure. When baked in a pie with the feet below the top crust, the steam escapes through the beak, keeping the savory juices permanently sealed in. Each bird shipped with explanatory tag giving full instructions.

COUNTER DISPLAY WITH EVERY ORDER
9" Diameter Display Pie and Bird with First Gross Order. Per dozen $6.60 plus 3% packing. Gross lots, per doz. $6.00 plus 3% packing
Minimum 3 dozen
IMMEDIATE DELIVERY
F. O. B. N. Y. CITY

Rubel & Company
225 FIFTH AVENUE   NEW YORK 10, N. Y.

Gift & Art Buyer, July 1944. This trade magazine reflects wholesale prices.

PB-202: *The "Pie-Chic" was given away as a premium inside packages of Pillsbury flour during the 1930s and 1940s. Both Morton and Shawnee Potteries are credited with their manufacture. Original apron-shaped tag reads, "DIRECTIONS FOR USE-Place Pie-Chic in the center of your pie and fit the upper crust snugly around the base above the slots. While the pie is baking, steam will escape thru Pie-Chic, the juices will be kept in and filling will not boil over." $50-60. Beware: this pie bird is being reproduced.*

PB-203: *This blue duck is also found in pink and yellow. $65-95.*

HE SAVES
THE JUICE

THE PIE DUCKLING

As every hostess knows, pies, when baking, have a tendency to spill the precious juices all over the oven. This is caused by the effort of trapped steam to escape. Now the PIE DUCKLING solves the problem — permits the steam to escape, thereby keeping the juices IN THE PIE . . . Just stand the PIE DUCKLING underneath top crust, and he does the rest.

PIE DUCKLING is $6.60 per dozen in sample package of three dozen assorted blue, yellow, rose, or 12 dozen lots at $6 per dozen—f.o.b. Philadelphia. Each PIE DUCKLING complete with tag illustrating and explaining his use, together with the following humorous jingle:

"I'm so proud, I blow off steam.
I keep your pies right 'on the beam.'
Bright smiles grace my lady's face—
No juices spill all o'er the place.

Just stand me 'near the upper crust
Your pies will never be a 'bust.'
And when the guests exclaim with glee
'Bout half the credit should go to me!"

5" high

A free pie display piece with a gross order. Prompt shipment.

EBELING & REUSS COMPANY

NEW YORK (10), N. Y.
225 Fifth Avenue

PHILADELPHIA (6), PA.
707 Chestnut Street

CHICAGO (54), ILL.
1157 Merchandise Mart

LOS ANGELES (14), CAL.
(Brack Shops) 527 W. Seventh Street

15 CROCKERY & GLASS JOURNAL for November, 1945

CROCKERY & GLASS JOURNAL for November, 1945

Crockery and Glass Journal, November 1945.

PB-205B: Benny with red buttons. $200+.

PB-204: We originally credited LePere for these hard-to-find pie birds. We've since discovered that Chic Pottery (Zanesville, Ohio) was the manufacturer, ca. 1930s-1960s. $150-200.

PB-205A: Cardinal China Co. of Carteret, New Jersey, was the distributor for "Benny the Baker," ca. 1951. This multi-purpose 5-1/4" pie bird came boxed with a pie crimper/cookie cutter and cake tester. Set: $150. Pie bird only: $120-130. (Add $20 for box.) Rumor has it that a shorter version of this model has been reproduced, but as of publication time we have yet to see an example.

Perched in the center of a fruit pie, Benny-the-Baker acts a capable air vent. Made by the Cardinal China Co. he will l a cheerful and useful addition to any household. Complete wi stainless steel cake tester and pie crimper. $1. M. J. Saltzma

Crockery and Glass Journal, November 1950. This trade magazine reflects wholesale prices.

PB-205C: This flesh-faced Benny with the pink cheeks was found in the original box. $250+.
PB-205D: The all black Benny is extremely rare. $350+.

PB-206: "Ralphies," or "Patricks," were produced in a variety of color combinations, Cleminsons of California, 4-1/4". $65-85.

PB-207/208: Rare "Ralphies." The small version on the left is 4-1/8". $100-150. The brown bird is 4-1/2". $400+.

PB-209: "Pie Boy" by Squire Pottery of California. $400+.

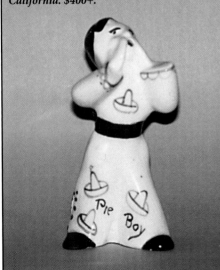

Meet Patrick the Pie Bird—a wee rooster who hatches the best pies you ever tasted. When you bake a pie place him in the middle of the crust so the juices won't escape. You see, the steam comes out through his beak. He's a mere $1.50 ppd. Robert Keith, Inc., 13th & Baltimore, Kansas City, Mo.

House and Garden, June 1944.

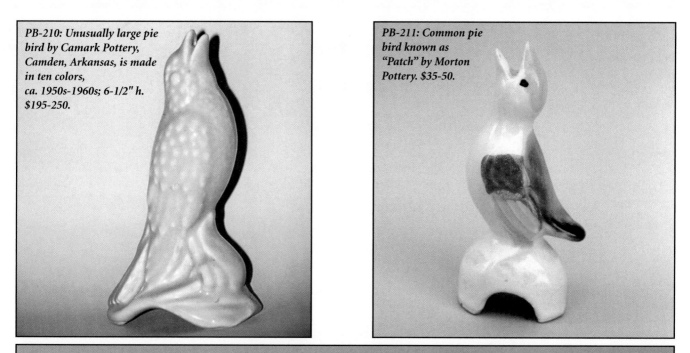

PB-210: Unusually large pie bird by Camark Pottery, Camden, Arkansas, is made in ten colors, ca. 1950s-1960s; 6-1/2" h. $195-250.

PB-211: Common pie bird known as "Patch" by Morton Pottery. $35-50.

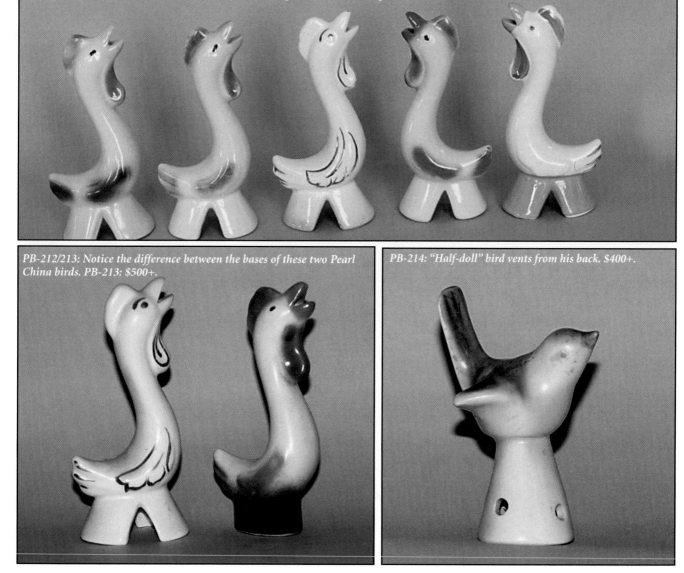

PB- 212: Pearl China's roosters, found in different colors, are one of the earliest pie birds made by an American company. Bird with blue base: $150. Other colors variations: $200. Beware: this pie bird has been reproduced.

PB-212/213: Notice the difference between the bases of these two Pearl China birds. PB-213: $500+.

PB-214: "Half-doll" bird vents from his back. $400+.

PB-215: Bird on nest with babies, sold by Artisian Galleries, Fort Dodge, Iowa. $750+.

Pie bird. You won't need four-and-twenty blackbirds to make your pies the talk of the town. Just this one lovely little ceramic bird, contentedly sitting on her nest, with her beak wide open to send forth her carol and the steam from your juicy fruit pie. $1.10 ppd. Artisan Galleries, Fort Dodge, Iowa.

Above: House and Garden, *October 1950.*

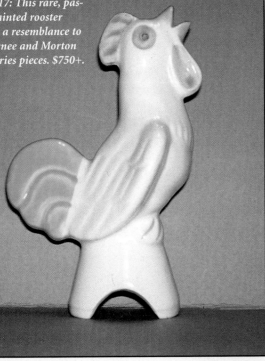

PB-217: This rare, pastel-painted rooster bears a resemblance to Shawnee and Morton Potteries pieces. $750+.

PB-218: Puff-chested bird is found in a variety of color combinabions, ca. 1940s. $500+.

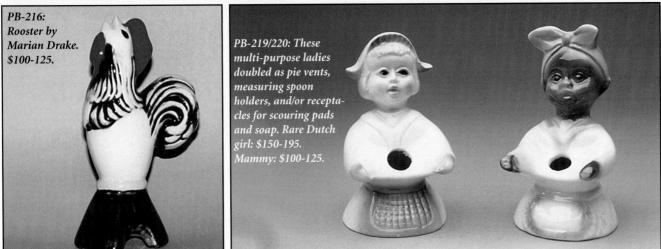

PB-216: Rooster by Marian Drake. $100-125.

PB-219/220: These multi-purpose ladies doubled as pie vents, measuring spoon holders, and/or receptacles for scouring pads and soap. Rare Dutch girl: $150-195. Mammy: $100-125.

❖ Mammy and Chef Pie Birds

Black memorabilia continues to rise in price, and the rare original Mammy pie bids are no exception. Beware: new Black pie vents continue to show up priced as old pieces.

PB-221: Newer vintage Mammy, $40.

PB-222: Made by Marian Drake in 1978, this Mammy matches the Luzianne cookie jar. $100-150.

PB-223: Another example of a newer vintage Mammy. $40

PB-224: Unusual black chef resembles "Pie-Aire." $200+.

PB-225A: 1940s "Pie-Aire the Chef" came in blue, yellow, and green. The original tag reads, "James Barry Products, Merchandise Mart Chicago, copyright JBP, 1945." Green: $175. Yellow: $80-100. Blue: $125-150.

PB-225B: Solid color "Pie-Aires" are not as common. $100+. Beware: This has been reproduced.

BELOW:
   PICTURE PIES are the responsibility of Pie-Aire the Chef. This porcelain figure is useful as well as attractive. Set inside the top crust of a fruit pie, it seals in the juices and lets out steam. Has yellow body, black face and hands, ruby red lips. Hand decorated, colors fired; 4½ inches high. Price in gross lots, $6.60 a dozen; in three dozen lots, $7.20 a dozen. A James Barry item distributed by Leon A. Bergsman, Merchandise Mart, Chicago.

House Beautiful, July 1945.

Gift & Art Buyer, May 1945. This trade magazine reflects wholesale prices.

❖ Original Disney Pie Bird

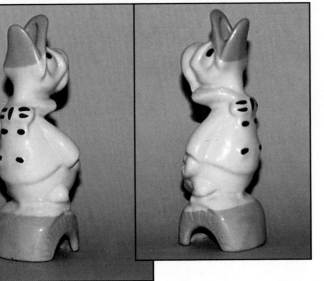

PB-226: Oh, to be the lucky owner of an original Disney "Donald Duck" pie bird. This piece has a "Walt Disney" mark on one side of base and "Donald Duck" on the other. $1000+. Beware: this pie bird is being reproduced with an unmarked base.

PB-227 reclassified as PB-159

❖ Recent Arrival Pie Birds

If we knew we didn't include all the American pieces in our first book, these birds wouldn't have ended up nesting in the south end of this chapter.

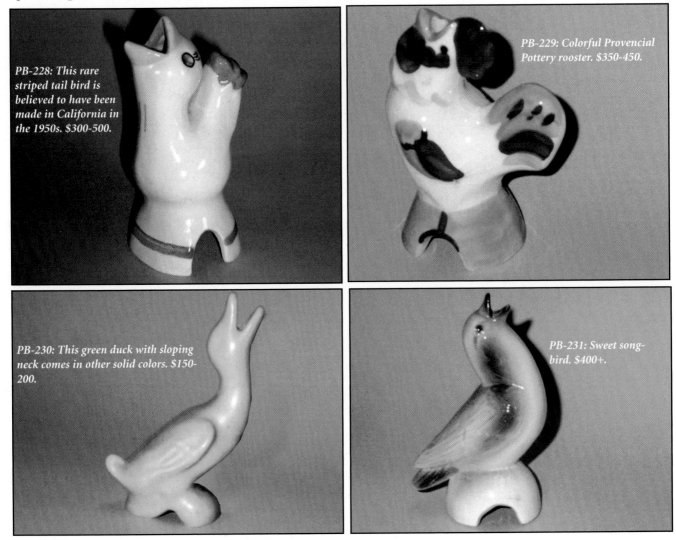

PB-228: This rare striped tail bird is believed to have been made in California in the 1950s. $300-500.

PB-229: Colorful Provencial Pottery rooster. $350-450.

PB-230: This green duck with sloping neck comes in other solid colors. $150-200.

PB-231: Sweet songbird. $400+.

PB-300: *Japanese blue bird (post-1960) with box. $20-30.*

PB-301: *"Yankee Pie Bird," Millford, New Hampshire, ca. 1960s. $40-50.*

PB-302/303/304/305: *Josef Originals pie birds from the 1980s were manufactured in the Far East. Original sticker reads, "A Lorrie Design, Japan." PB-302: $500+. PB-303/304/305: $95-125.*

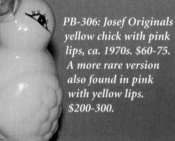

PB-306: *Josef Originals yellow chick with pink lips, ca. 1970s. $60-75. A more rare version also found in pink with yellow lips. $200-300.*

PB-310/311/312 and PB-313 reclassified as Wannabes.

PB-307/308: *The late ceramist Jackie Sammond of Holladay, Utah, was responsible for this owl and blackbird. The 3" bird was her first vent (early 1970s). Later, she designed and cast the owl, as well as an elephant and a howling hound dog. $125-150.*

PB-309: *Dolphin from the early 1970s, marked "Bermuda." Vents from back of neck. $300+.*

PB-314: *Rowe Pottery, two-piece pie bird with detachable base is no longer made but was offered for sale in their 1993 catalog. $20-40.*

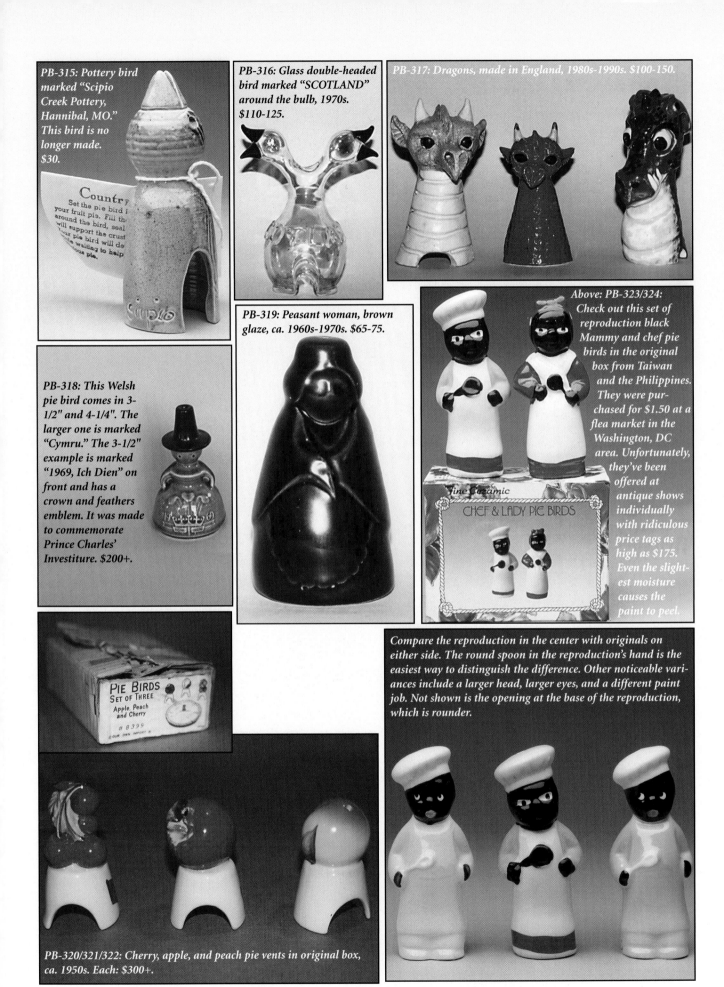

PB-315: Pottery bird marked "Scipio Creek Pottery, Hannibal, MO." This bird is no longer made. $30.

PB-316: Glass double-headed bird marked "SCOTLAND" around the bulb, 1970s. $110-125.

PB-317: Dragons, made in England, 1980s-1990s. $100-150.

PB-318: This Welsh pie bird comes in 3-1/2" and 4-1/4". The larger one is marked "Cymru." The 3-1/2" example is marked "1969, Ich Dien" on front and has a crown and feathers emblem. It was made to commemorate Prince Charles' Investiture. $200+.

PB-319: Peasant woman, brown glaze, ca. 1960s-1970s. $65-75.

Above: PB-323/324: Check out this set of reproduction black Mammy and chef pie birds in the original box from Taiwan and the Philippines. They were purchased for $1.50 at a flea market in the Washington, DC area. Unfortunately, they've been offered at antique shows individually with ridiculous price tags as high as $175. Even the slightest moisture causes the paint to peel.

Compare the reproduction in the center with originals on either side. The round spoon in the reproduction's hand is the easiest way to distinguish the difference. Other noticeable variances include a larger head, larger eyes, and a different paint job. Not shown is the opening at the base of the reproduction, which is rounder.

PB-320/321/322: Cherry, apple, and peach pie vents in original box, ca. 1950s. Each: $300+.

❖ Wannabes

The trunk of this elephant was designed to be a ring holder; the hole in his back is used for hatpins.

Mahoning Gifts catalog, Youngstown, OH.

Children's feeders are commonly mistaken for pie birds. The slot on the bottom, which allows the feeder to sit on a bowl, is the giveaway. Please see Chapter 6 to learn more about these.

Referred to as the "Howling Bear" pie bird, these bears are actually egg timers. Please see ET-130 in Chapter 5 to learn more about them.

These are pieces are actually incense burners, shown without their bases. The dog, seal, and bear are marked "Japan." The walrus is marked "Made in Japan." (Formerly PB-310-313.)

Teapot Whistler is showing up online auctions as a pie bird.

Avon's incense burner without the base is often misidentified as a pie bird. We've seen a new ceramic pie bird from England, made in the same image as this piece.

This 1940s photo of unpainted stringholders is courtesy of Miller Studio.

Decorative Stringholders

Have you ever been to an estate sale—one of those events held to liquidate a household's possessions? For the true collector these sales can mean hours of fun sifting through a treasure trove of bric-a-brac to junk.

The next time you attend a sale in an older home, be sure to check the drawers in the kitchen, laundry room, workshop or garage. Chances are you'll find balls of yellow twine, waxed lengths of rope or tangles of thin cotton string. If you get lucky enough to gain access to the attic, you might need a scissor or penknife to check out the contents. That's because most of the boxes will be tied up with string.

Long before adhesive tape became a common household fixture, string was king. It was used for all types of packages. Rather than have this household necessity jumbled in a drawer, the efficient and conscientious housewife kept it handy and neat on the countertop or hung on the wall, disguised behind the façade of a decorative stringholder.

At the height of popularity from the 1930s-1950s, these decorative novelties were mass produced by companies like Miller Studio (an innovator and leader of the era) and sold through the local five and dime stores or in the pages of catalogs such as Sears and Montgomery Ward.

Although many people more readily identify with the glass or cast iron stringholder of the old country store, this chapter focuses on the colorful chalkware and ceramic examples used in the everyday home—people, animals, flowers and vegetables seem to be the most popular designs.

While more stringholders seem to be becoming available on the market, finding vintage pieces in good shape has become difficult. Treated as inexpensive novelties, even the ceramic stringholders (which held up better than chalkware) are more elusive in mint or near mint condition, free of chips or cracks. No matter what any one tells you, *condition does count,* especially if it isn't a rare item. The good news is that prices seem to have settled down, and unless a piece is very unique, vintage stringholders are priced much more reasonably than they were a few years ago. You'll see these market changes in our values.

Although there hasn't been much new historical information unearthed since our last book, we've added some interesting vintage patents. If you're a seller of original stringholders, business is probably booming. But if you're just starting out as a collector, look out: the market is saturated by new ceramic and chalkware examples. Most of these are unmarked or had a label that was easily removed. Here are some other tips (remember they don't always apply) for distinguishing between the two: older stringholders are usually lighter in weight; look to see if the wire hanger looks old; and if the paint has a bright, almost shiny appearance you know its age may be questionable. There's nothing wrong with adding these new pieces to your collection—some are actually quite attractive. But a little knowledge can go a long way in ensuring that you pay a fair price for new versus old.

In the three years since our first book, there is definitely one thing that hasn't changed—those *exotic drink containers are still not stringholders*!

Birds

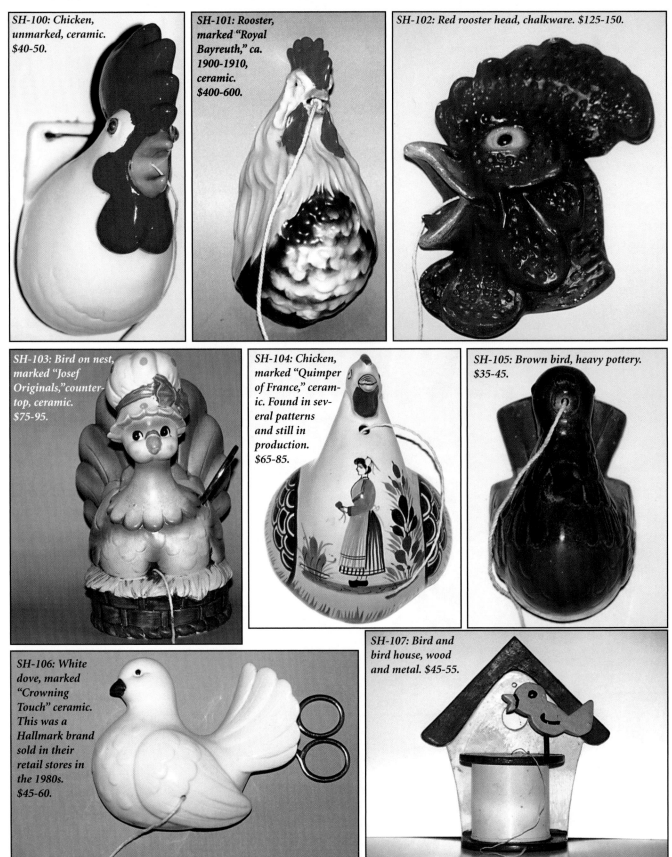

SH-100: Chicken, unmarked, ceramic. $40-50.

SH-101: Rooster, marked "Royal Bayreuth," ca. 1900-1910, ceramic. $400-600.

SH-102: Red rooster head, chalkware. $125-150.

SH-103: Bird on nest, marked "Josef Originals,"countertop, ceramic. $75-95.

SH-104: Chicken, marked "Quimper of France," ceramic. Found in several patterns and still in production. $65-85.

SH-105: Brown bird, heavy pottery. $35-45.

SH-106: White dove, marked "Crowning Touch" ceramic. This was a Hallmark brand sold in their retail stores in the 1980s. $45-60.

SH-107: Bird and bird house, wood and metal. $45-55.

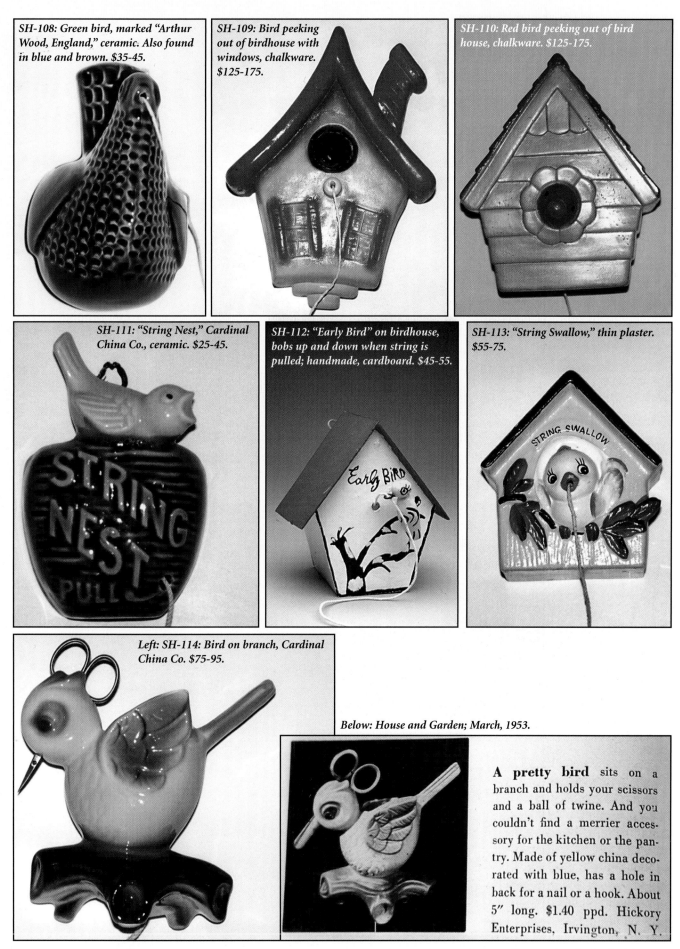

SH-108: Green bird, marked "Arthur Wood, England," ceramic. Also found in blue and brown. $35-45.

SH-109: Bird peeking out of birdhouse with windows, chalkware. $125-175.

SH-110: Red bird peeking out of bird house, chalkware. $125-175.

SH-111: "String Nest," Cardinal China Co., ceramic. $25-45.

SH-112: "Early Bird" on birdhouse, bobs up and down when string is pulled; handmade, cardboard. $45-55.

SH-113: "String Swallow," thin plaster. $55-75.

Left: SH-114: Bird on branch, Cardinal China Co. $75-95.

Below: House and Garden; March, 1953.

A pretty bird sits on a branch and holds your scissors and a ball of twine. And you couldn't find a merrier accessory for the kitchen or the pantry. Made of yellow china decorated with blue, has a hole in back for a nail or a hook. About 5" long. $1.40 ppd. Hickory Enterprises, Irvington, N. Y.

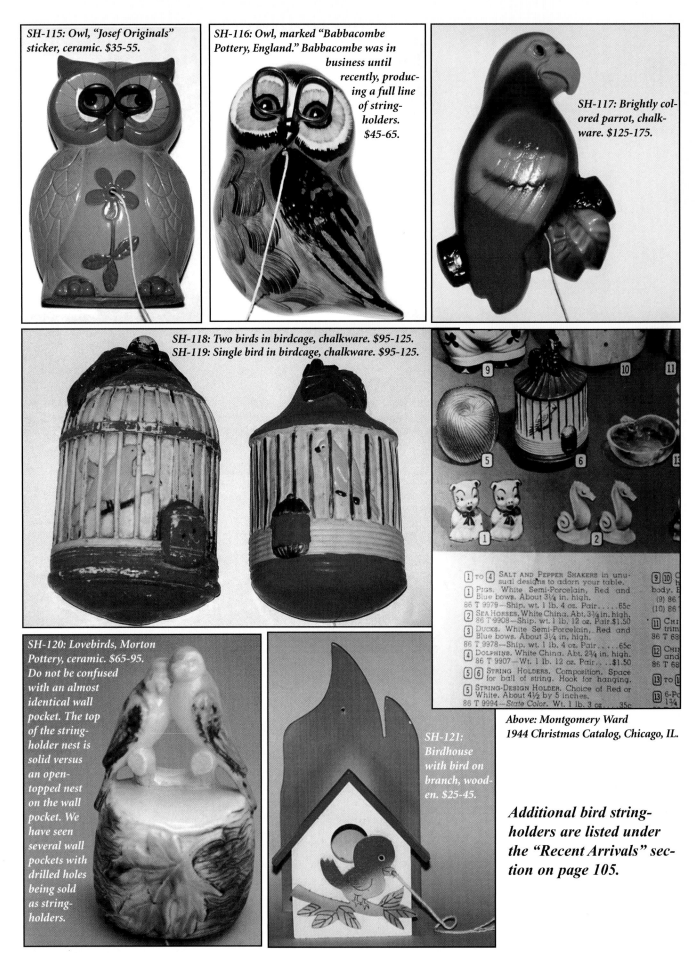

SH-115: Owl, "Josef Originals" sticker, ceramic. $35-55.

SH-116: Owl, marked "Babbacombe Pottery, England." Babbacombe was in business until recently, producing a full line of string-holders. $45-65.

SH-117: Brightly colored parrot, chalkware. $125-175.

SH-118: Two birds in birdcage, chalkware. $95-125.
SH-119: Single bird in birdcage, chalkware. $95-125.

SH-120: Lovebirds, Morton Pottery, ceramic. $65-95. Do not be confused with an almost identical wall pocket. The top of the string-holder nest is solid versus an open-topped nest on the wall pocket. We have seen several wall pockets with drilled holes being sold as string-holders.

SH-121: Birdhouse with bird on branch, wooden. $25-45.

① TO ④ SALT AND PEPPER SHAKERS in unusual designs to adorn your table.
① PIGS. White Semi-Porcelain. Red and Blue bows. About 3¼ in. high.
86 T 9979—Ship. wt. 1 lb. 4 oz. Pair.....65c
② SEA HORSES, White China. Abt 3¾ in. high.
86 T 9908—Ship. wt. 1 lb. 12 oz. Pair.$1.50
③ DUCKS. White Semi-Porcelain. Red and Blue bows. About 3¼ in. high.
86 T 9978—Ship. wt. 1 lb. 4 oz. Pair.....65c
④ DOLPHINS. White China. Abt. 2¾ in. high.
86 T 9907—Wt. 1 lb. 12 oz. Pair.....$1.50
⑤ ⑥ STRING HOLDERS. Composition. Space for ball of string. Hook for hanging.
⑤ STRING-DESIGN HOLDER. Choice of Red or White. About 4½ by 5 inches.
86 T 9994—State Color. Wt. 1 lb. 3 oz....35c

Above: Montgomery Ward 1944 Christmas Catalog, Chicago, IL.

Additional bird string-holders are listed under the "Recent Arrivals" section on page 105.

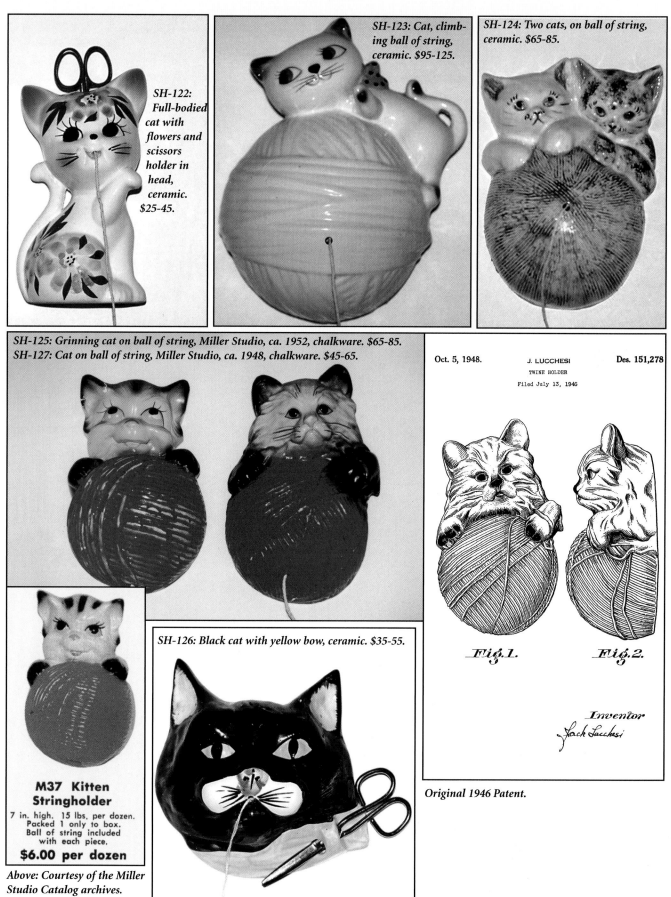

SH-122: *Full-bodied cat with flowers and scissors holder in head, ceramic. $25-45.*

SH-123: *Cat, climbing ball of string, ceramic. $95-125.*

SH-124: *Two cats, on ball of string, ceramic. $65-85.*

SH-125: *Grinning cat on ball of string, Miller Studio, ca. 1952, chalkware. $65-85.*
SH-127: *Cat on ball of string, Miller Studio, ca. 1948, chalkware. $45-65.*

Oct. 5, 1948.　　　　J. LUCCHESI　　　　Des. 151,278
TWINE HOLDER
Filed July 13, 1946

Fig.1.　　　*Fig.2.*

Inventor
Jack Lucchesi

Original 1946 Patent.

M37 Kitten Stringholder

7 in. high. 15 lbs. per dozen.
Packed 1 only to box.
Ball of string included
with each piece.
$6.00 per dozen

Above: Courtesy of the Miller Studio Catalog archives.

SH-126: *Black cat with yellow bow, ceramic. $35-55.*

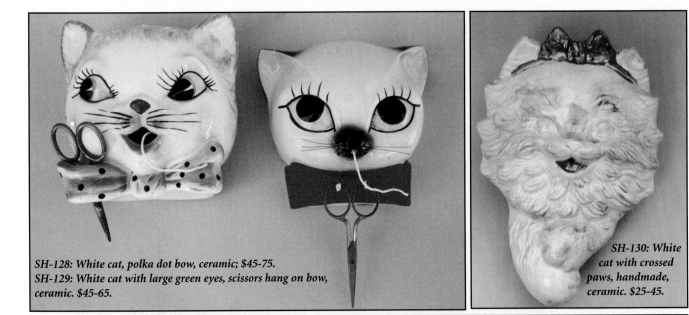

SH-128: *White cat, polka dot bow, ceramic; $45-75.*
SH-129: *White cat with large green eyes, scissors hang on bow, ceramic. $45-65.*

SH-130: *White cat with crossed paws, handmade, ceramic. $25-45.*

SH-131: *Black cat face with slanted eyes, ceramic. $65-85.*

SH-132: *Handmade cat holding ball of string, found in many color combinations, ceramic. REPRODUCTION ALERT: This cat is being reproduced in cast resin and sold in a mail order catalog for $31.99. $25-45.*

SH-133: *Black and white cat face, chalkware. $95-125.*

SH-134: *"Tom Cat," marked "Takahashi, San Francisco, Made in Japan," ceramic. $55-75.*

SH-135: Cat with bow holding ball of string, chalkware. $45-75.

SH-136: Full-figured cat on top of ball of string, ceramic. $55-85.

SH-137: Cat with matching wall pocket, ceramic. $55-75.

SH-138: Cat with plaid bow, ceramic. $45-65.

SH-139: Cat with scissors in collar, marked "Babbacombe Pottery, England," ceramic. $25-50.

SH-140: Full-figured sitting cat, marked "Horton Ceramics," ceramic. $35-55.

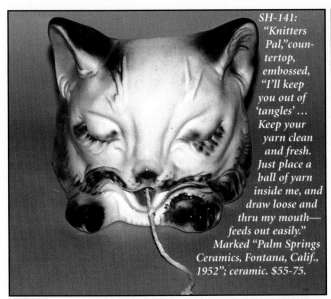

SH-141: "Knitters Pal," countertop, embossed, "I'll keep you out of 'tangles' … Keep your yarn clean and fresh. Just place a ball of yarn inside me, and draw loose and thru my mouth—feeds out easily." Marked "Palm Springs Ceramics, Fontana, Calif., 1952"; ceramic. $55-75.

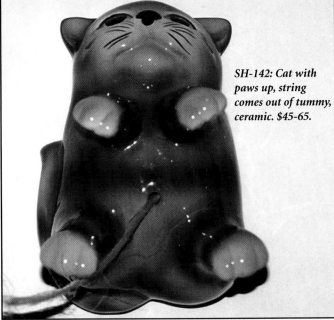

SH-142: Cat with paws up, string comes out of tummy, ceramic. $45-65.

SH-143A: Cat, marked "Holt Howard, 1958," ceramic. This piece originally sold for $1.00. $35-55.

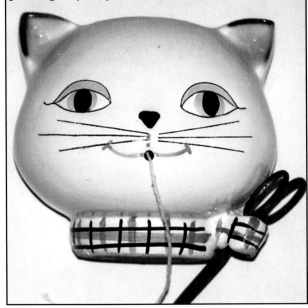

SH-143B: Notice how the eyes on this cat are glancing to one side, marked "Holt Howard, 1959": ceramic. $35-55.

SH-144: Spatterware sleeping cat, ceramic. $35-55.

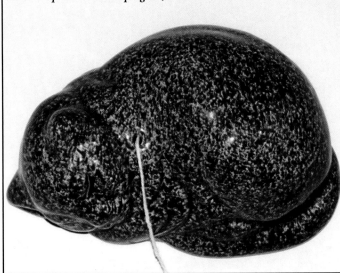

SH-145: Handmade cat with gold bow, ceramic. $50-75.

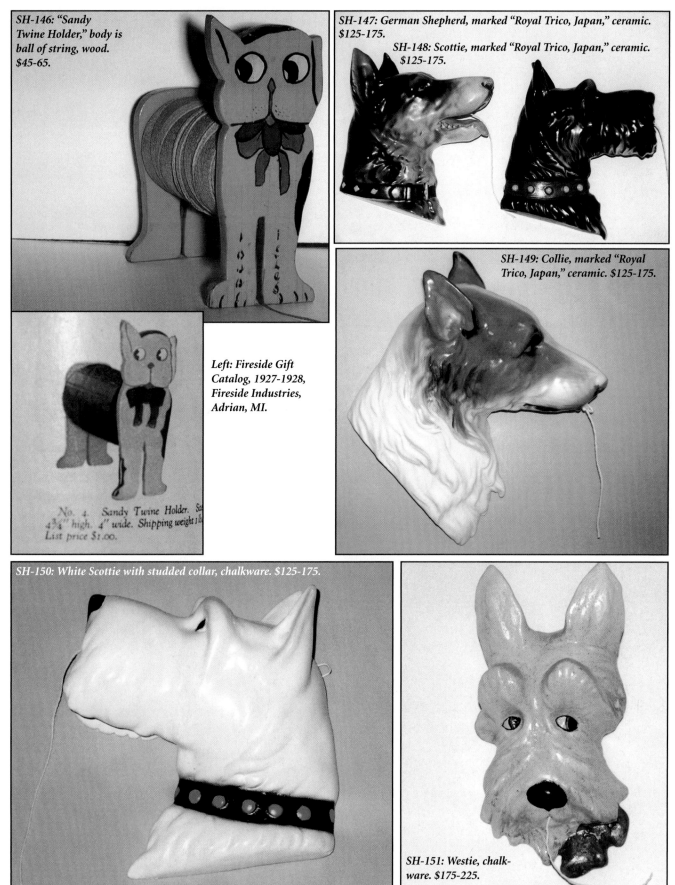

SH-146: "Sandy Twine Holder," body is ball of string, wood. $45-65.

SH-147: German Shepherd, marked "Royal Trico, Japan," ceramic. $125-175.

SH-148: Scottie, marked "Royal Trico, Japan," ceramic. $125-175.

SH-149: Collie, marked "Royal Trico, Japan," ceramic. $125-175.

Left: Fireside Gift Catalog, 1927-1928, Fireside Industries, Adrian, MI.

No. 4. Sandy Twine Holder. Size 4¾" high. 4" wide. Shipping weight 1 lb. List price $1.00.

SH-150: White Scottie with studded collar, chalkware. $125-175.

SH-151: Westie, chalkware. $175-225.

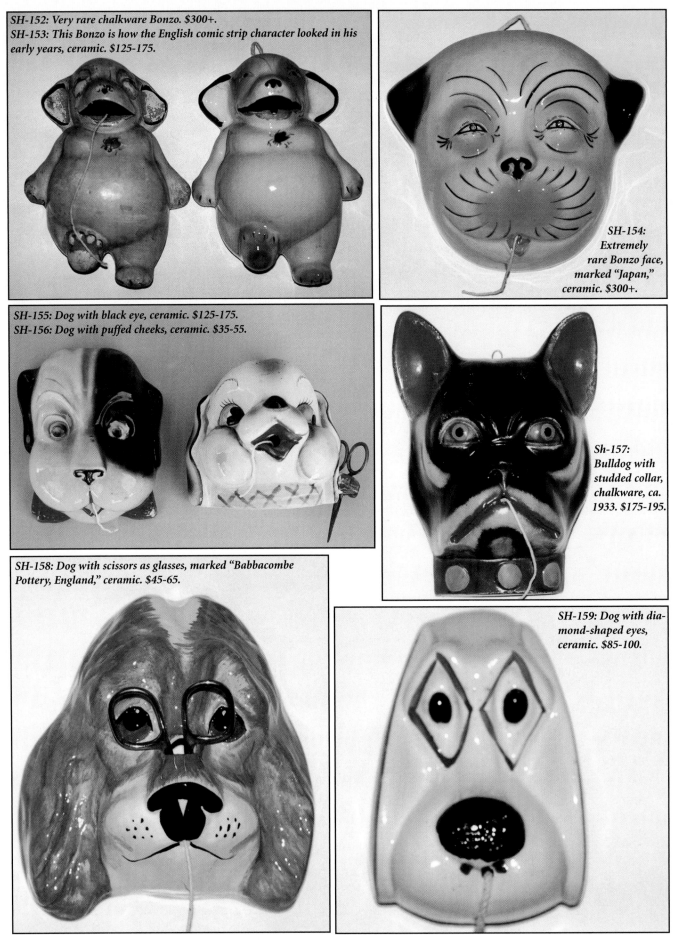

SH-152: Very rare chalkware Bonzo. $300+.
SH-153: This Bonzo is how the English comic strip character looked in his early years, ceramic. $125-175.

SH-154: Extremely rare Bonzo face, marked "Japan," ceramic. $300+.

SH-155: Dog with black eye, ceramic. $125-175.
SH-156: Dog with puffed cheeks, ceramic. $35-55.

Sh-157: Bulldog with studded collar, chalkware, ca. 1933. $175-195.

SH-158: Dog with scissors as glasses, marked "Babbacombe Pottery, England," ceramic. $45-65.

SH-159: Dog with diamond-shaped eyes, ceramic. $85-100.

SH-160: Boxer, ceramic. $95-135.
SH-161: Scottie, ceramic. $95-135.

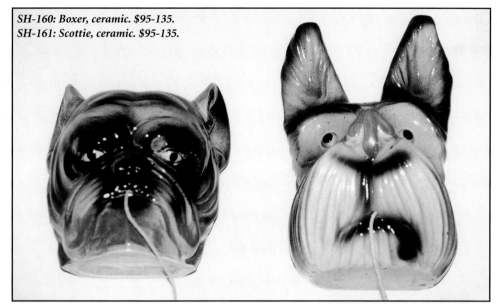

Additional dog stringholders are listed under the "Recent Arrivals" section on page 105.

SH-162A: Dog with red collar for scissors, marked "Arthur Wood, England," ceramic. $45-65.
SH-163: Holt Howard-style dog, ceramic. $95-125.

Dog String Holder with Scissors. Keeps string (not incl.) handy. Ceramic—5x4½ in. Wt. 1 lb.
86 B 7012D–Import.**$1.00**

Above: Montgomery Ward 1960 Spring/Summer Catalog, Chicago, Illinois.

SH-162B: A similar dog only with a black circle around one eye, ceramic. $55-75.

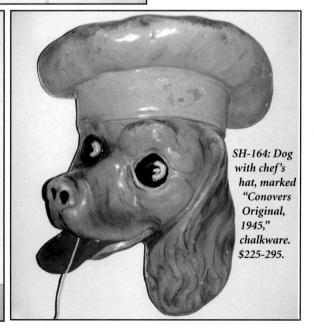

SH-164: Dog with chef's hat, marked "Conovers Original, 1945," chalkware. $225-295.

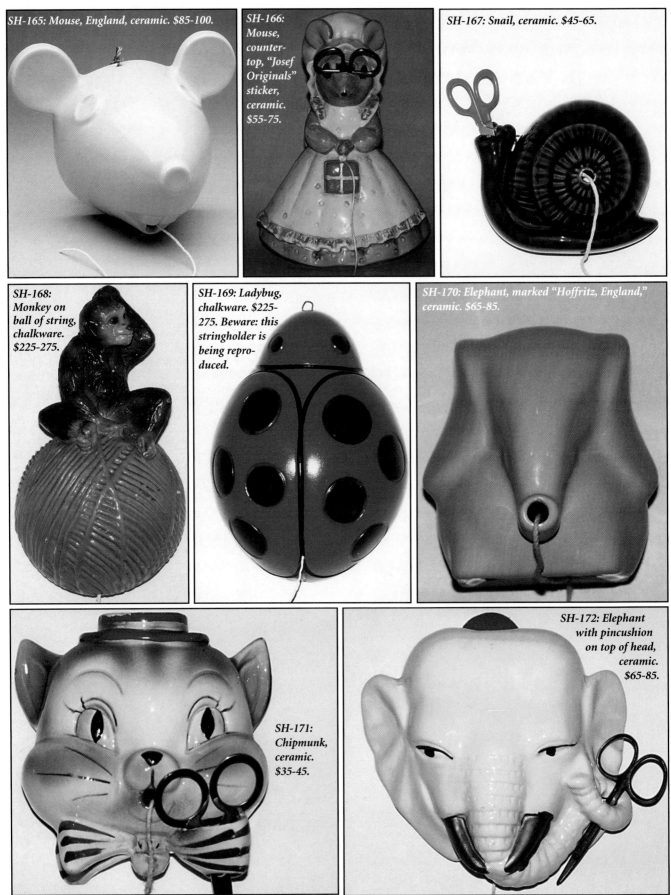

SH-165: Mouse, England, ceramic. $85-100.

SH-166: Mouse, countertop, "Josef Originals" sticker, ceramic. $55-75.

SH-167: Snail, ceramic. $45-65.

SH-168: Monkey on ball of string, chalkware. $225-275.

SH-169: Ladybug, chalkware. $225-275. Beware: this stringholder is being reproduced.

SH-170: Elephant, marked "Hoffritz, England," ceramic. $65-85.

SH-171: Chipmunk, ceramic. $35-45.

SH-172: Elephant with pincushion on top of head, ceramic. $65-85.

SH-173: "Susie Sunfish," Miller Studio, ca. 1948, chalkware. REPRODUCTION ALERT: this stringholder has been reproduced. In most cases, the hook on the reproductions is positioned on the top rather than on the back as it is on the original pieces. $225-275.

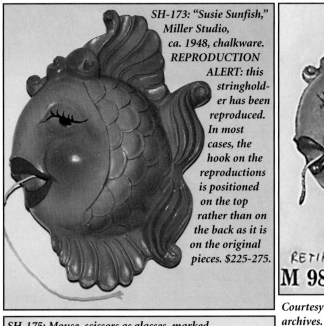

RETIRED JAN, 1950
M 98 Susie Sunfish
Courtesy of the Miller Studio Catalog archives.

SH-174: Elephant, scissors as glasses, bisque. $75-95.

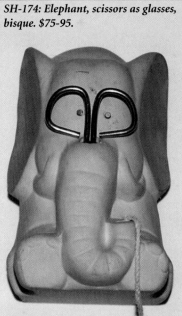

SH-175: Mouse, scissors as glasses, marked "Babbacombe, England," ceramic. $45-65.

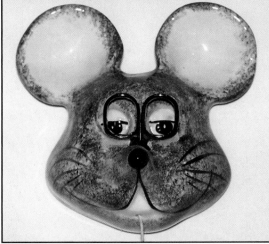

SH-176: Brown bear, marked "Babbacombe, England," ceramic. $45-65.
SH-177: Bear, scissors as glasses, ceramic. $45-65.

SH-178: Mole, scissors as glasses, England, ceramic. $45-65.

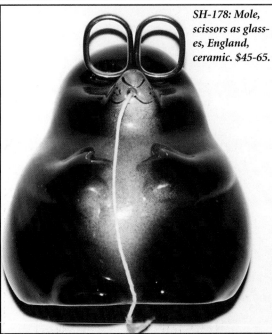

SH-179: Fox with mane, scissors as glasses, marked "Babbacombe, England," ceramic. $45-65.
SH-180: Fox without mane, scissors as glasses, marked "Babbacombe, England," ceramic. $65-85.

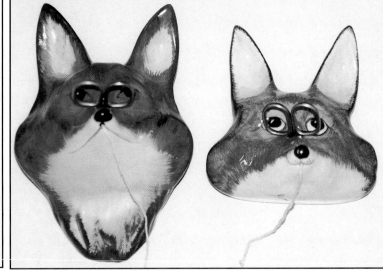

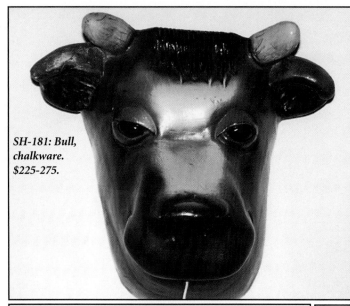

SH-181: Bull, chalkware. $225-275.

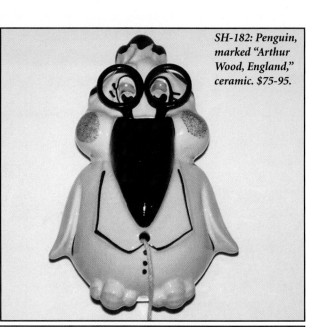

SH-182: Penguin, marked "Arthur Wood, England," ceramic. $75-95.

SH-183: Handmade Christmas bear, ceramic. $65-85.

SH-184: Full-bodied red pig, chalkware. $175-225.

SH-185: "Posie Pig," Miller Studio, 1948, chalkware. $175-225.

M 100 Posie Pig
Retired Jan. 54

Left: Courtesy of Miller Studio Catalog archives

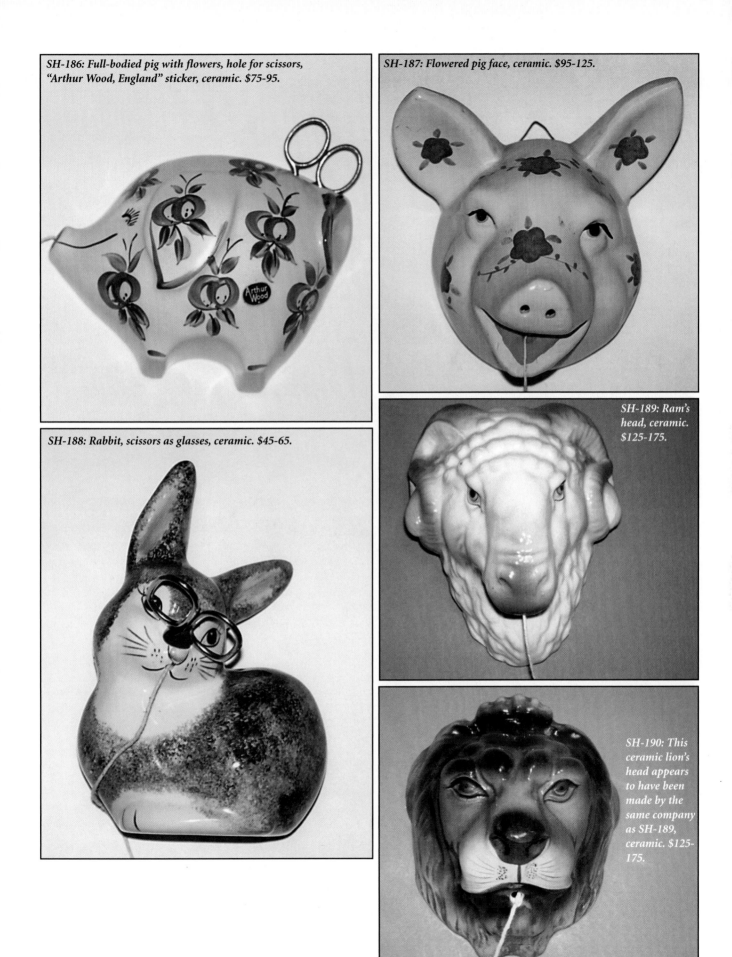

SH-186: Full-bodied pig with flowers, hole for scissors, "Arthur Wood, England" sticker, ceramic. $75-95.

SH-187: Flowered pig face, ceramic. $95-125.

SH-188: Rabbit, scissors as glasses, ceramic. $45-65.

SH-189: Ram's head, ceramic. $125-175.

SH-190: This ceramic lion's head appears to have been made by the same company as SH-189, ceramic. $125-175.

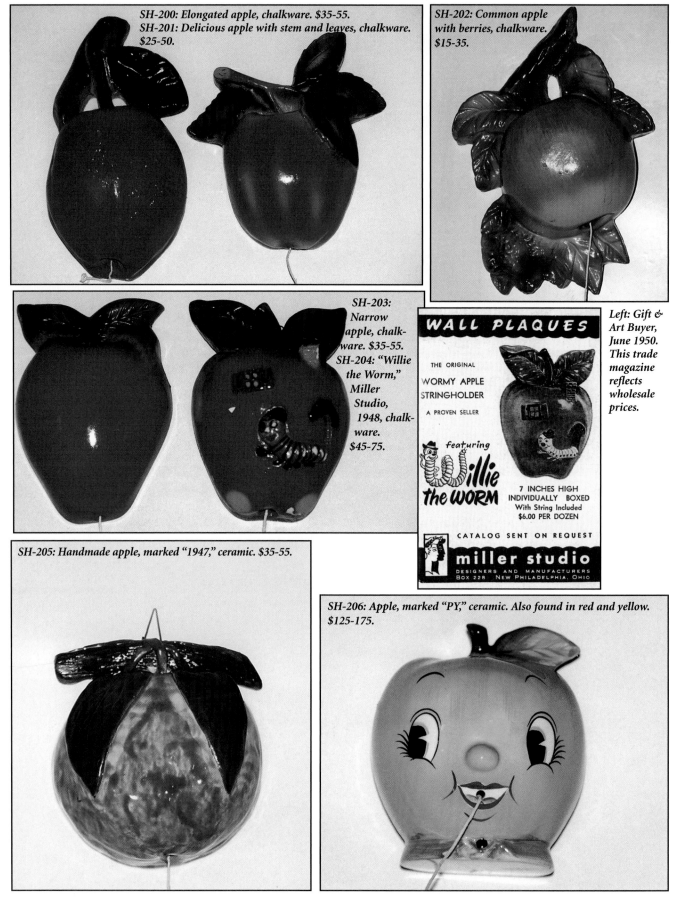

SH-200: Elongated apple, chalkware. $35-55.
SH-201: Delicious apple with stem and leaves, chalkware. $25-50.

SH-202: Common apple with berries, chalkware. $15-35.

SH-203: Narrow apple, chalkware. $35-55.
SH-204: "Willie the Worm," Miller Studio, 1948, chalkware. $45-75.

Left: Gift & Art Buyer, June 1950. This trade magazine reflects wholesale prices.

WALL PLAQUES

THE ORIGINAL
WORMY APPLE
STRINGHOLDER
A PROVEN SELLER

featuring
Willie the WORM

7 INCHES HIGH
INDIVIDUALLY BOXED
With String Included
$6.00 PER DOZEN

CATALOG SENT ON REQUEST

miller studio
DESIGNERS AND MANUFACTURERS
BOX 228 NEW PHILADELPHIA, OHIO

SH-205: Handmade apple, marked "1947," ceramic. $35-55.

SH-206: Apple, marked "PY," ceramic. Also found in red and yellow. $125-175.

SH-207: Yellow and red apple, "Rego" sticker, ceramic. $95-125.

SH-208: Cherries, chalkware. $125-150.

SH-209: Gourd, chalkware. $125-150.

SH-210: Bananas, ca. 1980s to present, chalkware. $25-50.

SH-211: Black grapes with large leaves, chalkware. $125-150.

SH-212: Embossed white grapes reads, "STRING," marked "California, U.S.A., #662," ceramic. $35-55.

SH-213: Bunch of fruit, chalkware. $150-200.

SH-214: Purple grapes, chalkware. $125-150.

SH-215: Grapes with fruit, chalkware. $125-150.

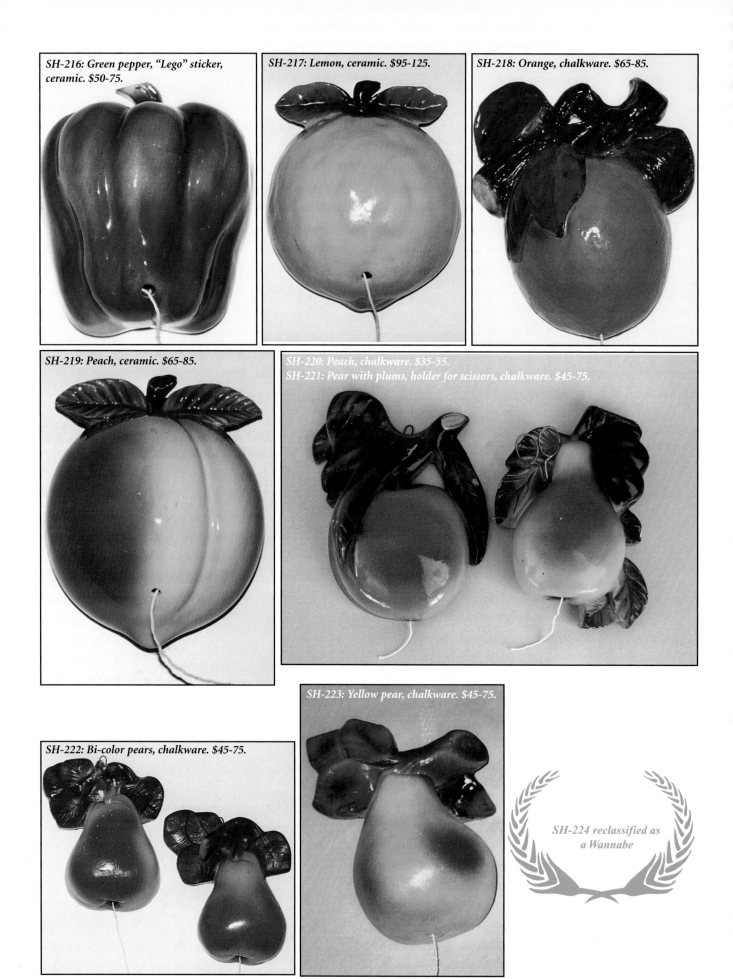

SH-216: Green pepper, "Lego" sticker, ceramic. $50-75.

SH-217: Lemon, ceramic. $95-125.

SH-218: Orange, chalkware. $65-85.

SH-219: Peach, ceramic. $65-85.

SH-220: Peach, chalkware. $35-55.
SH-221: Pear with plums, holder for scissors, chalkware. $45-75.

SH-222: Bi-color pears, chalkware. $45-75.

SH-223: Yellow pear, chalkware. $45-75.

SH-224 reclassified as a Wannabe

SH-225: Pineapple, chalkware. $150-175.

SH-226: "Miss Strawberry," Miller Studio, 1950, chalkware. $55-95.

M99 Miss Strawberry Stringholder
7 in. high. 15½ lbs. per dozen.
Packed 1 only to box.
Ball of string included
with each piece.
$6.00 per dozen

Courtesy of the Miller Studio Catalog archives.

SH-227: Strawberry, chalkware. $55-95.

SH- 228: "Prince Pineapple," by Miller Studio, 1948, chalkware. $225-250. Beware: this stringholder is being reproduced.

Right: Courtesy of the Miller Studio Catalog archives.

M98 Prince Pineapple
RETIRED JAN. 53

SH-229: Tomato, Japan, ceramic. $35-55.

SH-230: Strawberry with white flower and green leaves, chalkware. The original sticker reads "Genuine Hand Painted, Devon Ware, Made In Canada." $35-55.

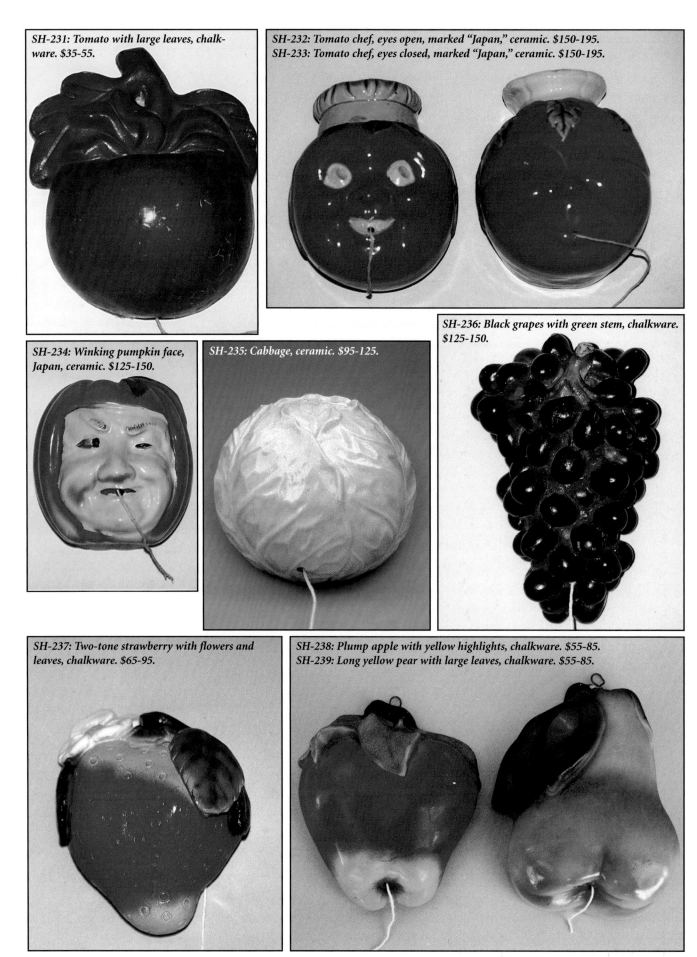

SH-231: Tomato with large leaves, chalk-ware. $35-55.

SH-232: Tomato chef, eyes open, marked "Japan," ceramic. $150-195.
SH-233: Tomato chef, eyes closed, marked "Japan," ceramic. $150-195.

SH-236: Black grapes with green stem, chalkware. $125-150.

SH-234: Winking pumpkin face, Japan, ceramic. $125-150.

SH-235: Cabbage, ceramic. $95-125.

SH-237: Two-tone strawberry with flowers and leaves, chalkware. $65-95.

SH-238: Plump apple with yellow highlights, chalkware. $55-85.
SH-239: Long yellow pear with large leaves, chalkware. $55-85.

❖ People Stringholders
Black Memorabilia

The popularity of collecting vintage Black memorabilia continues to rise. Stringholders are among the most coveted items. While the older stringholders are the more valuable, do not overlook some of the newer models.

❖ Black Men

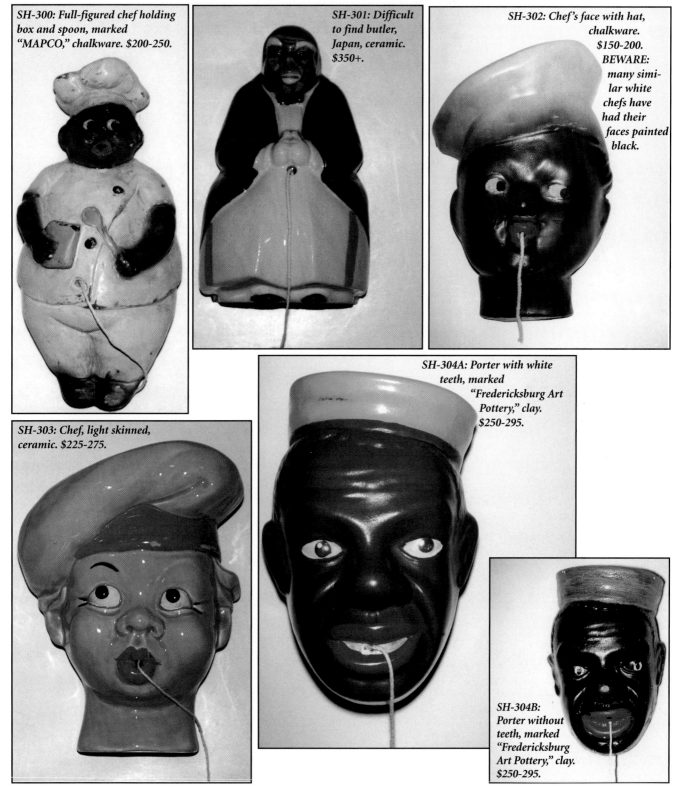

SH-300: Full-figured chef holding box and spoon, marked "MAPCO," chalkware. $200-250.

SH-301: Difficult to find butler, Japan, ceramic. $350+.

SH-302: Chef's face with hat, chalkware. $150-200. BEWARE: many similar white chefs have had their faces painted black.

SH-303: Chef, light skinned, ceramic. $225-275.

SH-304A: Porter with white teeth, marked "Fredericksburg Art Pottery," clay. $250-295.

SH-304B: Porter without teeth, marked "Fredericksburg Art Pottery," clay. $250-295.

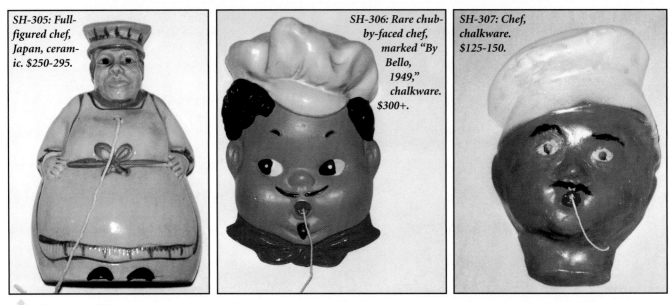

SH-305: Full-figured chef, Japan, ceramic. $250-295.

SH-306: Rare chubby-faced chef, marked "By Bello, 1949," chalkware. $300+.

SH-307: Chef, chalkware. $125-150.

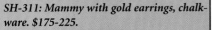

❖ Black Women

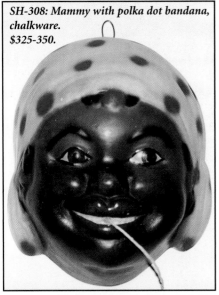

SH-308: Mammy with polka dot bandana, chalkware. $325-350.

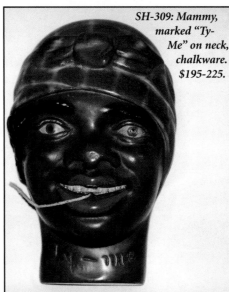

SH-309: Mammy, marked "Ty-Me" on neck, chalkware. $195-225.

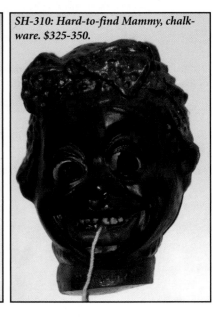

SH-310: Hard-to-find Mammy, chalkware. $325-350.

SH-311: Mammy with gold earrings, chalkware. $175-225.

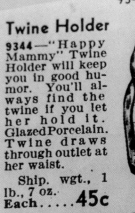

SH-312: Mammy, plaid and polka dot dress, Japan, ceramic. $125-175.

Below: Fall & Winter 1937 Herrschner Company Catalog, Chicago, IL.

9344   45ᶜ

Twine Holder

9344—"Happy Mammy" Twine Holder will keep you in good humor. You'll always find the twine if you let her hold it. Glazed Porcelain. Twine draws through outlet at her waist.

Ship. wgt., 1 lb., 7 oz.
Each.....**45c**

SH-313: Full-figured Mammy holding ball of twine, marked "Nadine Wenden, made in U.S.A., 1941," composition. REPRODUCTION ALERT: A resin copy, painted red and wearing a yellow bandana, is now selling in a mail order catalog for $32. $150-195.

SH-314A/314B: Although these Mammies appear to be the same mold with different paint combinations, notice the size difference, chalkware. $175-225.

SH-314C: This version appears to be white, chalkware. $175-225.

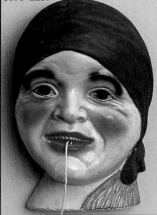

TWINE HOLDERS
3 styles, aver. 7 in. high, asstd. Dutch girl, mammy and chef, colorfully painted. '90R-8215—1 doz. in carton, 20 lbs. Not stocked Baltimore
Doz 2.00

Butler Brothers catalog - Spring 1940.

SH-315: Mammy wearing blue and yellow bandana, chalkware. $175-225.

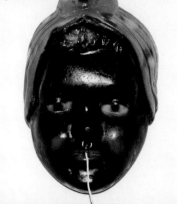

SH-316: Full-figured Mammy holding sock, ceramic. $250-295.
SH-317: Full-figured Mammy holding flowers, Japan, ceramic. $150-195.

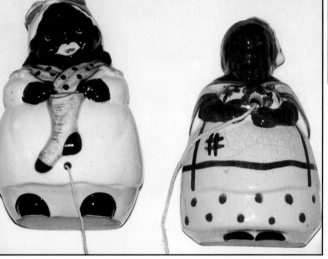

SH-318: Young girl with surprised look, Japan, ceramic. $250-295.

SH-319A: Full-figured Mammy holding flowers, marked "MAPCO," chalkware. $250-295.

SH-319B: Full-figured Mammy holding flowers with potholder hooks, chalkware. $250-295.

SH-320: Full-figured mammy with arms up, ceramic. $195-250. Compare the original (left) to the reproduction on the right. The primary noticeable difference is the deeper grooves in the original Mammy's skirt.

SH-321: Luzianne Mammy, newer vintage, ceramic. $35-55.

SH-322: Newer vintage full-figured Mammy with cake, marked "Adrian Pottery," ceramic. $35-55.

SH-323: Rare cloth-faced Mammy, includes card that says, "I'm smiling Jane, so glad I came, to tie your things, with nice white strings," marked "Simone." $150-195.

SH-324: Full-figured cloth Mammy, "My name is Handy Mandy, for string I am just dandy." $65-85.

MY NAME IS
HANDY MANDY
FOR STRING I AM
JUST DANDY

SH-325: Child, cloth and wood. $50-75.

SH-326: Mammy, cloth and wood. $50-75.

Gift & Art Buyer, February 1937. This trade magazine reflects wholesale prices.

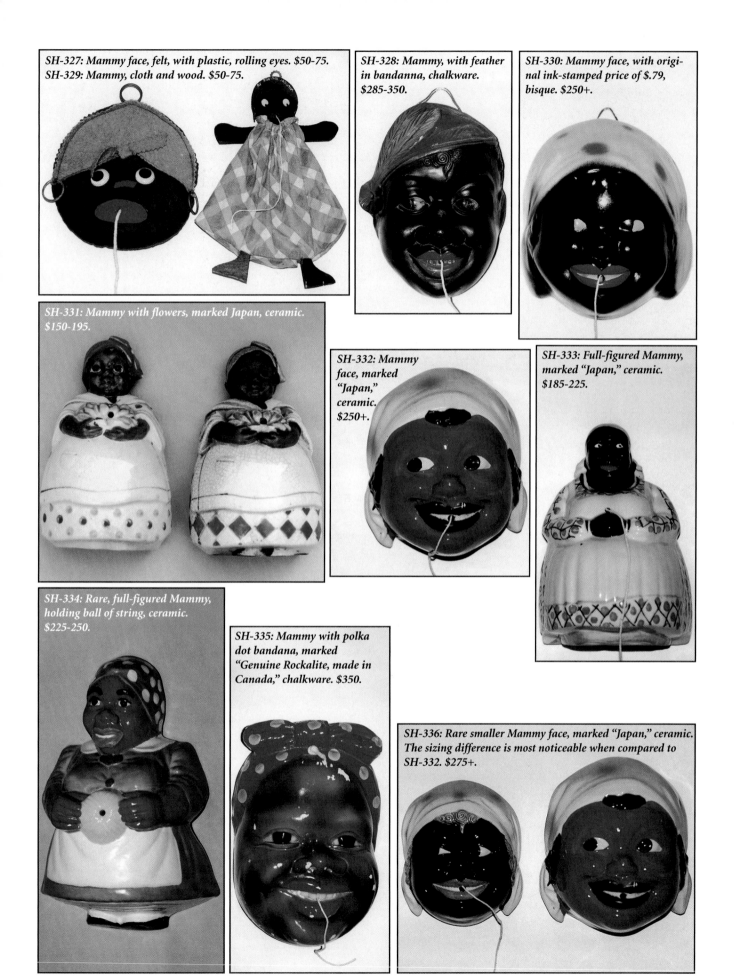

SH-327: Mammy face, felt, with plastic, rolling eyes. $50-75.
SH-329: Mammy, cloth and wood. $50-75.

SH-328: Mammy, with feather in bandanna, chalkware. $285-350.

SH-330: Mammy face, with original ink-stamped price of $.79, bisque. $250+.

SH-331: Mammy with flowers, marked Japan, ceramic. $150-195.

SH-332: Mammy face, marked "Japan," ceramic. $250+.

SH-333: Full-figured Mammy, marked "Japan," ceramic. $185-225.

SH-334: Rare, full-figured Mammy, holding ball of string, ceramic. $225-250.

SH-335: Mammy with polka dot bandana, marked "Genuine Rockalite, made in Canada," chalkware. $350.

SH-336: Rare smaller Mammy face, marked "Japan," ceramic. The sizing difference is most noticeable when compared to SH-332. $275+.

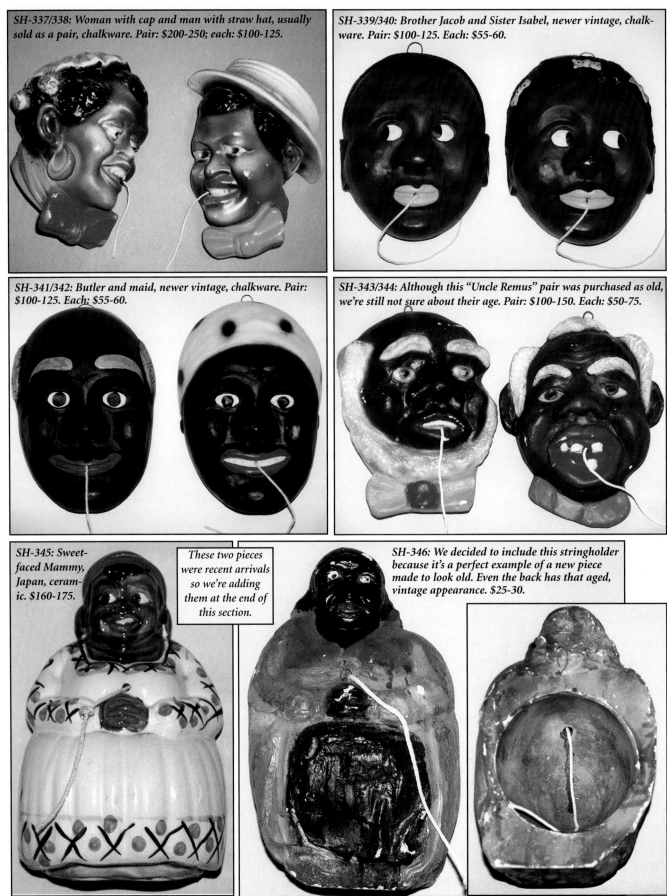

SH-337/338: Woman with cap and man with straw hat, usually sold as a pair, chalkware. Pair: $200-250; each: $100-125.

SH-339/340: Brother Jacob and Sister Isabel, newer vintage, chalkware. Pair: $100-125. Each: $55-60.

SH-341/342: Butler and maid, newer vintage, chalkware. Pair: $100-125. Each: $55-60.

SH-343/344: Although this "Uncle Remus" pair was purchased as old, we're still not sure about their age. Pair: $100-150. Each: $50-75.

SH-345: Sweet-faced Mammy, Japan, ceramic. $160-175.

These two pieces were recent arrivals so we're adding them at the end of this section.

SH-346: We decided to include this stringholder because it's a perfect example of a new piece made to look old. Even the back has that aged, vintage appearance. $25-30.

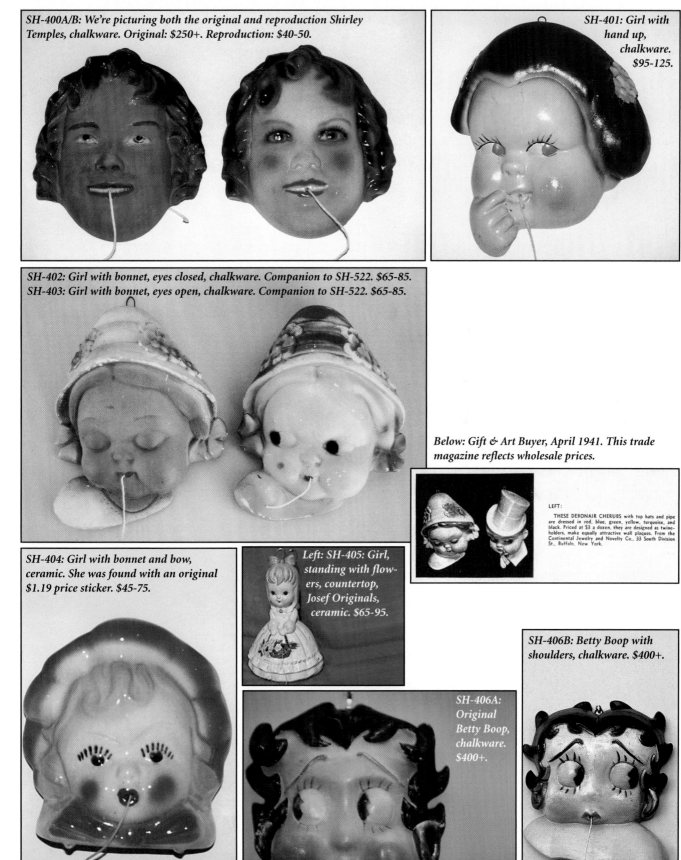

SH-400A/B: We're picturing both the original and reproduction Shirley Temples, chalkware. Original: $250+. Reproduction: $40-50.

SH-401: Girl with hand up, chalkware. $95-125.

SH-402: Girl with bonnet, eyes closed, chalkware. Companion to SH-522. $65-85.
SH-403: Girl with bonnet, eyes open, chalkware. Companion to SH-522. $65-85.

Below: Gift & Art Buyer, April 1941. This trade magazine reflects wholesale prices.

LEFT:
THESE DEBONAIR CHERUBS with top hats and pipe are dressed in red, blue, green, yellow, turquoise, and black. Priced at $3 a dozen, they are designed as twine-holders, make equally attractive wall plaques. From the Continental Jewelry and Novelty Co., 33 South Division St., Buffalo, New York.

SH-404: Girl with bonnet and bow, ceramic. She was found with an original $1.19 price sticker. $45-75.

Left: SH-405: Girl, standing with flowers, countertop, Josef Originals, ceramic. $65-95.

SH-406B: Betty Boop with shoulders, chalkware. $400+.

SH-406A: Original Betty Boop, chalkware. $400+.

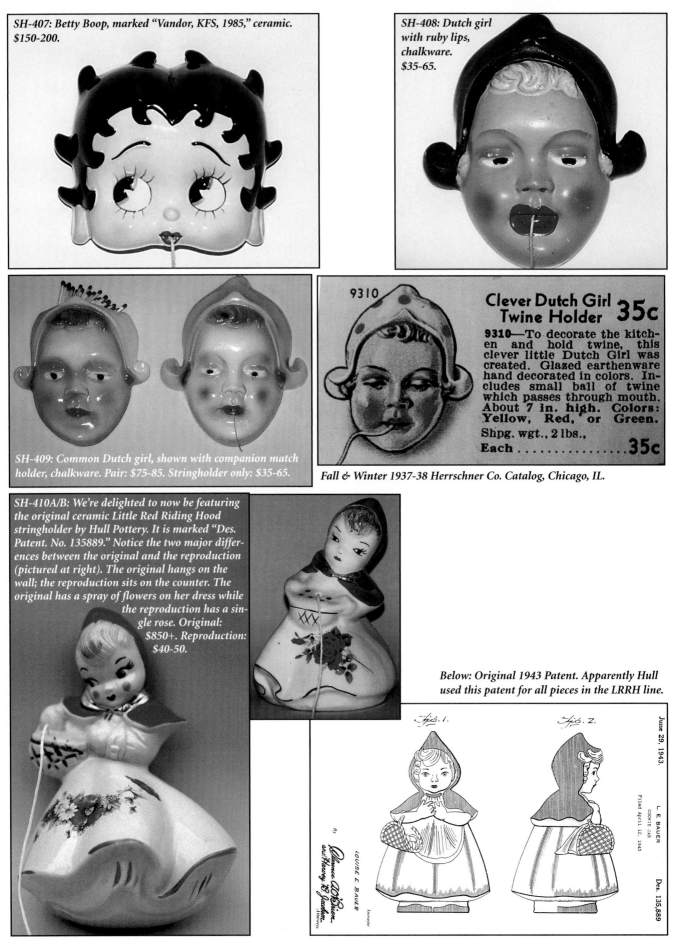

SH-407: Betty Boop, marked "Vandor, KFS, 1985," ceramic. $150-200.

SH-408: Dutch girl with ruby lips, chalkware. $35-65.

SH-409: Common Dutch girl, shown with companion match holder, chalkware. Pair: $75-85. Stringholder only: $35-65.

9310

Clever Dutch Girl Twine Holder 35c

9310—To decorate the kitchen and hold twine, this clever little Dutch Girl was created. Glazed earthenware hand decorated in colors. Includes small ball of twine which passes through mouth. About 7 in. high. Colors: Yellow, Red, or Green. Shpg. wgt., 2 lbs.,
Each 35c

Fall & Winter 1937-38 Herrschner Co. Catalog, Chicago, IL.

SH-410A/B: We're delighted to now be featuring the original ceramic Little Red Riding Hood stringholder by Hull Pottery. It is marked "Des. Patent. No. 135889." Notice the two major differences between the original and the reproduction (pictured at right). The original hangs on the wall; the reproduction sits on the counter. The original has a spray of flowers on her dress while the reproduction has a single rose. Original: $850+. Reproduction: $40-50.

Below: Original 1943 Patent. Apparently Hull used this patent for all pieces in the LRRH line.

June 29, 1943.

L. E. BAUER
COOKIE JAR
Filed April 12, 1943

Des. 135,889

LOUISE E. BAUER

Fig. 1.   Fig. 2.

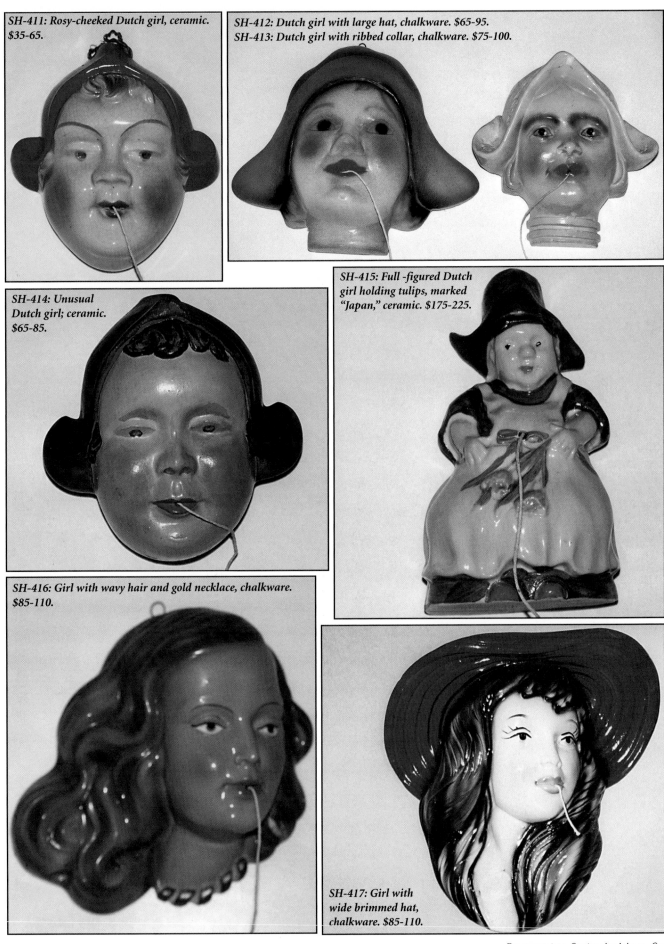

SH-411: Rosy-cheeked Dutch girl, ceramic. $35-65.

SH-412: Dutch girl with large hat, chalkware. $65-95.
SH-413: Dutch girl with ribbed collar, chalkware. $75-100.

SH-414: Unusual Dutch girl; ceramic. $65-85.

SH-415: Full-figured Dutch girl holding tulips, marked "Japan," ceramic. $175-225.

SH-416: Girl with wavy hair and gold necklace, chalkware. $85-110.

SH-417: Girl with wide brimmed hat, chalkware. $85-110.

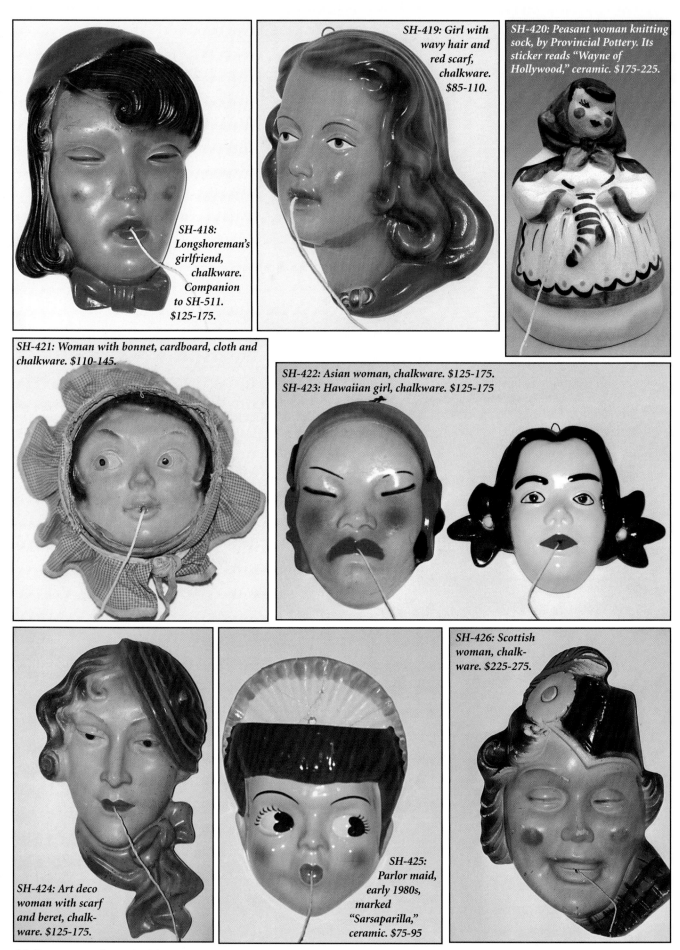

SH-418: Longshoreman's girlfriend, chalkware. Companion to SH-511. $125-175.

SH-419: Girl with wavy hair and red scarf, chalkware. $85-110.

SH-420: Peasant woman knitting sock, by Provincial Pottery. Its sticker reads "Wayne of Hollywood," ceramic. $175-225.

SH-421: Woman with bonnet, cardboard, cloth and chalkware. $110-145.

SH-422: Asian woman, chalkware. $125-175.
SH-423: Hawaiian girl, chalkware. $125-175

SH-426: Scottish woman, chalkware. $225-275.

SH-424: Art deco woman with scarf and beret, chalkware. $125-175.

SH-425: Parlor maid, early 1980s, marked "Sarsaparilla," ceramic. $75-95

SH-427: Little "White" Riding Hood, marked "Universal Statuary Co., Artist Bello," chalkware. Also found in red and blue. $225-275.

SH-428: Art deco woman with golden hair, chalkware. $85-110.

SH-429/ 430: Art deco women, chalkware. $85-110.

SH-433: Woman with fancy bonnet, chalkware. $95-135.

SH-431: Victorian woman, ceramic. $45-65.

SH-432: Prayer Lady by Enesco, ceramic. $200-300.

SH-434: English maid, Japan, ceramic. $95-125.

SH-435: Woman with arched eyebrows, ceramic. $135-175.

SH-436: *Full-figured woman with flowered dress. Also found in yellow and green, ceramic. $95-125.*
SH-437: *Bride, marked "Japan," ceramic. $75-125.*

SH-438: *Victorian woman sitting in chair, marked "Japan," ceramic. $75-95.*

SH-439: *"Sailor Girl," commonly known as "Rosie the Riveter" by collectors, chalkware. Companion to SH-515. $135-175*

Here are a few of our fast selling novelties

For our Complete Line of Gift Goods, see our Pricelist B sent to any Gift Shop on application.

Three Stringholder Wallplacques, Most Attractively Colored

Made of terra cotta composition.

No. 4385B Sailor Boy   No. 4386B Sailor Girl   No. 4279B Apple

5 ¾ inches x 7 ¼ inches, 2 ¾ inches deep. 12 lbs. to the doz. Packed ½ doz. in box. $9.00 per doz. In 3 doz. lots $8.40 per doz.

6 ¼ x 7 ¾ inches, 3 ¾ inches deep, 15 lbs. to the doz. $9.00 per doz. In 3 doz lots $8.40 per doz.

7 inches wide, 7 inches long, 3 inches deep. 12 lbs. to the doz. Packed ½ doz. in box. $7.80 per doz. In 3 doz. lots $7.20 per doz.

Gift & Art Buyer, February 1945. This trade magazine reflects wholesale prices.

SH-440: *Bride with bridesmaids, marked "Japan," ceramic. $75-125.*
SH-442: *Groom with bridesmaids, marked "Japan," ceramic. $75-125.*

.25

Imported earthenware twine holders, pierced for hanging with inside construction to hold ball of twine and small aperture in front for end of string. Cost $1.65 per dozen in case lots of 18 dozen—delivery from stock in New York.

Pottery, Glass & Brass Salesman, November 1939. This trade magazine reflects wholesale prices.

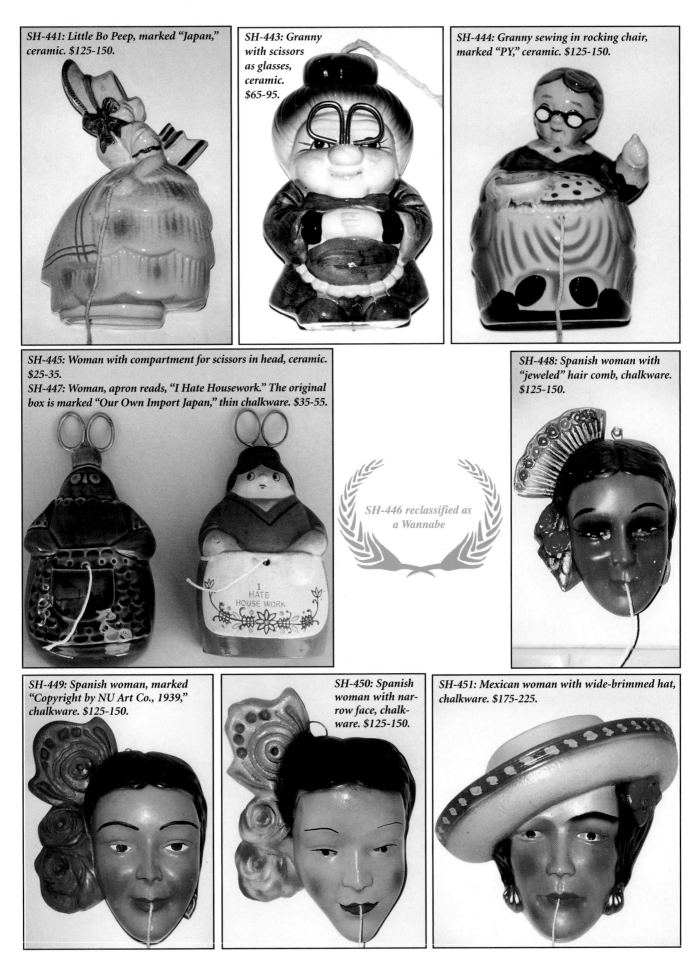

SH-441: Little Bo Peep, marked "Japan," ceramic. $125-150.

SH-443: Granny with scissors as glasses, ceramic. $65-95.

SH-444: Granny sewing in rocking chair, marked "PY," ceramic. $125-150.

SH-445: Woman with compartment for scissors in head, ceramic. $25-35.

SH-447: Woman, apron reads, "I Hate Housework." The original box is marked "Our Own Import Japan," thin chalkware. $35-55.

I HATE HOUSE WORK

SH-446 reclassified as a Wannabe

SH-448: Spanish woman with "jeweled" hair comb, chalkware. $125-150.

SH-449: Spanish woman, marked "Copyright by NU Art Co., 1939," chalkware. $125-150.

SH-450: Spanish woman with nar-row face, chalk-ware. $125-150.

SH-451: Mexican woman with wide-brimmed hat, chalkware. $175-225.

SH-452: Mexican woman wearing pointy sombrero, chalkware. $175-225.

SH-453 reclassified as a Wannabe

SH-454: Mexican woman with sombrero, marked "© The Universal Stat. Co., copyright 1941," chalkware. $75-100
SH-455: Mexican woman with braids and sombrero, chalkware. $125-150.

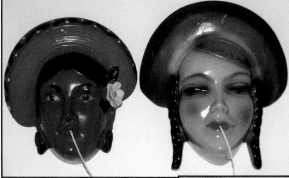

SH-456/457: Pirate couple. Found in an old sewing box filled with thin balls of sewing thread, marked "M & N Novelty Co., N.Y.C., U.S.A.," composition. Each: $65- 85.

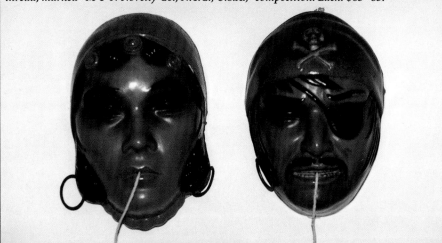

MEXICAN TWINE HOLDERS

2 Styles—8 in., composition, asstd. Mexican Man and Mexican Girl, colorfully decorated.
90R-8307—1 doz in carton, 16½ lbs.
Doz 2.00

Right: Butler Brothers catalog - Spring 1940.

SH-458: Lady in apron wearing glasses, ceramic. $40-60.

SH-459: German lady, hand-painted, wood. $40-50.

little twine girl in Figure 24 will help you reform quickly and painlessly, for she conceals beneath her voluminous decorative skirts a ball of twine which is inserted from the base and may be pulled out, as needed, through the flower basket she carries on her arm. Another service which she renders gladly is to hold securely a ball of wool for knitting, so that it cannot roll away, and although playful kittens will grieve at being deprived of a favorite sport, the knitter herself will welcome such a convenience. The little figure is made of wood, 6″ high; she has sunshiny yellow hair and a gay colored dress —

Fig. 24

pale green, soft blue, or rose — and she costs but $2.75, postpaid, without the twine. — RENA ROSENTHAL, 520 Madison Avenue, N. Y. C.

Mary Jackson Lee

Right: House Beautiful, June 1931.

SH-500: *Frowning baby, chalkware. $225-275.*

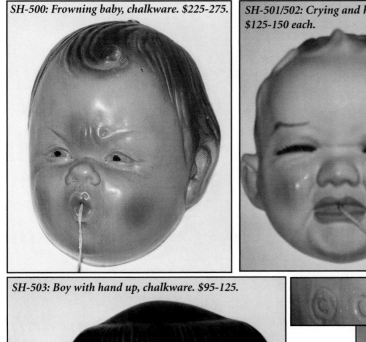

SH-501/502: *Crying and happy babies, marked "Lefton," early 1950s, ceramic. $125-150 each.*

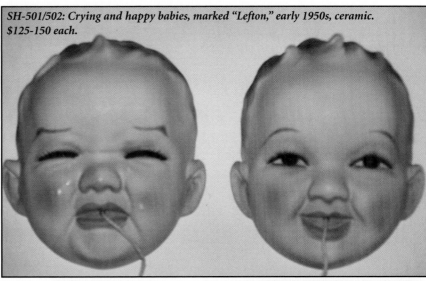

SH-503: *Boy with hand up, chalkware. $95-125.*

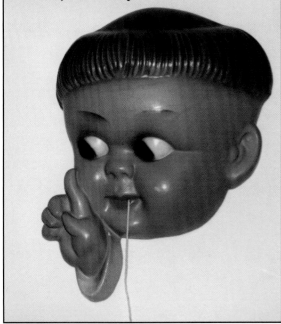

SH-504: *Campbell's Soup boy, chalkware, $350+. The Campbell copyright mark is embossed under the chin.*

Right: Gift & Art Buyer, February 1939. This trade magazine reflects wholesale prices.

SH-505/506/507: *Variety of Mexican men with sombreros, marked "© The Universal Stat. Co., copyright 1941," chalkware. $55-75.*

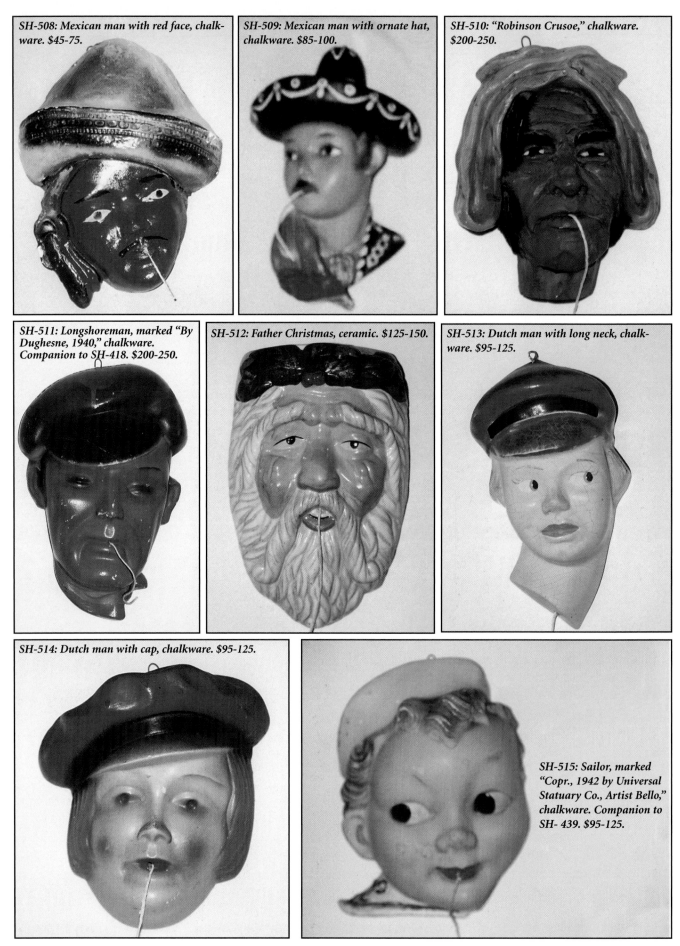

SH-508: *Mexican man with red face, chalk-ware. $45-75.*

SH-509: *Mexican man with ornate hat, chalkware. $85-100.*

SH-510: *"Robinson Crusoe," chalkware. $200-250.*

SH-511: *Longshoreman, marked "By Dughesne, 1940," chalkware. Companion to SH-418. $200-250.*

SH-512: *Father Christmas, ceramic. $125-150.*

SH-513: *Dutch man with long neck, chalk-ware. $95-125.*

SH-514: *Dutch man with cap, chalkware. $95-125.*

SH-515: *Sailor, marked "Copr., 1942 by Universal Statuary Co., Artist Bello," chalkware. Companion to SH- 439. $95-125.*

SH-516: Soldier with pipe, chalkware. $45-65.
SH-517: Soldier without pipe, chalkware. $45-65.

SH-518: Oriental man, marked "Japan," ceramic. $175-225.

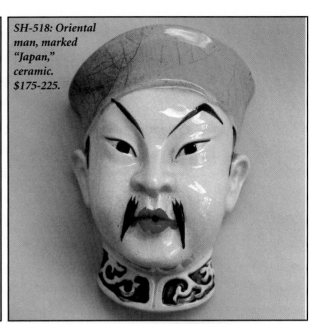

SH-519: Oriental man with coolie hat, marked "Abingdon," ceramic. $175-225.
SH-520: 'Drunk' man designed by and marked "Elsa," ceramic. Although this was originally thought to be a product of Pfaltzgraff, there is no accurate information to substantiate this claim. $95-135.

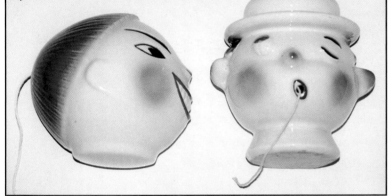

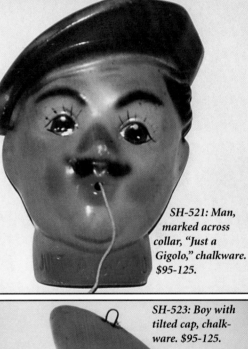

SH-521: Man, marked across collar, "Just a Gigolo," chalkware. $95-125.

SH-522: Boy with top hat and pipe, signed "H. Belo," chalkware. Companion to SH-402 and SH-403. $45-65.

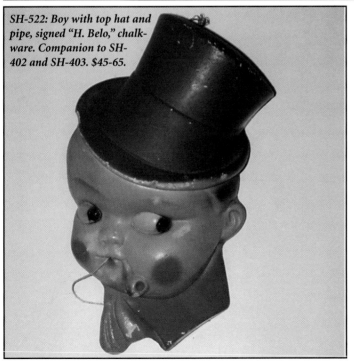

SH-523: Boy with tilted cap, chalkware. $95-125.

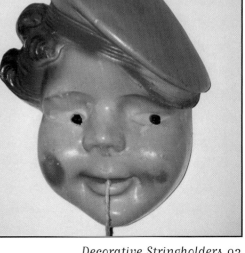

SH-524: Indian with headband, chalkware. $225-250.

SH-525: Indian chief with headdress, chalkware. $225-250.

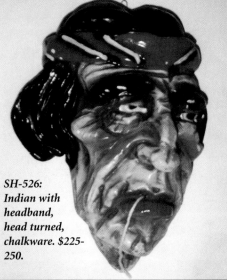

SH-526: Indian with headband, head turned, chalkware. $225-250.

SH-527: Rare sailor man, chalkware. $225-275.

SH-528: Indian chief with headdress and full collar, chalkware. $225-250.

SH-529: "Pancho Villa," chalkware. $250-275.

Right: SH-530: "Fred the Flour Man," top unscrews to put in the string, marked "Spillers," plastic. He's part of a complete line of accessories issued by the English company Homepride Flour. See companion pie bird, PB-160, on page 45. $55-65.

SH-600: Boy with chef's hat, chalkware. $175-225.

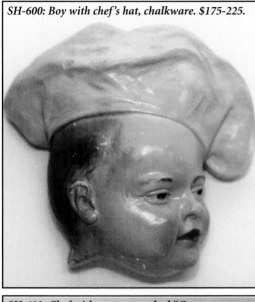

SH-601: Whimsical chef, composition. $145-175.

SH-602: Chef with rolling pin, marked "Nadine Wenden, 1941, Made in USA," composition. $65-95.

SH-603: Chef with goatee, marked "Conover Originals, 1945," chalkware. $125-175.

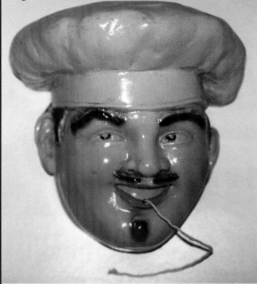

SH-605: Chef with rolling pin and potholders, chalkware. $65-95.

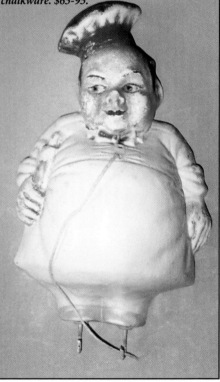

SH-604/606: Smaller version of the same chef, marked "Japan," ceramic. $75-100.

SH-607: "Little Chef," Miller Studio, 1950, chalkware. $175-225.

WALL PLAQUES

ANOTHER PAIR OF MILLER ORIGINAL

STRINGHOLDERS

M99 Miss Strawberry

7 inches high
Individually boxed
with string included
$6.00 per dozen

M100 Little Chef

CATALOG SENT ON REQUEST

miller studio

DESIGNERS AND MANUFACTURERS
BOX 228   NEW PHILADELPHIA, OHIO

Above: Gift & Art Buyer, March 1950. This trade magazine reflects wholesale prices.

SH-608: Chef with glass and bottle, Japan, ceramic. $175-225.

SH-609: Chef with scissors holder in head, marked "Gift Ideas Creation, Phila, Pa.," ceramic. $35-65.

SH-610: Chef with bushy eyebrows, marked "Made in Japan," ceramic. $65-95.

SH-611: Common chef with polka dot hat, chalkware, ca. 1939. $45-65.

SH-612: Common chef, chalkware. $45-65.

SH-613: Unusual chalkware version of chef with bushy eyebrows, smaller than SH-610. $95-125.

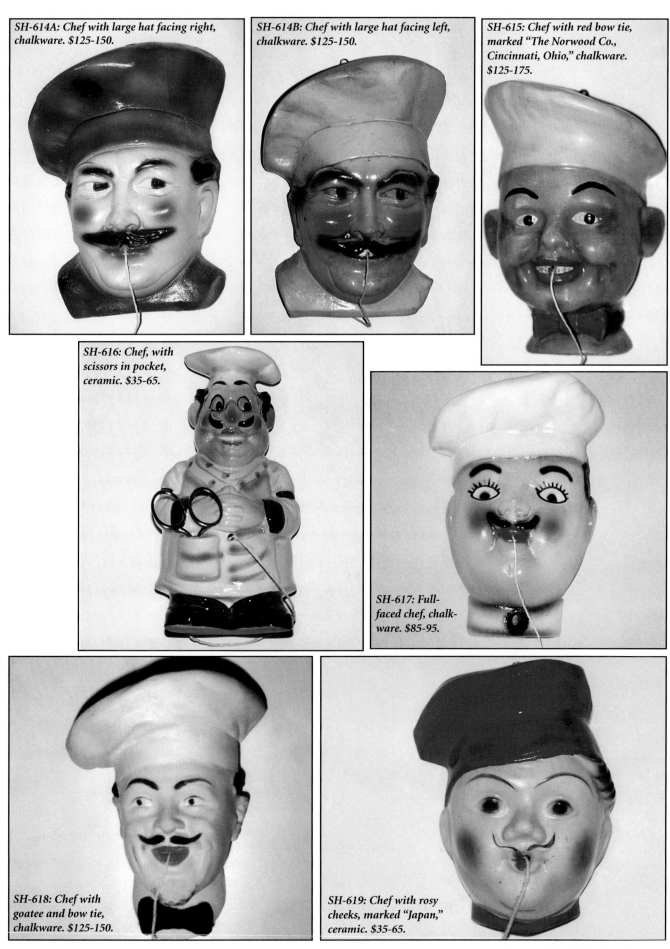

SH-614A: Chef with large hat facing right, chalkware. $125-150.

SH-614B: Chef with large hat facing left, chalkware. $125-150.

SH-615: Chef with red bow tie, marked "The Norwood Co., Cincinnati, Ohio," chalkware. $125-175.

SH-616: Chef, with scissors in pocket, ceramic. $35-65.

SH-617: Full-faced chef, chalkware. $85-95.

SH-618: Chef with goatee and bow tie, chalkware. $125-150.

SH-619: Chef with rosy cheeks, marked "Japan," ceramic. $35-65.

Decorative Stringholders 97

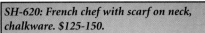

SH-620: *French chef with scarf on neck, chalkware. $125-150.*

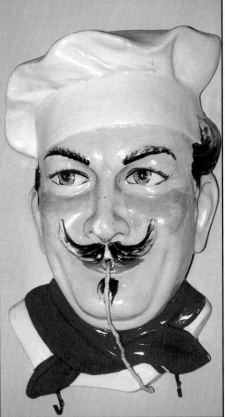

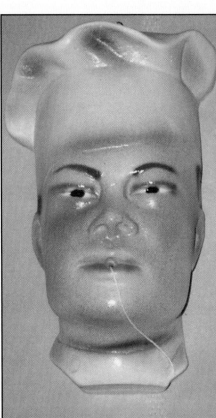

SH-621: *Pug-nosed chef, chalkware. $125-150.*

SH-622: *Robust-faced chef, string pulls from collar, chalkware. $150-175.*

SH-623: *Rotund chef, marked "Fitz and Floyd, ©MCMLXXXFF," ceramic. $45-65.*

SH-624: *Chef holding "String Saver" towel, chalkware. $55-65.*

SH-625: *Newer vintage French chef with compartment for scissors in head, ceramic. $35-40.*

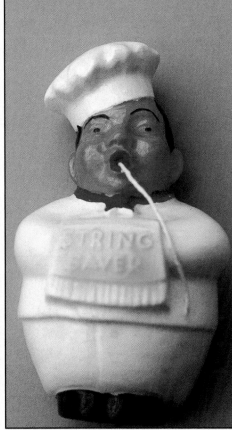

SH-700: *Feathered tulip, chalkware.* $125-175.

SH-701: *Wooden box with flowers and poem.* $35-65.

STRING.
WASTE NOT YOUR TIME
BUT STRING ALONG WITH ME
YOU'LL FIND ME VERY HANDY
WHEN YOU'RE BUSY AS A BEE

SH-702: *Wooden teapot with chef decal.* $35-65.

SH-703: *Rose, chalk-ware.* $125-150.

SH-704: *Teapot with parakeet, Japan, ceramic.* $85-125.

SH-705: *Stringholder with Oriental person, ceramic.* $85-125.

ME UNTWINEY TWINE

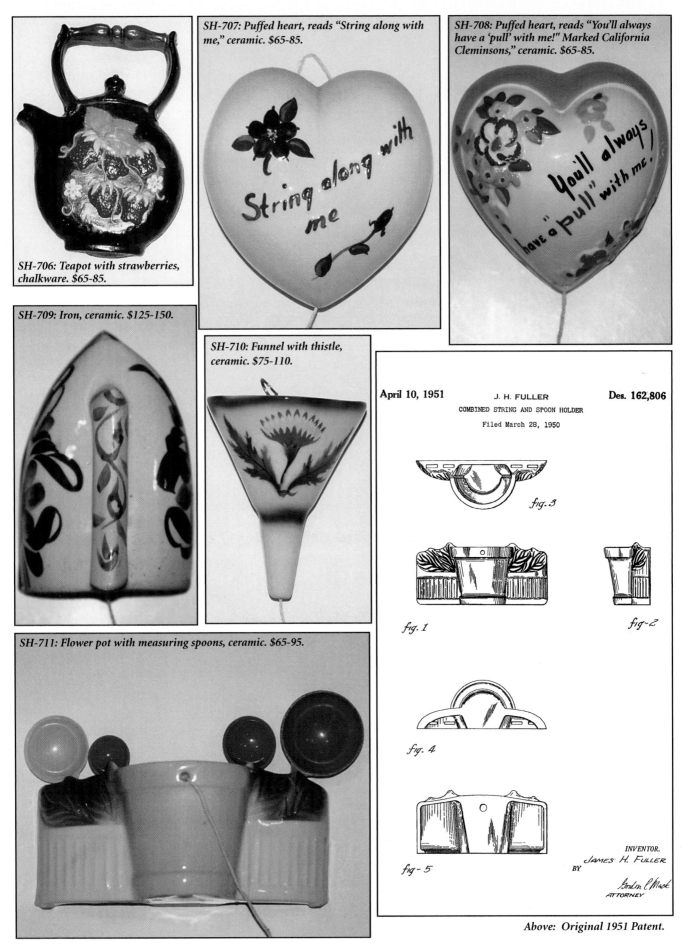

SH-706: Teapot with strawberries, chalkware. $65-85.

SH-707: Puffed heart, reads "String along with me," ceramic. $65-85.

SH-708: Puffed heart, reads "You'll always have a 'pull' with me!" Marked California Cleminsons," ceramic. $65-85.

SH-709: Iron, ceramic. $125-150.

SH-710: Funnel with thistle, ceramic. $75-110.

SH-711: Flower pot with measuring spoons, ceramic. $65-95.

April 10, 1951   J. H. FULLER   Des. 162,806
COMBINED STRING AND SPOON HOLDER
Filed March 28, 1950

fig. 3

fig. 1   fig. 2

fig. 4

fig. 5

INVENTOR.
JAMES H. FULLER
BY
Gordon C Mack
ATTORNEY

Above: Original 1951 Patent.

SH-712: *Funnel with cat and yarn, ceramic.* $75-110.

SH-713: *Ivy covered bowl, ceramic.* $30-50.

SH-714: *"Pumpkin Cottage," countertop, marked "Manorware, England," pottery.* $45-75.

SH-715: *Thatched-roof cottage, ceramic.* $45-75.

SH-716: *House, reads "Friends from afar and nearabout will find our Latchstring always out!" California Cleminsons, ceramic.* $125-150.

SH-717: *Balls of twine, chalkware, ca. 1944.* $35-75.

SH-718: *Single balloon, ceramic.* $35-65. SH-719: *Bunch of balloons, marked "FF © Fitz and Floyd, 1983," ceramic.* $45-75.

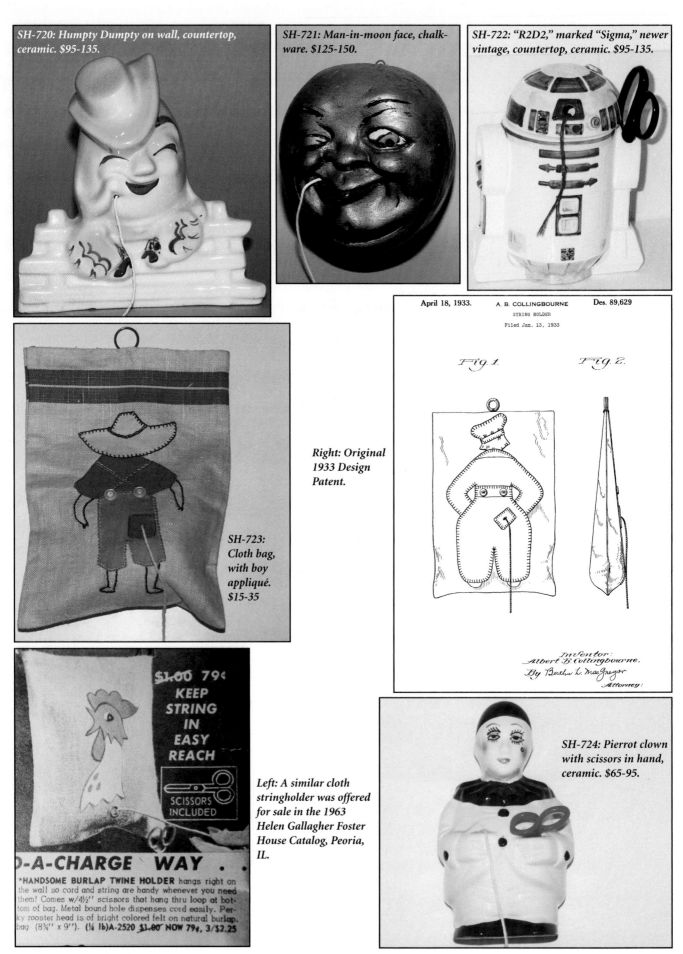

SH-720: *Humpty Dumpty on wall, countertop, ceramic. $95-135.*

SH-721: *Man-in-moon face, chalkware. $125-150.*

SH-722: *"R2D2," marked "Sigma," newer vintage, countertop, ceramic. $95-135.*

April 18, 1933.   A. B. COLLINGBOURNE   Des. 89,629

STRING HOLDER

Filed Jan. 13, 1933

Fig. 1.   *Fig. 2.*

Inventor:
Albert B. Collingbourne,
By Bertha L. MacGregor
Attorney:

Right: Original 1933 Design Patent.

SH-723: *Cloth bag, with boy appliqué. $15-35*

$1.00 79¢
KEEP
STRING
IN
EASY
REACH

SCISSORS
INCLUDED

O-A-CHARGE WAY . .

HANDSOME BURLAP TWINE HOLDER hangs right on the wall so cord and string are handy whenever you need them! Comes w/4½'' scissors that hang thru loop at bottom of bag. Metal bound hole dispenses cord easily. Perky rooster head is of bright colored felt on natural burlap. bag (8¾'' x 9''). (¼ lb)A-2520 $1.00 NOW 79¢, 3/$2.25

Left: A similar cloth stringholder was offered for sale in the 1963 Helen Gallagher Foster House Catalog, Peoria, IL.

SH-724: *Pierrot clown with scissors in hand, ceramic. $65-95.*

SH-725A/B: Court jester, found in many color combinations, chalkware. Notice the difference in size between the two pieces. $125-150.

SH-726: "Jo-Jo" the clown, Miller Studio, 1948, chalkware. $175-225.

SH-727 reclassified as a Wannabe

SH-728: Clown, with cloth-ruffled collar and hat, ceramic. $100-135.

RETIRED JAN. 1950
M 97 Jo-Jo the Clown

Courtesy of the Miller Studio Catalog archives.

SH-729: "The Darned String Caddy," marked "Fitz and Floyd, MCMLXXVI," ceramic. $35-55.

SH-730: Notice that the ruffle on this 6" court jester does not surround the entire head and the facial features are more pronounced than SH-725A&B, chalkware. $225-250.

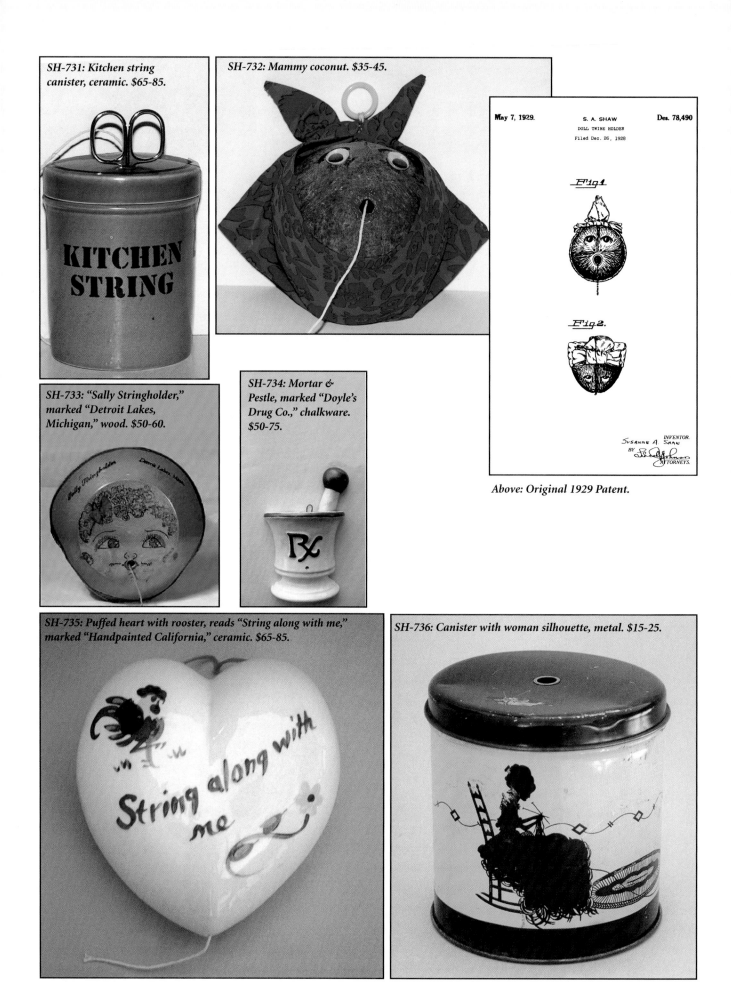

SH-731: Kitchen string canister, ceramic. $65-85.

KITCHEN STRING

SH-732: Mammy coconut. $35-45.

May 7, 1929.
S. A. SHAW
Des. 78,490
DOLL TWINE HOLDER
Filed Dec. 26, 1928

Fig.1.

Fig.2.

INVENTOR.
SUSANNE A. SHAW
BY
ATTORNEYS.

Above: Original 1929 Patent.

SH-733: "Sally Stringholder," marked "Detroit Lakes, Michigan," wood. $50-60.

SH-734: Mortar & Pestle, marked "Doyle's Drug Co.," chalkware. $50-75.

RX

SH-735: Puffed heart with rooster, reads "String along with me," marked "Handpainted California," ceramic. $65-85.

String along with me

SH-736: Canister with woman silhouette, metal. $15-25.

❖ Recent Arrival Stringholders

Who knew we would write another book ... certainly not us! As a result, in some sections we just continued the numbering system without any thought about adding more stringholders to that category at a later date. So we created "Recent Arrivals" to accommodate these additional pieces.

SH-800: Chicken, resembles Quimper SH-104, ceramic. $45-55.

SH-801: French chicken with scissors in tail, ceramic. $95-125.

SH-802: Sitting cat with ball of string, marked "Lorrie Design, Japan," composition. $25-35.

SH-803: Cat head, chalkware, newer vintage. $30-40.

SH-804: Warner Bros. Studios issued this Tweety & Sylvester stringholder a few years ago. It originally sold for $12.99, ceramic. $20-30.

SH-805: Fish with scissors in tail, ceramic. $45-65.

SH-806: Bulging-eyed bulldog, thin chalkware. $160-175.

SH-807: Bulldog profile, ceramic. $175-195.

SH-808: Hound dog, marked "Babbacombe Pottery, England," countertop, ceramic. $45-65.

SH-809: "Elsie the Cow," chalkware. $450.

SH-810: Elephant with scissors for glasses, marked "Babbacombe Pottery, England," countertop, ceramic. $45-65.

SH-811: Cat on haunches holding a ball of string, ceramic. $45-65.

SH-812: "String Mouse," pottery. $30-40.

SH-813: Cross-legged fishing frog, marked "Babbacombe Pottery, England," countertop, ceramic. $45-65.

Above: SH-814: Kangaroo, Josef Originals, chalkware. $35-45.

SH-815: Pig string and memo holder, marked "Holt Howard," ceramic. $65-75.

SH-816: Mouse, marked "Abingdon USA," pottery. $250-275.

SH-817: Pink pig, hanger or countertop, ceramic. $40-50.

SH-818: White elephant, ceramic. $30-40.

❖ Wannabe Stringholders

The popularity of decorative stringholders has dramatically increased in the last few years. As with so many collectibles, trying to distinguish the authentic versions has become difficult. The following are presented as stringholder "Wannabes." However, as so many of these items were mass-produced by machine, it could be possible that some were made into stringholders, while others from the same mold were not. When purchasing a stringholder, check carefully around the hole where the string comes out. If the hole looks tampered with, it is different color than the area surrounding it, or if it just looks like it was drilled yesterday, be leery.

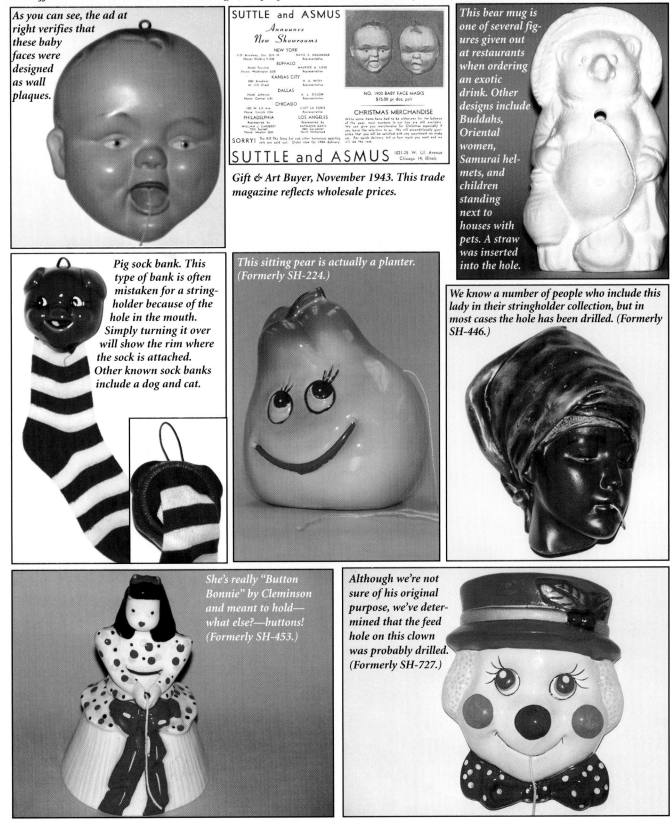

As you can see, the ad at right verifies that these baby faces were designed as wall plaques.

Gift & Art Buyer, November 1943. This trade magazine reflects wholesale prices.

This bear mug is one of several figures given out at restaurants when ordering an exotic drink. Other designs include Buddahs, Oriental women, Samurai helmets, and children standing next to houses with pets. A straw was inserted into the hole.

Pig sock bank. This type of bank is often mistaken for a stringholder because of the hole in the mouth. Simply turning it over will show the rim where the sock is attached. Other known sock banks include a dog and cat.

This sitting pear is actually a planter. (Formerly SH-224.)

We know a number of people who include this lady in their stringholder collection, but in most cases the hole has been drilled. (Formerly SH-446.)

She's really "Button Bonnie" by Cleminson and meant to hold—what else?—buttons! (Formerly SH-453.)

Although we're not sure of his original purpose, we've determined that the feed hole on this clown was probably drilled. (Formerly SH-727.)

United States Patent Office

Des. 198,469
Patented June 16, 1964

198,469

LAUNDRY SPRINKLER

Morris Friedman, New York, N.Y., and Andrey V. Mackey, Ambler, Pa., assignors to Minerware, Inc., New York, N.Y., a corporation of New York, and H.M.S. Associates Co., Willow Grove, Pa., a corporation of Pennsylvania

Filed Apr. 17, 1963, Ser. No. 74,488

Term of patent 14 years

(Cl. D49—1)

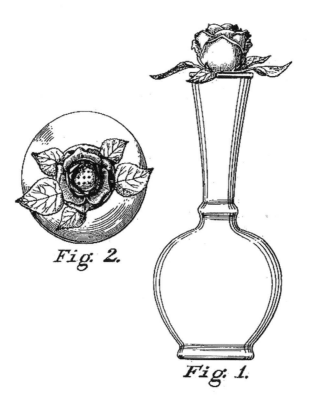

Fig. 2.

Fig. 1.

FIG. 1 is a side elevational view of a laundry sprinkler showing our new design; and

FIG. 2 is a top plan view of the laundry sprinkler of FIG. 1.

The side not shown is substantially the same as the side shown except as indicated.

We claim:

The ornamental design for a laundry sprinkler, substantially as shown.

References Cited in the file of this patent

UNITED STATES PATENTS

D. 102,768	Rossman	Jan. 19,	1937
273,666	Carleton	Mar. 6,	1883

OTHER REFERENCES

Tebor Crownford China, Rubel & Fenton, New York, received July 22, 1948, page 3, item 2021.

Tebor Crownford China, Rubel & Fenton, New York, received July 22, 1948, page 6, item 2003.

Housewares Review, May 1939, page 51, water sprinkler.

Original 1964 Patent for SB-806.

Laundry Sprinkler Bottles

A sprinkle on ironing day kept the wrinkles away … much to the delight of the diligent housewife! Of course that was in the days when household chores were relegated to specific days of the week—Monday was laundry, Tuesday was ironing … and so forth.

In the early to middle part of the twentieth century the average homemaker did just that—stayed at home and took care of the family. Their success and self-worth were often judged by their family's appearance. Remember June Cleaver? I'm sure Beaver's mom never let his father leave for work without a smoothly pressed, snowy white shirt and immaculate trousers with a sharp crease down the front. Imagine how tough it was to iron out the wrinkles after the wringing the clothes got in the old washer agitator. One of June's most trusted household helpers was probably the laundry sprinkler bottle.

Growing up in the 1950s, we remember thinking that our mothers were crazy—they ironed sheets, pillowcases, even dad's underwear and hankies. When we were old enough to be pressed into service (no pun intended), we were handed a soda bottle with a sprinkler top and told to dampen the clothing to get out the most difficult creases.

As baby boomers, we count ourselves lucky to have come of age during the reign of steam irons and polyester. You remember *that* miracle fabric—you could even sleep in your shirt and it still didn't need ironing. Fast-forward to the millennium where cotton and natural fibers are "in," the kind of materials that spawn wrinkles from merely hanging in the closet. So while we may no longer follow the household regimen of days gone by, ironing seems to be back in our routines, and in vogue—even some of the new irons have a retro look about them.

In a *Washington Post* article last year on the fine art of ironing, it offered this helpful suggestion, "Keep a spray bottle of water or a damp sponge on hand for spot dampening in case you accidentally iron in an unwanted crease." That's probably the same advice you'd find in the household hints column of a magazine from the 1930s or 1940s.

In the late 1940s and early 1950s, sprinkler bottles took on the shapes of irons, clothespins, elephants and humans. Although politically incorrect in the twenty-first century, the stereotype of the Oriental laundry boy produced by Cleminson and Cardinal China are probably the most affordable and plentiful figural sprinklers found in today's market. Conversely, the uniquely decorated homemade versions and the much sought after Emperors by Holland Mold are commanding high prices. The recent discovery of the Cardinal China Clothespin (SB-204) has been one of the most exciting finds in the world of laundry sprinklers. Ask any collector, however, and he or she will tell you that Cleminson's Fireman continues to be elusive, and remains in a class by itself.

In our first book, we only provided a few samples of the plastic sprinklers that gained prominence in the 1950s. We've expanded this section; for many people, the skyrocketing prices of the ceramics and older glass models have prompted an increased interest in plastics. Many collectors who once turned up their noses at these 1950s "upstarts" have finally accepted them as legitimate parts of their collection.

It seems that there is a direct correlation between the rise in sprinkler bottle prices and the number of "Wannabes" offered for sale. If a sprinkler top fits in the top of a fancy bottle, decorative decanter or even a vintage soda bottle, some people think the piece is magically transformed into a *bona fide* laundry sprinkler. Most purists don't want to clutter their collection with these "marriages," nor are they willing to pay the exorbitant price usually associated with such "rare" examples. Before you get all steamed up about being sold a "Wannabe," be sure to deal with only reputable sellers who stand behind their wares.

You will notice the large range in values for this chapter. That's because so many sprinkler bottles were homemade and the value is often dictated by the craftsmanship of the artist. Rather than provide an average, we decided to give you the full range you can expect to pay.

If you haven't purchased a laundry sprinkler bottle in the past, we hope this chapter will whet your appetite to sprinkle a few among your future collections.

❖ Animal Sprinkler Bottles

Cats

SB-100: The American Bisque Company cat has marble eyes, 7-1/2". $295-395.

SB-101: The Siamese cat on left is marked "Cardinal USA" and bears the original price tag of $.98. The others are unmarked. $150-200.

SB-102: These handmade Siamese cats (heights vary from 8" to 8-1/2") were all made from the same mold. Values are determined by skill and complexity of the decorative finish.

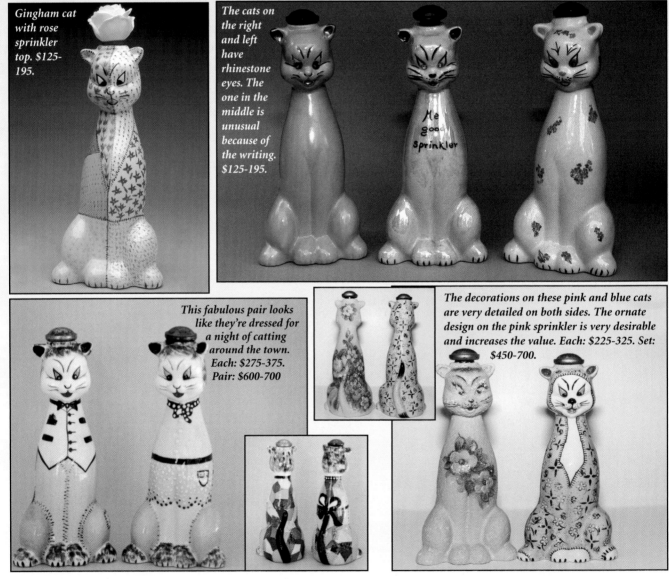

Gingham cat with rose sprinkler top. $125-195.

The cats on the right and left have rhinestone eyes. The one in the middle is unusual because of the writing. $125-195.

Me good Sprinkler

This fabulous pair looks like they're dressed for a night of catting around the town. Each: $275-375. Pair: $600-700

The decorations on these pink and blue cats are very detailed on both sides. The ornate design on the pink sprinkler is very desirable and increases the value. Each: $225-325. Set: $450-700.

❖ Dogs

SB-103: These poodles are found in gray, pink, and white, 8". $225-325.

SB-104: White poodle, 8-1/4", has a flat head. The bottom is marked "Cardinal USA," ca. 1956. $225-325.

❖ Elephants

SB-105: The trunk on this American Bisque 6-1/4" chubby elephant serves as a handle. $575-750.

SB-106: This unmarked 7" gray and pink elephant is by Cardinal China. $60-95.

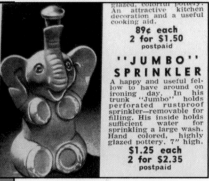

glazed, colorful pottery. An attractive kitchen decoration and a useful cooking aid.

89¢ each
2 for $1.50
postpaid

"JUMBO" SPRINKLER

A happy and useful fellow to have around on ironing day. In his trunk "Jumbo" holds perforated rustproof sprinkler—removable for filling. His inside holds sufficient water for sprinkling a large wash. Hand colored, highly glazed pottery, 7" high.

$1.25 each
2 for $2.35
postpaid

House and Garden, March 1953.

SB-107: White elephant with the shamrock on his tummy is probably Japanese. It has a "3328" ink mark. $100-150.

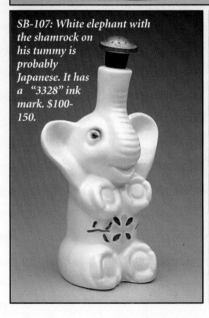

SB-108: This 7" handmade elephant with rough finish is "in the pink." $50-75.

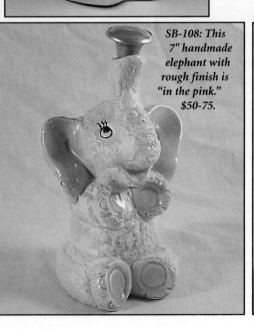

SB-109: Unusual pink and gray 7" elephant, has "#" signs on all four feet. $75-100.

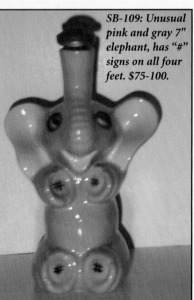

❖ Roosters

SB-110A: *Sierra Vista rooster, 9", is commercially made. $145-175.*

Original Sierra Vista label. Notice that the sprinkler was designed to be multi-purpose.

SB-111: *These handmade roosters each measure 8-1/8". Value varies according to the artistic appearance.*

SB-110B: *New rooster produced from the original Sierra Vista mold. $45-75.*

No hen-pecked rooster — this barn-yard dignitary earns his keep. Fill his 9″ tall ceramic body with water and he'll be custodian of all your sprinkling chores. After his job is done, give the brightly colored fellow the perch of honor on a kitchen shelf. Comes with cork to use as cruet. $2.25 ppd. Dan Rocklin Gifts, Dept. R, 600 New York Ave., Bklyn. 3, N.Y.

Redbook, August 1953.

Deep green. $100-125.

Brown with red highlights. $75-95.

❖ Clothespin Sprinkler Bottles

SB-200: *Factory manufactured yellow and turquoise clothespins, 7-3/4". $250-325*

SB-201/202: *Each of these handmade clothespins is quite unique. The flowers on the 7-3/4" example are quite colorful. Its companion is complete with painted hair, 7-1/2". $200-350.*

SB-203: *This very unusual commercially manufactured clothespin is underglazed, 7-3/4". $275-325.*

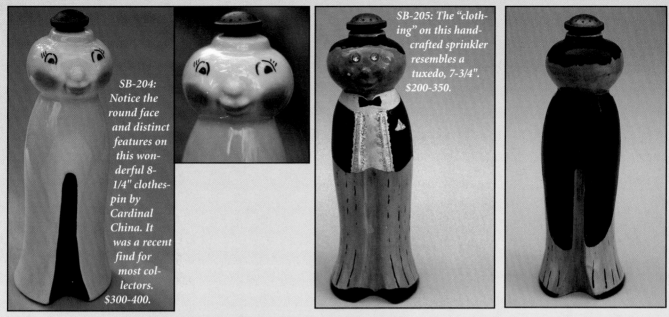

SB-204: Notice the round face and distinct features on this wonderful 8-1/4" clothespin by Cardinal China. It was a recent find for most collectors. $300-400.

SB-205: The "clothing" on this hand-crafted sprinkler resembles a tuxedo, 7-3/4". $200-350.

❖ Iron Sprinkler Bottles

These irons all appear to be commercially made, varying from 6" to 6-1/2" unless otherwise noted.

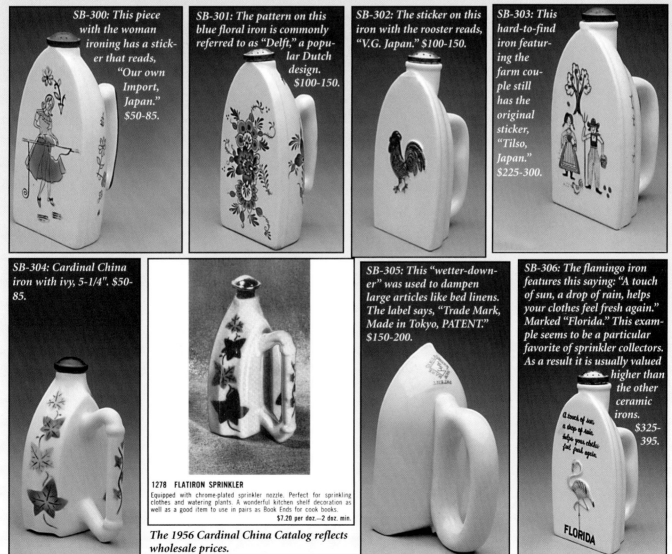

SB-300: This piece with the woman ironing has a sticker that reads, "Our own Import, Japan." $50-85.

SB-301: The pattern on this blue floral iron is commonly referred to as "Delft," a popular Dutch design. $100-150.

SB-302: The sticker on this iron with the rooster reads, "V.G. Japan." $100-150.

SB-303: This hard-to-find iron featuring the farm couple still has the original sticker, "Tilso, Japan." $225-300.

SB-304: Cardinal China iron with ivy, 5-1/4". $50-85.

1278 FLATIRON SPRINKLER
Equipped with chrome-plated sprinkler nozzle. Perfect for sprinkling clothes and watering plants. A wonderful kitchen shelf decoration as well as a good item to use in pairs as Book Ends for cook books.
$7.20 per doz.—2 doz. min.

The 1956 Cardinal China Catalog reflects wholesale prices.

SB-305: This "wetter-downer" was used to dampen large articles like bed linens. The label says, "Trade Mark, Made in Tokyo, PATENT." $150-200.

SB-306: The flamingo iron features this saying: "A touch of sun, a drop of rain, helps your clothes feel fresh again." Marked "Florida." This example seems to be a particular favorite of sprinkler collectors. As a result it is usually valued higher than the other ceramic irons. $325-395.

Iron sprinklers wre popular souvenir items judging from this variety:

SB-307: Six Flags Amusement Park. $275-350.

SB-308: Aquarena Springs, San Marcos, Texas, marked "Hand painted, Made in Japan." $275-350.

SB-309: "Wonder Cave, San Marcos, Texas." $275-375.

SB-310: This 4-1/2" iron appears to be a wetter-downer, but even the owner didn't have any definite information on its background. The entire foot or base is black glazed. $45-75.

❖ People Sprinkler Bottles

Oriental

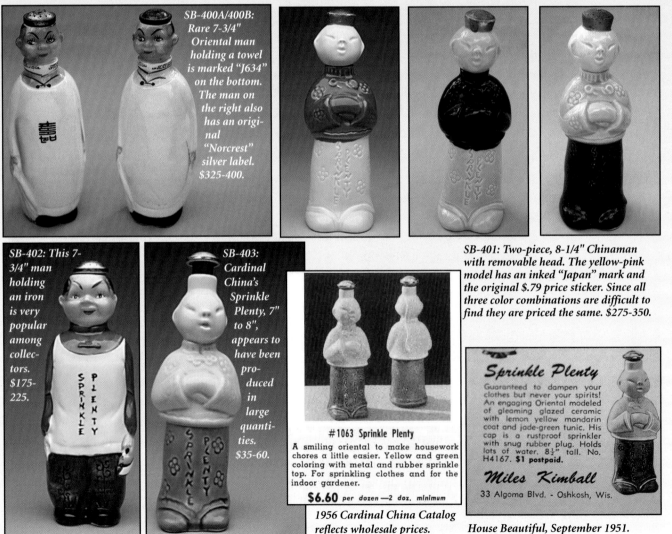

SB-400A/400B: Rare 7-3/4" Oriental man holding a towel is marked "J634" on the bottom. The man on the right also has an original "Norcrest" silver label. $325-400.

SB-402: This 7-3/4" man holding an iron is very popular among collectors. $175-225.

SB-403: Cardinal China's Sprinkle Plenty, 7" to 8", appears to have been produced in large quantities. $35-60.

SB-401: Two-piece, 8-1/4" Chinaman with removable head. The yellow-pink model has an inked "Japan" mark and the original $.79 price sticker. Since all three color combinations are difficult to find they are priced the same. $275-350.

#1063 Sprinkle Plenty

A smiling oriental to make housework chores a little easier. Yellow and green coloring with metal and rubber sprinkle top. For sprinkling clothes and for the indoor gardener.

$6.60 per dozen—2 doz. minimum

1956 Cardinal China Catalog reflects wholesale prices.

Sprinkle Plenty

Guaranteed to dampen your clothes but never your spirits! An engaging Oriental modeled of gleaming glazed ceramic with lemon yellow mandarin coat and jade-green tunic. His cap is a rustproof sprinkler with snug rubber plug. Holds lots of water. 8½" tall. No. H4167. **$1** postpaid.

Miles Kimball

33 Algoma Blvd. - Oshkosh, Wis.

House Beautiful, September 1951.

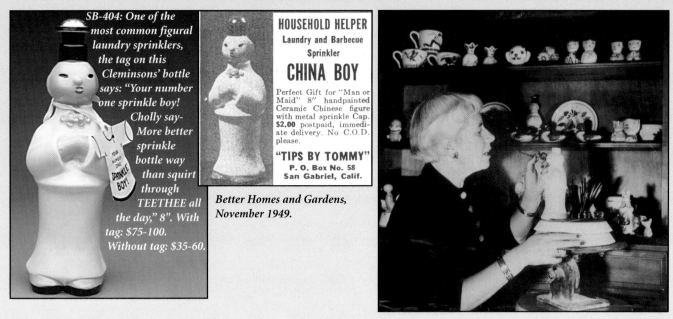

SB-404: *One of the most common figural laundry sprinklers, the tag on this Cleminsons' bottle says: "Your number one sprinkle boy! Cholly say- More better sprinkle bottle way than squirt through TEETHEE all the day," 8". With tag: $75-100. Without tag: $35-60.*

Better Homes and Gardens, November 1949.

This is a wonderful photo of Betty Cleminson decorating one of her sprinklers. Notice the finished sprinkler on the second shelf and the blade bank on the top.

SB-405: *All these handmade Oriental men were made from mold #104 of an unknown company, 7-3/4". Complexity of design affects value. $75-150.*

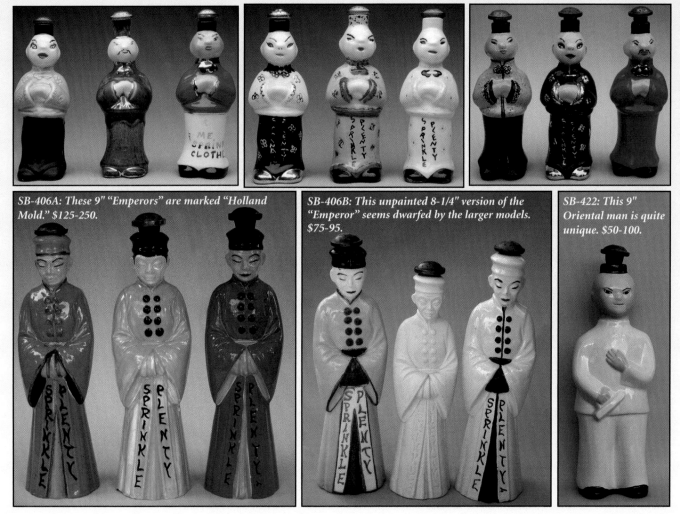

SB-406A: *These 9" "Emperors" are marked "Holland Mold." $125-250.*

SB-406B: *This unpainted 8-1/4" version of the "Emperor" seems dwarfed by the larger models. $75-95.*

SB-422: *This 9" Oriental man is quite unique. $50-100.*

❖ Dutch

SB-407A: Homemade Dutch lady. $200-300.

The Dutch ladies in these two photos vary in height from 7-3/4" to 8". Although we always assumed that these were all hand-made pieces, the finish on the SB-407B girls indicates that they are probably commercially manufactured.

SB-407B: The painted finish distinguishes these pieces from the homemade versions. $250-350.

SB-410 reclassified as SB-800

SB-408/409: This unusual 8" Dutch couple features a man sprinkler and a girl "wetter-downer." She was found with this label, "Cleanser cans are ugly things, besides they're never handy. So fill me with your favorite brand, I'll do the job, I'm handy. I can also be used for powdered sugar, dishwasher detergent, coarse salt, etc. In fact for anything that was to be poured. My goodness with all the jobs that I can do, every kitchen should have at least two." Because this girl was obviously one of those multi-purpose gadgets, we debated whether to keep her in this section or move her to the "Wannabes." Since she has been known and used as a wetter-downer for so long, we left her with her male companion. Each: $150-200.

❖ Special People

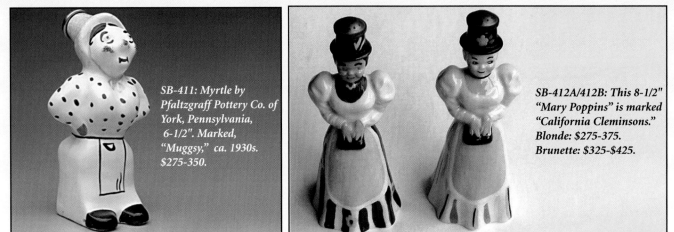

SB-411: Myrtle by Pfaltzgraff Pottery Co. of York, Pennsylvania, 6-1/2". Marked, "Muggsy," ca. 1930s. $275-350.

SB-412A/412B: This 8-1/2" "Mary Poppins" is marked "California Cleminsons." Blonde: $275-375. Brunette: $325-$425.

SB 413: "Dearie is Weary" by Enesco is part of a complete line of kitchenware. Her head comes off to fill the bottle, 7". $350-500.

SB-414: Lucky is the collector who owns the "Prayer Lady" sprinkler by Enesco, 6-1/2". The adage on her base reads: "A mother's work is never done." One of the most difficult-to-find pieces in the "Prayer Lady" line of kitchen accessories, her head removes to fill the bottle. $500-750.

SB-415: This will be the first glimpse many collectors have of the rare Fireman by California Cleminsons, 6-1/4". $1,500+.

SB-416: The original sticker on this 6-5/8" peasant woman reads, "To dampen your laundry, use this sprinkler maid and she's not only pretty, she's a handy kitchen aid. Provincial Pottery, California." Since each piece was hand decorated, the dress designs are all usually different. $275-375.

SB-417: Handmade 6-3/4" Mammy. $175-225.

SB-418: Mammy sprinkler, 6-3/4", and matching clothespin holder, 7" h. x 9-1/4" w. $275-350 each.

MAMMY SPRINKLER

Throw away that old pop bottle —here's a clothes sprinkler that is so trickily designed, with the perforated metal cap in the back, that it becomes an attractive figurine when not busily dampening clothes. Glazed ceramic; natural skin color with red trim. About 6½" high.

(No. 682) Each.............$1.39

Mahoning Giftware Catalog, Youngstown, OH.

SB-419 reclassified as SB-803

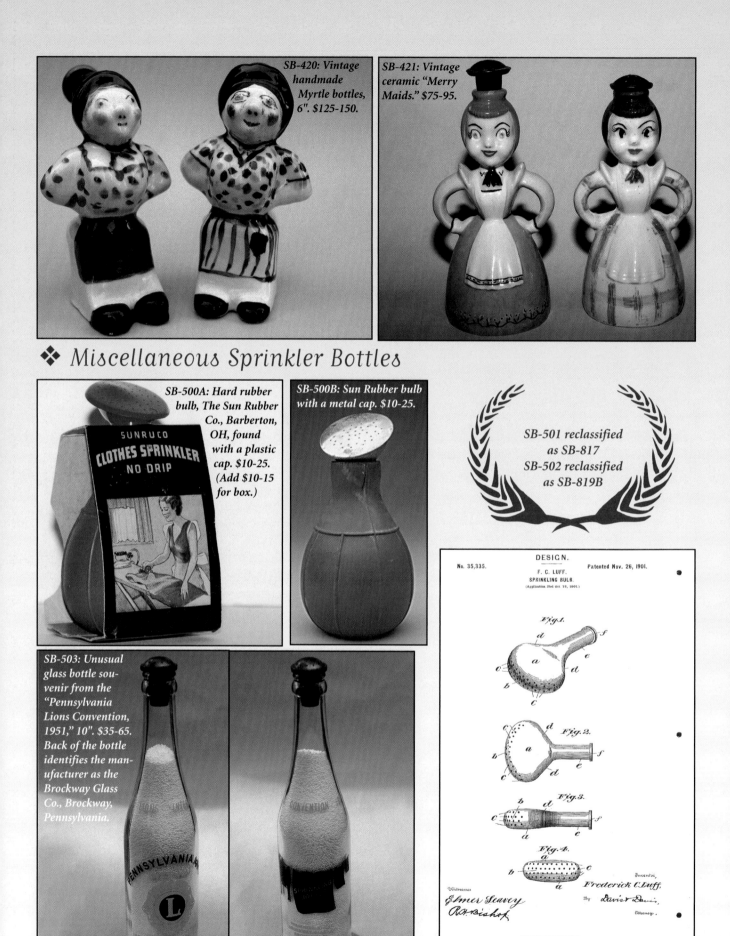

SB-420: Vintage handmade Myrtle bottles, 6". $125-150.

SB-421: Vintage ceramic "Merry Maids." $75-95.

❖ Miscellaneous Sprinkler Bottles

SB-500A: Hard rubber bulb, The Sun Rubber Co., Barberton, OH, found with a plastic cap. $10-25. (Add $10-15 for box.)

SB-500B: Sun Rubber bulb with a metal cap. $10-25.

SB-501 reclassified as SB-817
SB-502 reclassified as SB-819B

SB-503: Unusual glass bottle souvenir from the "Pennsylvania Lions Convention, 1951," 10". $35-65. Back of the bottle identifies the manufacturer as the Brockway Glass Co., Brockway, Pennsylvania.

Original 1901 Patent.

Sprinkler bulbs were an early 20th century invention.

SB-504:
Glass with
screw top,
7-1/4" l.
$60-70.

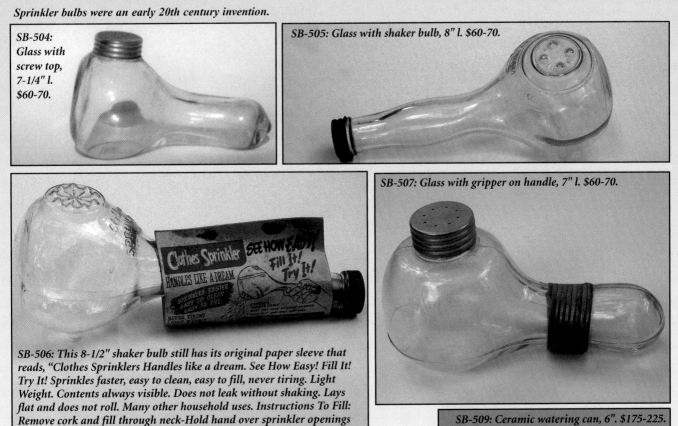

SB-505: Glass with shaker bulb, 8" l. $60-70.

SB-507: Glass with gripper on handle, 7" l. $60-70.

SB-506: This 8-1/2" shaker bulb still has its original paper sleeve that reads, "Clothes Sprinklers Handles like a dream. See How Easy! Fill It! Try It! Sprinkles faster, easy to clean, easy to fill, never tiring. Light Weight. Contents always visible. Does not leak without shaking. Lays flat and does not roll. Many other household uses. Instructions To Fill: Remove cork and fill through neck-Hold hand over sprinkler openings until cork is replaced. When not in use lay flat as above. This sprinkler is excellent for sprinkling floors, watering plants and for sprinkling insecticides on flowers and shrubs as well as for dampening clothes. To clean just rinse in warm water, K.R. Haley Glassware Company Inc., Greensburg, Pa." $80-100.

SB-509: Ceramic watering can, 6". $175-225.

SB-508: The green color makes
this piece more valuable, 7-1/4" l.
Also found in crystal. $100-125.

SB-511: Green rubber
bulb, marked "made in
USA." $35-55.

SB-510 reclassified
as SB-806

SB-512 reclassified
as SB-818
SB-513 reclassified
as SB-805

Here are some other rubber-ball-style sprinklers. They range from 4-1/2" to 6". The size of the sprinkling apparatus can add up to 2" to the total height.

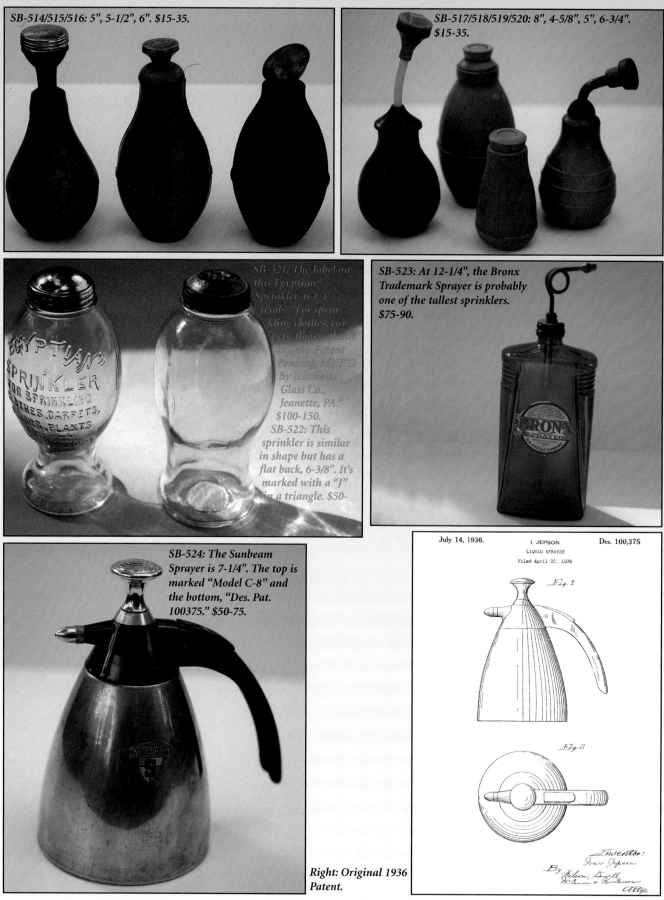

SB-514/515/516: 5", 5-1/2", 6". $15-35.

SB-517/518/519/520: 8", 4-5/8", 5", 6-3/4". $15-35.

SB-521: The label on this Egyptian Sprinkler, 6-1/4", reads: "For sprinkling clothes, carpets, floors, plants, etc., etc. Patent Pending, MNF'D By Jeannette Glass Co., Jeanette, PA." $100-150.
SB-522: This sprinkler is similar in shape but has a flat back, 6-3/8". It's marked with a "J" in a triangle. $50-

SB-523: At 12-1/4", the Bronx Trademark Sprayer is probably one of the tallest sprinklers. $75-90.

SB-524: The Sunbeam Sprayer is 7-1/4". The top is marked "Model C-8" and the bottom, "Des. Pat. 100375." $50-75.

Right: Original 1936 Patent.

SB-525: We thought this 7-1/8" bottle was probably a "Wannabe" until we turned it over and saw the original label. $40-60.

Right: House Beautiful, October 1949.

SB-526: The label on the 9-1/2" multi-purpose Wilkins Clothes Sprayer says: "The Wilkins Clothes Sprayer is also equally effective for spraying disinfectants of all types, cleaning windows, etc.". $35-75.

Right: House Beautiful, November 1953.

SB-527: The white milk glass color of this shaker makes it highly desirable, 6-1/4". $125-175.

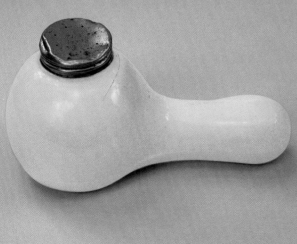

SB-528: This canister style metal sprinkler with its original box is unique, 6". It's marked "Made & PTD. In USA." $40-65. (Add $10-20 for box.)

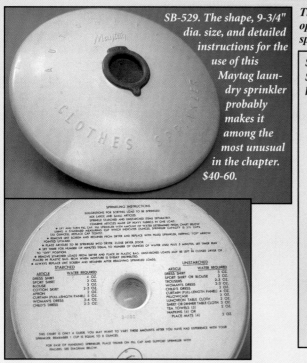

SB-529. The shape, 9-3/4" dia. size, and detailed instructions for the use of this Maytag laundry sprinkler probably makes it among the most unusual in the chapter. $40-60.

These two sprinklers are old Chinese brass models. We've been told that the operator propelled the water by spitting or blowing into the open end of the spout, $50-$75.

SB-530: The spout on this 5-1/2" sprinkler is a long 7-5/8".
SB-531: The unique feature of this other sprinkler is the 4-1/2" w. x 1-7/8" h. size.

❖ Newer Vintage Sprinkler Bottles

SB-600: The same ceramist made the first of these 12" ladies in 1980. $50-125.

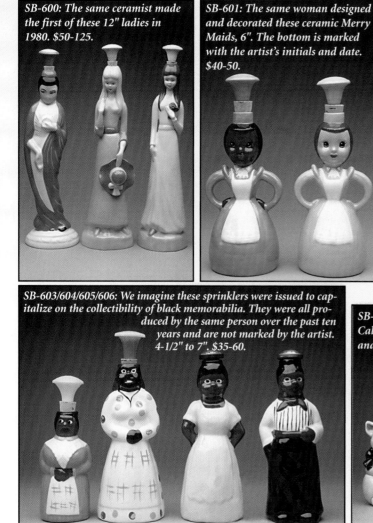

SB-601: The same woman designed and decorated these ceramic Merry Maids, 6". The bottom is marked with the artist's initials and date. $40-50.

SB-602: New, unmarked 6-3/4" glass Merry Maid from Taiwan is also found in emerald green. $10-20.

SB-603/604/605/606: We imagine these sprinklers were issued to capitalize on the collectibility of black memorabilia. They were all produced by the same person over the past ten years and are not marked by the artist. 4-1/2" to 7". $35-60.

SB-607/608/609/610/611: A variety of characters made in California, ranging from 5" to 6". Signed with artist's initials and date. $35-60.

❖ Sprinkler Bottle Tops

Although not much to look at, when inserted in any bottle, the homemaker had an inexpensive and functional laundry sprinkler. Unless found with original packaging, most individual tops sell for $5-$15.

SB-700: This top with the rubber stopper is the oldest.

CLOTHES SPRINKLERS

OK CLOTHES SPRINKLER

MOISTENS CLOTHES

BRASS
Rustless CAP
RUBBER CORK

The finest quality product of its kind. Lustre finish brass cap, black rubber stopper. Twelve in a counter display box. Length 1⅜ inches.

Each
No. DU48—Per Display (12)   ₹ cnt $0.15
One Display in a Carton

Left: 1955 Bostwick & Braun Company Wholesale Catalog No. 55, Toledo, Ohio.

SB-701: Production on this aluminum top with cork stopper has recently been discontinued.

LAUNDRY SPRINKLER TOP

FITS ANY BEVERAGE BOTTLE

15¢

minerware inc.
MADE IN U.S.A.
NO. 3123

SB-702: Whimsical rose top on original card, Minerware, Inc., NY. $15. This top was also sold as part of a complete set; see SB-806.

SB-703: This plastic top with cork stopper is still being made.

Feb. 16, 1937.   C. E. ANDERSON   2,071,101
SPRINKLER FOR RECEPTACLES
Filed Nov. 13, 1935

Fig. 1

Fig. 2   *Fig. 3*

INVENTOR
Carl E. Anderson.
BY
Wm. H. Camfield.
ATTORNEY.

Original 1937 Patent.

FOR SPRINKLING CLOTHES · SETTLING DUST · SPRAYING FLOWERS · FRESHENING VEGETABLES

LOXON
TRADE MARK

SPRINKLER
BOTTLE CAP

IT LOCKS ON THE BOTTLE

Can't "Pop" off
WHEN YOU ARE SPRINKLING

Use the Small Handy Size Beverage Bottle

"EASY OFF-EASY ON"
IT "LOXON"

5¢ EACH

Right: SB-704: Original display of Loxon Sprinkler Tops, copyright 1946. $85.

SB-707: This blue ceramic top is quite unusual. It's marked "Made In U.S.A."

SB-705: Chiltonware's sprinkler top.

SB-706: Sprinkler top by Luster Chrome.

❖ Plastic Sprinkler Bottles

SB-800/801: The boy on this pair of Dutch people is difficult to find, 6-1/2". Girl: $40-50. (Formerly SB-410.) Boy: $50-85.

SB-802: Collectors have nicknamed this sprinkler the "Ladybug." This hard-to-find piece is 7". Courtesy of the Walker Collection. $60-75.

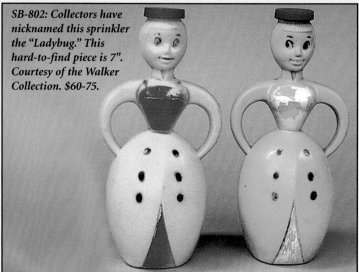

SB-803: The 6-1/2" "Merry Maid" comes in a wide variety colors and is the mostly commonly found plastic sprinkler in today's collectibles market. The original label says, "Merry Maid Clothes Sprinkler, Many Practical Uses … Brightens up the kitchen, a RELIANCE product No. 535, pat. pend." (Formerly SB-419.) SB-804: At first glance the "Merry Maid" on the right appears to be like all the others … that is until you hold her and realize that she's made of a heavier grade plastic. This Australian model is 6-7/8". American: $20-35. Australian: $25-35.

SB-805: For obvious reasons, this piece is called Mr. Clothespin, 6-3/4". $25-30. (Formerly SB-513.)

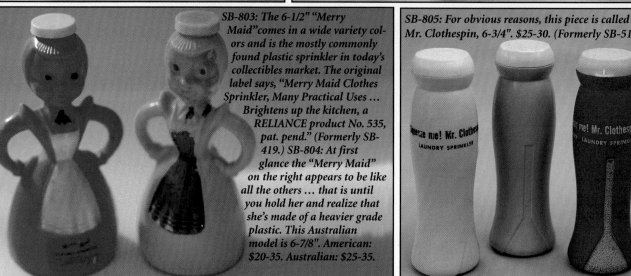

SB-806: The rose top on these vase-style sprinklers came in different colors. The bottom is marked "Made in USA, Minerware Inc., NY 10, NY," 8-1/4". $25-50. (Formerly SB-510.)

Minerware label.

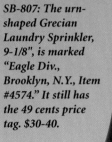

SB-807: The urn-shaped Grecian Laundry Sprinkler, 9-1/8", is marked "Eagle Div., Brooklyn, N.Y., Item #4574." It still has the 49 cents price tag. $30-40.

SB-808: Sally Sprinkler, marked "U.S.A., Pat. Pend.," "SPS" in a star, 8-1/4", still has its 39 cents tag. $40-60.

SB-809: This 7" Tupperware sprinkler was sold with a set of tops to perform different functions. The bottom is marked "US Pat. 28859786, Copyright 1954, Tupper Corporation." $10-20.

SB-810A: Sprinklers in the shape of clothespins were an obvious favorite—Sprinklepin, 7", is just one of the many plastic clothespin examples featured here. The top is marked "Sprinklepin, Pat. Pend. Hollywood, Calif." $30-50.

SB-810B: This 7" Sprinklepin is still marked 39 cents (apparently this was a common price for plastic sprinklers). $30-50.

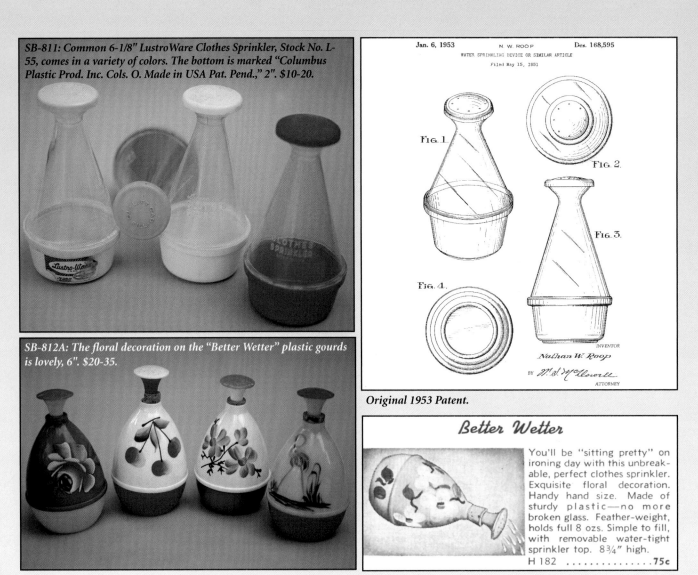

SB-811: Common 6-1/8" LustroWare Clothes Sprinkler, Stock No. L-55, comes in a variety of colors. The bottom is marked "Columbus Plastic Prod. Inc. Cols. O. Made in USA Pat. Pend.," 2". $10-20.

Original 1953 Patent.

SB-812A: The floral decoration on the "Better Wetter" plastic gourds is lovely, 6". $20-35.

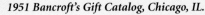

Better Wetter

You'll be "sitting pretty" on ironing day with this unbreakable, perfect clothes sprinkler. Exquisite floral decoration. Handy hand size. Made of sturdy plastic—no more broken glass. Feather-weight, holds full 8 ozs. Simple to fill, with removable water-tight sprinkler top. 8¾" high.
H 182 ....75¢

1951 Bancroft's Gift Catalog, Chicago, IL.

SB-812B: Minus the flowers, the 6" Clo-Spray gourds are more functional than decorative. The bottom is marked, "Clospray Plas.-Tex Corp., L.A., Calif., Made in U.S.A." $10-20.

CLOSPRAY

No. 13B308.....Price $2.00 doz. Colorful sparkling water sprinklers, in 2-color combinations. Feather-weight. 8¾" high, 3" wide. Colors, red and white, blue and white, green and white. Pkd. 1 doz. asst.

No. 13B309.....Price $2.00 doz. Pkd. 1 doz. Sprinkler complete, with clothespin shape. Assorted colors.

No. 13B312.....Price $ .75 doz. Pkd. 4 doz. Plastic clothes sprinkler head.

Right: 1957 NYMCO Wholesale Catalog, New York, NY.

SB-813: *These white plastic sprinklers were plain yet functional, 5-1/4". $8-20.*

SB-814: *The Bolta Sprinkler clothespin is 7-7/8" with decorated baskets of laundry design. The bottom is marked "The Bolta Co., No. 000, Lawrence, Mass." $10-30.*

Only Frigidaire Washers have the 3 Ring "Pump" Agitator . . .

Bathes deep dirt out without beating!
Your sprinkler is a miniature of the patented 3 Ring "Pump" Agitator—heart of the Frigidaire washer. No blades, no beating, pumps up and down, surges water through the fabric 330 times a minute. Actually bathes even deep dirt out of every fabric, blue jeans to woolens, gently yet thoroughly.
Ask your Frigidaire dealer about today's most advanced washing action now!

The Exclusive Frigidaire 3 Ring "Pump" Agitator . . .

LINT CHASER

CIRCULATOR

ENERGY RING

Dispenses All Laundry Aids . . . AUTOMATICALLY! Releases detergent, bleach or dye, liquid or powder, under water!

Removes Lint . . . AUTOMATICALLY! Lint Chaser Ring sweeps lint, dirt and scum out of the tub, without draining through clothes. No traps to empty.

Bathes Out Deep Dirt! Energy Ring puts suds and water to work fast—keeps them working. Pumps them through every piece and fold, for cleanest wash ever!

Guards Against Twisting, Tangling! Circulator Ring opens every fold, keeps clothes separate. No catching, no stretching.

EXCLUSIVE FROM F FRIGIDAIRE

SB-816: *The Ironees, 6-3/4", is marked on the bottom: "Wisk Product, Made in U.S.A., Pat. Pend.," with the letters "PCO" in a circle. $30-45.*

39¢
PLUS SALES TAX/WHERE APPLICABLE
IRONEES LAUNDRY SPRINKLER No. 99

DECOLITE
LAUNDRY **SPRINKLER** also used for WATERING PLANTS

SB-815: *We were surprised that this is the only plastic sprinkler in the shape of an iron that we've found so far, 6-7/8". $45-65.*

SB-817: *The insert found with this 5-1/4" Frigidaire Agitator sprinkler indicates that it was a premium given away with the purchase of a washing machine. We've seen ads for the actual machine from the early 1960s so we assume this piece is from the same era. $45-75. (Formerly SB-501.)*

The range of plastic sprinklers seems to be endless. Some are pretty basic in design, others more colorful—all have the common purpose of dampening clothes to make ironing easier.

SB-818: *Mr. Sprinkle, 6-1/2". $15-30. (Formerly SB-512.)*

SB-819A: *Another representation of 1950s laundry sprinklers, 6-1/2". $15-30.*

SB-819B: *The clothesline of laundry adds a nice touch to this otherwise common bottle, 6-1/2". $15-25.*

SB-820: This "Laundry Sprinkler" is marked "A Lucky Wish Product, pat. Pend., Made in USA," 6-1/2". $15-25.

SB-821: Canadian version of SB-820, 5-7/8". $20-35.

SB-822: The "Basket Weave" laundry sprinkler gets its name from the surface design, 6-7/8". $15-25.
SB-823: The top on this 6-3/4" sprinkler reads, "Lift cap to fill." $10-20.
SB-824: The bottom of this 7" sprinkler has a simulated laundry basket weave. The bottom is marked "Royal-Pacific Co., Inc., San Fer. Sprgs., Cal., 90670." $15-30.

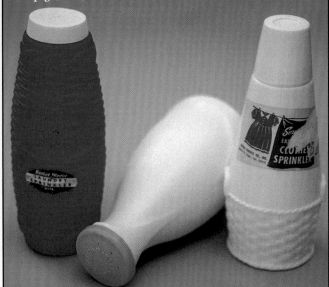

SB-825: This piece is marked, "Bi-Cor Chicago, Bloomfield, IN, Inc.," 5-1/2". $10-20.
SB-826: This Life Sprinkler still has the original 25 cents price sticker, 5-3/4". $10-20.
SB-827: Unmarked red sprinkler with clear top, 4-7/8". $10-20.

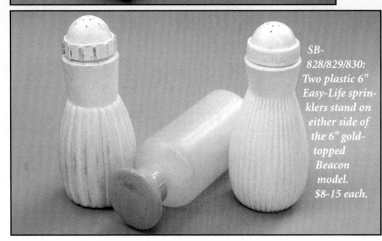

SB-828/829/830: Two plastic 6" Easy-Life sprinklers stand on either side of the 6" gold-topped Beacon model. $8-15 each.

SB-831: These 8-1/4" sprinklers have an angular, hourglass shape. The bottom is marked "USA, Minerware, Inc., NY 10, NY." $35-50.

SB-832: Gothamware sprinklers, 5-1/2", are marked, "Made In USA." $8-15.

SB-833: This round, hard plastic canister has a nice sailboat painted on the front, 6". The person who has this one in their collection could not verify that this is definitely a sprinkler, but we decided to include it and let you be the judge! $15-25.

❖ Wannabes

The Carrie Nation vinegar bottle is the biggest offender in this category. Patented in the 1930s, it was produced by the Owens-Illinois Bottle Company of Huntington, West Virginia. We've been told that the vinegar company ran a promotion offering a sprinkler top that could be used once the liquid was gone. While that would certainly explain the large numbers of these being sold as sprinkler bottles, we have been unable to turn up any concrete information to substantiate this claim.

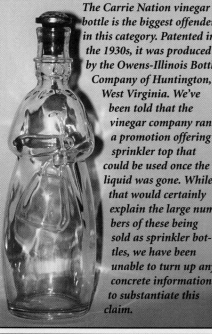

Shown with the original red cork stopper nose, this "Booze Hound" liquor bottle was offered for sale as a laundry sprinkler for $600. In the 1950s it originally sold for $2.95.

This "queen," marked "Tilso, Japan," looks like a salt shaker to us.

A coffee pot-shaped cleanser dispenser by Cardinal China Co., Carteret, New Jersey. Since the sticker on the back label matches the Dutch girl "wetter-downer" (SB-409), it too could be used as a sprinkler.

Imagine how excited we were to find this "unlisted" ceramic sprinkler. Luckily it was unused and still had the original contents and label—it actually holds talcum powder!

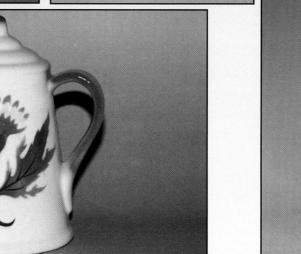

Gebrüder Plein O.H.G., Germany, ca. 1930s.

130 Figural Egg Timers

Figural Egg Timers

Chapter 5

We imagine that the person who coined the phrase "Time flies when you're having fun" must have been an egg timer collector! These are the kind of folks who would tell you that they're having the time of their lives. After all, what could be a better way to mark time—collecting cute figurines with an attached sand vial that ticks off the three minutes necessary to boil the perfect egg or make a phone call without extra charges.

Once a household necessity, vintage egg timers are now considered timeless treasures. Replaced by plastic wind-ups or the automatic timer on the stove or microwave, these lovely and sometimes whimsical pieces are now more likely to be found behind the doors of display cases.

The majority of the egg timers featured in this chapter measure between three to five inches, and are made of some sort of ceramic material. We have also featured some really unusual metal, composition, chalkware, and wood examples. Take a look at ET-720—this Welsh woman is plastic. People (either in the form of occupational figures or fictional characters) and animals such as dogs, cats, rabbits and chicks, are still the dominating themes. Other types like windmills and lighthouses are sometimes marked as souvenirs from a particular attraction or location. The telephone timers were most likely multi-purposed, often used to time the telephone calls in boarding houses.

There still seems to be confusion on how to distinguish between German, Japanese and American examples. The timers with maker marks (almost all Goebel timers bear their distinctive trademark) or an inked country of origin helps on some examples. Many of the German pieces have incised manufacturer numbers as well. Pay close attention to the joints attaching the sand glass to the figure. The Germans preferred a brass joint while their Japanese and American counterparts sport a less expensive wire-type connector. The workmanship on German ceramics tends to be more detailed; don't, however, discount some of the intricately painted Japanese models. The Goebel figures, especially the "doubles," continue to be on the top of most collectors' want lists.

The value of egg timers varies according to condition of the figure, country of origin (German pieces are usually more costly) or maker, and even the geographic region where you live. The Goebel ETs shown in the 900 series are highly desirable to both Goebel and egg timer collectors, and therefore are among the priciest. Black chefs and Mammy pieces also rank on top of the collectibility scale since they're also of interest to black memorabilia collectors.

While market values have remained fairly steady over the past three years, the variety of vintage timers has increased dramatically. Antique shows and flea markets continue to be good sources, but the international reach of online auctions have surfaced some great examples from Europe and Australia. We're delighted to be including some of these hard-to-find pieces among the more than seventy timers added to this chapter.

Remember that although it's preferable to purchase egg timers complete with the original sand vial, this piece can be easily replaced. The condition of the actual figure is the most important consideration. As with any ceramic collectible, chips, cracks, paint loss, and crazing are the main detractors, and you can expect to pay less if the piece has any sort of damage.

We think the pages in this chapter will definitely tempt you to take your sweet time with this collection!

❖ Animal Egg Timers

These egg timers are ceramic, unless otherwise noted.

ET-100: Lady mouse, "Josef Originals" sticker. $35-55.
ET-101: Bird on nest, "Josef Originals" sticker. $30-50.

ET-102: Dog, marked "Japan." $45-75.
ET-103: Double Scotties, marked "Germany." $75-95.
ET-104: Pekingese, marked "Germany." $75-95.

ET-105: Dog, holding timer in mouth, marked "Germany." $65-85.
ET-106: Dog, marked "Germany." $65-85.
ET-107: Black poodle, marked "Germany." $65-95.

ET-108: Elephant, marked "Germany." $65-85.
ET-109: Penguin, marked "Manorware, England," glazed chalkware. $45-65.
ET-110: Frog, marked "Japan." $45-75.

ET-111: Cat, marked "Germany." $65-85.
ET-112: Cat by fireplace, marked "Manorware, England," glazed chalkware. $45-65.

ET-113: Bird by post, marked "Germany." $55-75.
ET-114: Cat by clock, marked "Germany." $55-75.

ET-115: Chick, marked "Japan." $65-85.
ET-116: Chicken, marked "Germany." $75-95.

ET-117: Rabbit, marked "Germany." $95-125.
ET-118: Rabbit by egg, marked "Germany," wood. $35-55.
ET-119: Rabbit, marked "Germany." $95-125.

ET-120/121: Two roosters, wood. $35-55.

ET-122: Chicken, holding timer in beak, marked "Germany." $75-95.
ET-123: Chicken, flat back, marked "Japan." $45-65.
ET-124: Chicken, marked "Germany." $75-95.

9020   9018   8702   8597   8972

8191   8264   7957   7954   8595

8914   8939   8971   9023   8596

German Catalog, ca. 1930s.

ET-125: Green dog looking at his tail.
$55-85.

ET-126: White
Scottie, chalkware.
$45-65.

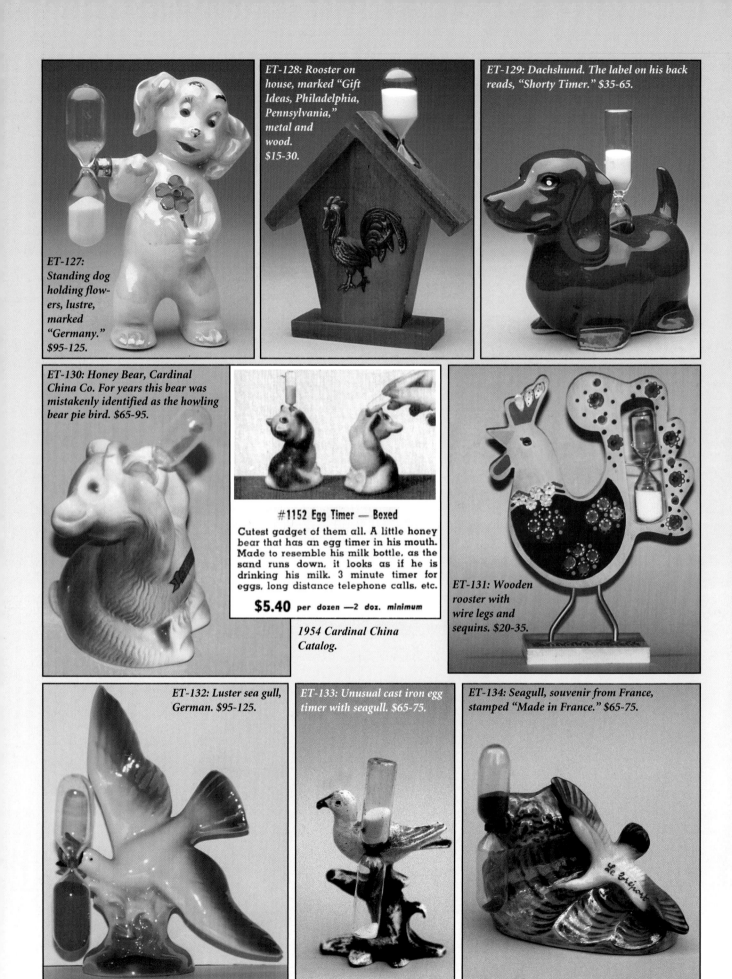

ET-127: Standing dog holding flowers, lustre, marked "Germany." $95-125.

ET-128: Rooster on house, marked "Gift Ideas, Philadelphia, Pennsylvania," metal and wood. $15-30.

ET-129: Dachshund. The label on his back reads, "Shorty Timer." $35-65.

ET-130: Honey Bear, Cardinal China Co. For years this bear was mistakenly identified as the howling bear pie bird. $65-95.

#1152 Egg Timer — Boxed

Cutest gadget of them all. A little honey bear that has an egg timer in his mouth. Made to resemble his milk bottle, as the sand runs down, it looks as if he is drinking his milk. 3 minute timer for eggs, long distance telephone calls, etc.

$5.40 per dozen —2 doz. minimum

1954 Cardinal China Catalog.

ET-131: Wooden rooster with wire legs and sequins. $20-35.

ET-132: Luster sea gull, German. $95-125.

ET-133: Unusual cast iron egg timer with seagull. $65-75.

ET-134: Seagull, souvenir from France, stamped "Made in France." $65-75.

ET-135: Kiwi tending egg on nest. $75-95.

ET-136: Colorful lusterware fish, marked "Germany." $75-95.

ET-137: Rabbit holding ear of corn. $65-75.

ET-138: Tommie the Timer, metal. $25-35.

CUTE KITTENS. Original kitchen plaques in black metal hold your shopping memos or time your eggs. Whimsical plaques are about 5½" long. Choose Jenny Jot, with memo pad, or Tommie the Timer, the egg-timer. Nice gifts. $1 ea. ppd. Nancy Norman, Dept. FC, 422 Washington St., Brighton 35, Mass.

Family Circle, November 1957.

ET-139: Small wooden black cat, "Japan" sticker. $35-45.

ET-140: Smiling mouse with chef's apron, Josef Originals. $30-50.

ET-141: Beatrice Potter type rabbit with cap holding a carrot, "Made in Japan" sticker. $45-65.

ET-142: Dog sitting on a ball, marked "Germany." $75-95.

ET-143: Large lusterware Scottie, German. $95-125.

ET-144: Little red dog with bone, German. $75-95.

ET-145: Spotted dog, timer in head, marked "Foreign." $75-95.

ET-146: Standing rabbit. $55-65.
ET-147: Donkey. $45-65.

ET-148: Sitting dog with hat. $60-70.
ET-149: Standing Terrier, stamped "Made in Japan," on tummy. $65-75.

ET-150: Bonzo, stamped "Pfeffer Porzellan, 5699." $85-95.

ET-151: Owl, Josef Originals, with "Japan" sticker. $55-65.

❖ Character Egg Timers

ET-200: Humpty Dumpty, marked "California Cleminsons." He stands on his head to activate the sand. $45-75.

ET-201: Golliwog, marked "FOR-EIGN." $150-200.

ET-202/203/204: "Happy," made by the Maw Co., England. $125-150. ET-203: Huckleberry Finn, marked "Japan." $95-125. ET-204: Oliver Twist, marked "Germany." $95-125.

6287 TOOTHPICK HOLDER
1 dz. Min., 4½" Tall .... 4.80 dz.

6288 EGG TIMER
½ dz. Min., 6½" Tall .... 7.20 dz.

Lugene's Wholesale Souvenir and Gifts, Branson, MO, 1966.

ET-205: Santa Claus, holding timer, unmarked. $50-75.
ET-206: Santa Claus, label reads, "SONSCO," marked "Japan." $50-75.

ET-207: Mrs. Claus with Santa's sack embossed with company name, however only "Enterprises 19__" is visible. $55-65.

ET-208: Little Bo Peep, marked "Japan." $95-125.

ET-209: "Grumpy" made by Maw Co., England. $125-150.

ET-210: Father Time marked on the front of the base and "11599" on the back of the base. Probably German. $95-110.

ET-211: Little Red Riding Hood and the wolf, stamped "Germany" on the base and "7879" on the back. $115-135.

ET-212: Tommy Tucker, marked "Japan." $75-85.

ET-213: Rare "Flip the Frog" (pre-dates Mickey Mouse). Sticker on bottom reads, "Trademark Flip the Frog by arrangements with Showman Films, LTD., 167 Wardour Street, WI RD 758233, Foreign." $500.

❖ Chef Egg Timers

ET-300: Black chef with potholder hooks, composition board. $75-95.

ET-301: Mammy cooking, with potholder hooks, tin lithographed. $125-150.

ET-302: Chef with eggcup, wood. $45-65. Stand him on his head to reveal eggcup.

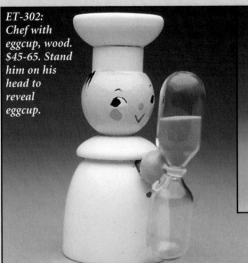

ET-303: Chef holding egg, wood. $35-45.

ET-304: Chef carrying cake, marked "Germany," composition. $85-100.

Adolf Röhring Porzellan-Atelier German Catalog, ca. 1930s.

ET-305: Chef with platter and knife, metal. $50-75.

ET-306: Little Black Sambo chef, wood. $85-100.

POHLSON GALLERIES

The line of thoughtfully assembled gifts for every-day selling. Let us send you a $25.00 shipment of these quick selling kitchen shower gifts, and include adorable gifts for children and other prize items. All attractively boxed and all to retail for $1.00 and under. Illustrated.

No. 66 Sambo egg or telephone timer....$6.00 dz.
No. 67 Rolling-pin pot holder set..........$7.20 dz.
No. 65 Rastus memo pad with pencil.......$6.00 dz.

Gift & Art Buyer, January 1950. This trade magazine reflects wholesale prices.

ET-307: Black chef with built-in timer, new. $15-20. Turn him on his head to activate sand.

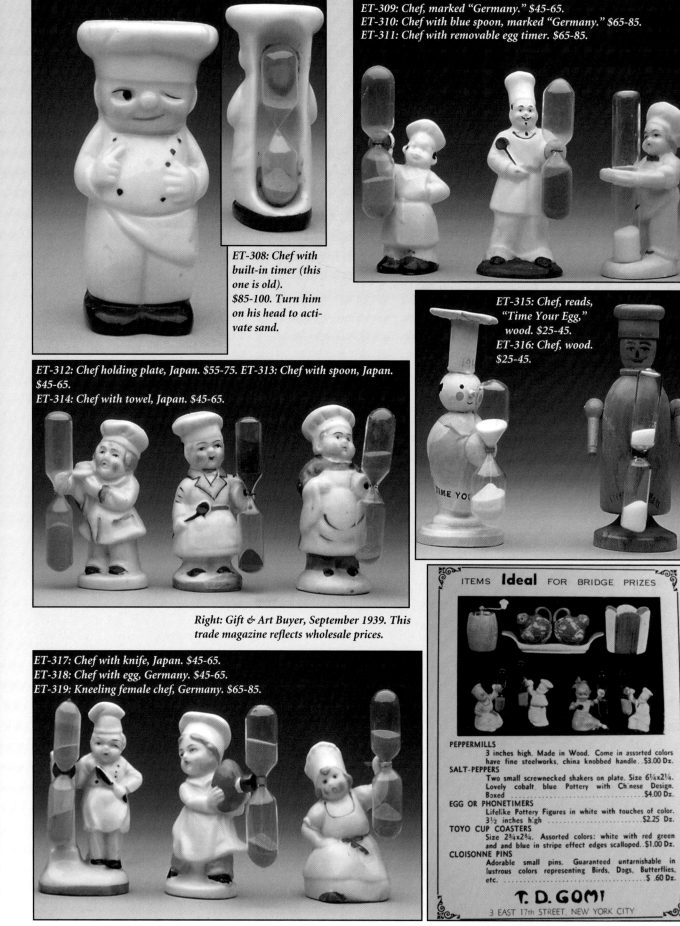

ET-308: Chef with built-in timer (this one is old). $85-100. Turn him on his head to activate sand.

ET-309: Chef, marked "Germany." $45-65.
ET-310: Chef with blue spoon, marked "Germany." $65-85.
ET-311: Chef with removable egg timer. $65-85.

ET-312: Chef holding plate, Japan. $55-75. ET-313: Chef with spoon, Japan. $45-65.
ET-314: Chef with towel, Japan. $45-65.

ET-315: Chef, reads, "Time Your Egg," wood. $25-45.
ET-316: Chef, wood. $25-45.

Right: Gift & Art Buyer, September 1939. This trade magazine reflects wholesale prices.

ET-317: Chef with knife, Japan. $45-65.
ET-318: Chef with egg, Germany. $45-65.
ET-319: Kneeling female chef, Germany. $65-85.

ET-320A: White chef holding fish, Japan. $95-125.
ET-320B: Black chef holding fish, Japan. $95-125.

ET-321: Black chef, souvenir of Llangollen, Wales is marked "Germany." $95-125.

ET-322: Black chef, Japan. $95-125.
ET-323: Black chef holding yellow spoon, Japan. $95-125.

ET-324/325/326: Sitting black male chefs holding up timers, various sizes, Germany. $95-125.

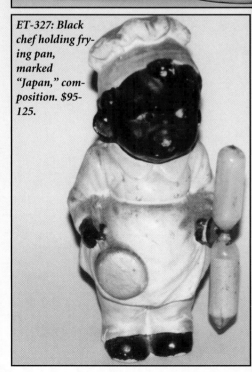

ET-327: Black chef holding frying pan, marked "Japan," composition. $95-125.

ET-328: Sitting black lady chef, marked "Germany 9300." $95-125.

ET-329: Sitting white male chef, marked "Germany." $95-125.

ET-330: Black chef, ink marked "Japan." $75-95.
ET-331: Mammy girlfriend, marked "Japan." $75-95.

ET-332: Lady chef holding spoon, wood. $30-40.

ET-333: Cute chef with mustache, sticker on bottom "Italy," wood. $25-35.

ET-334: Musical chef with original box. Spoon turns to wind music box. Box marked "Handmade and handpainted in the Italian Tyrol. Genuine Swiss Musical Works." $175 (including box).

ET-335: Chef with tall hat, stamped "Germany" on inside of base. $110-120.
ET-336: Chef on ball holding an egg, stamped "Japan" on bottom. $100-125.
ET-337: Black lady chef holding spoon. Base marked "Japan" on the base. Decal on apron "Souvenir of Lake Huntington, NY." $90-100.

❖ Children Egg Timers

ET-400: Boy skiing, marked "Germany." $75-95.
ET-401: Boy with rifle, marked "Germany." $75-95.
ET-402: Boy playing guitar, marked "Germany." $75-95.

Gebrüder Plein O.H.G. German Catalog, ca. 1930s.

ET-403: Girl with yellow dress and pigtails, marked "Germany." $85-95.
ET-404: Sitting girl with legs to side, marked "Germany." $75-95.
ET-405: Girl holding ball, marked "Germany." $75-95.

ET-406: Girl with watering can, marked "Germany." $75-95.
ET-410: Boy with pail, marked "Germany." $75-95.

ET-407: Boy in Swiss outfit, marked "Germany." $75-95.
ET-408: Girl holding cup, marked "Germany." $75-95.
ET-409: Girl sitting with telephone, marked "Germany." $75-95.

ET-411: Boy with large red bow, marked "Germany." $95-125.

ET-412: Boy with guitar sitting on stump, "Germany." $75-95.

ET-413: Little girl with basket of apples, marked "Foreign," however, her appearance in a German catalog confirms her origin. $75-95.

ET-414: Black baby, composition. $75-95.

Gebrüder Plein O.H.G. German Catalog.

ET-418: Little boy in Swiss outfit. Paper label on bottom marked "Germany 39 cents." Composition material, $85-100.

ET-415: Little boy with bow tie, stamped "Germany" on bottom. $85-95. ET-416: Little girl with pinafore and cap, stamped "Germany 60" on bottom and marked "7060" on back. $85-95. ET-417: Little girl on telephone, marked "8914" on back. $85-95.

❖ Dutch Egg Timers

ET-500: *Windmill, marked "Germany." $55-75.* **ET-501:** *Windmill with kissing Dutch couple, marked "Japan." $55-75.* **ET-502:** *Windmill with Dutch shoes, candleholder, unmarked. $45-65.*

ET-503: *Bird sitting atop windmill, marked "Germany." $50-75.* **ET-504:** *Windmill, marked "Japan." $50-75.* **ET-505:** *Goose sitting atop windmill, marked "Germany." $50-75.*

ET-506: *Windmill with dog standing on base, marked "Japan." $85-100.*
ET-507: *Windmill with pigs standing on base, marked "Japan." $85-100.*

ET-508: *Windmill, yellow and green, removable timer, Cardinal China Co., New Jersey. $35-50.*

ET-509: *Windmill with kissing Dutch couple. $50-75.*

Right: House Beautiful, April 1951. The sand glass on this version of the windmill egg timer is attached with a wire.

ET-510: *Dutchman with pipe, Japan. $55-75.*
ET-511: *Dutch boy, kneeling, Japan. $50-70.*
ET-512: *Dutch boy, Japan. $55-75.*

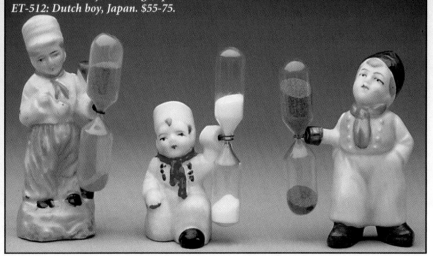

ET-513: Dutch girl on telephone, Japan. $45-65.
ET-514: Dutch girl, kneeling, Japan. $45-65.
ET-515: Dutch girl, Germany. $65-85.

ET-516: Dutch girl, walking, Germany, composition, companion to ET-522. $65-85. ET-517: Dutch girl, kneeling, Germany. $50-75.

ET-518: Tall Dutch boy, Japan. $45-65.
ET-519: Small Dutch boy, Germany. $65-85.
ET-520: Dutch girl with heart on apron, Germany. $65-85.

The Gift & Art Buyer, September 1939. This trade magazine reflects wholesale prices.

ET-521: Little Dutch girl, smaller than ET-516, marked "Germany." $65-$85.

ET-522: Little Dutch boy, Germany, composition, companion to ET-516. $65-75.

ET-523: Dutch girl in yellow, ceramic. $45-65.

EGG and telephone timers in delft blue reproduction porcelain. 1¾ by 4¼ inches, and 2 x 4½ inches. One dozen to a box asst., retail at 50c to 59c each. M. B. Daniels & Co., Inc., 31-37 West 27th St., New York.

Crockery and Glass Journal, August 1952. This trade magazine reflects wholesale prices.

❖ Boys and Men Egg Timers

ET-600: English Bobby, Germany. $80-100

ET-601: Sitting boy chef with raised arm, Germany. $65-85.
ET-602: Butler, Germany. $75-95.
ET-603: Dutch boy, Japan. $45-65.

ET-604: Colonial man, Japan. $65-85.
ET-605: Minuteman, Germany. $75-95.
ET-606: Colonial man, Japan. $45-65.

ET-607: Chimney sweep, Germany. $80-100.
ET-608: Newspaper boy, Germany. $75-95.
ET-609: Garden boy, Germany. $75-95.

ET-610: Native, Japan. $95-125.

ET-611: Boy with cap and kerchief, wood. $25-45.

Weiss, Kuhnert & Co. German Catalog.

ET-612: "Timothy Timer," label reads "Cooley Lilley, Cape May, N.J., Chester, Pa." $45-65. Stand "Timothy" on his head and he fills with sand.

House Beautiful, November 1948.

ET-613: Clown with ball on head, marked "Japan." $45-65. ET-614: Standing clown on telephone, marked "Japan." $55-75. ET-615: Sitting Pierrot with legs to side, marked "Germany." $95-125.

ET-616: Boy holding blackbird, unmarked. $65-85.
ET-617: Men playing checkers, wood. $25-45.
ET-618: Bear in chef's outfit, marked "Japan." $65-85.

ET-622: Sailor with sailboat, marked "Germany." $85-115.
ET-623: Sailor, marked "Germany." $65-85.

ET-619: Bellhop with flowers, marked "Germany," composition. $85-115. ET-620: Tall bellhop, marked "Japan." $65-85. ET-621: Oriental bellhop, marked "Germany." $65-85.

ET-624: Kneeling Indian with head-dress, marked "Germany." $95-125.

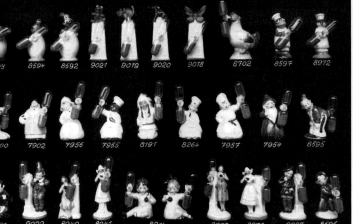

Left: Hertwig German Catalog, ca. 1932.

ET-625: Oriental bellhop, kneeling, marked "Germany." $65-85.
ET-626: Bellhop, marked "Germany." $65-85.
ET-627: Bellhop on telephone, marked "Japan." $35-55.

ET-628: Swami, white skin, marked "Japan." $75-95. ET-629: Swami, dark skin, marked "Germany." $75-95.

ET-630: Leprechaun by wishing well, marked "Manorware," glazed chalkware, England. $35-65. ET-631: Leprechaun, marked "Manorware," glazed chalkware, England. $35-65.

ET-632: Minuteman, marked "Enesco" and "Japan." $25-45. ET-633: Pixie, marked "Enesco" and "Japan." $25-35.

ET-634: Scotsman, "A Casdon Product, British made," plastic. $45-75.
ET-635: Leprechaun, brass. $35-55.

ET-636: English Bobby, Germany. $75-95.

ET-637: Fisherman with fish over shoulder, marked "Foreign." $75-95.

ET-638: Clown bent over and timer attached to bottom, marked "Germany." $95-125.

ET-639: Little boy holding towel. $55-65.

ET-640: Little boy with beret on the phone, marked "Germany." $55-65.

ET-641: Large genie egg timer, 6-1/2", recipe holder in the back, with matching lady ashtray. Timer only: $75-95.

ET-642: Black Swami marked "Germany 8520 and 8620." $125-135.

ET-644: Black boy sitting on chamber pot, marked "Foreign." $85-110.

ET-643: Double monks with casks on composition base. $55-65.

ET-645: Sitting white Swami. $125-135. ET-646: British soldier, stamped "Japan" on bottom. $75-95.

❖ Girls and Women Egg Timers

ET-700: Colonial lady, marked "Germany." $75-95. ET-701: Tall colonial woman with bonnet, marked "Germany." $75-95. ET-702: Colonial lady, marked "Germany." $75-95.

ET-703: Victorian lady, marked "Germany." $65-85.
ET-704: Peasant woman, marked "Germany." $75-95.
ET-705: Peasant woman with basket, marked "Germany." $75-95.

**ET-706: Parlor maid, marked "Japan." $45-65.
ET-707: Parlor maid carrying food, marked
"FOREIGN." $65-85.**

**ET-708: Maid, marked "Japan." $45-65. ET-709: Parlor maid, marked "Japan."
$45-65. ET-710: Parlor maid with cat by side, marked "Japan." $45-65. Also
comes in a German version. $65-80.**

**ET-711: Maid on telephone, marked "Japan." $35-45.
ET-712: Sitting woman, on telephone,
marked "Japan." $35-45. ET-713: Standing
woman, on telephone, marked "Japan."
$45-65.**

**ET-714: Welsh woman, marked "Japan." $50-70. ET-715: Swiss
woman, marked "Germany." $65-85. ET-716: Welsh woman,
marked "Germany." $65-85.**

**ET-717: Prayer Lady, Enesco.
$95-125.**

ET-718: Mammy holding potholders, wood. $75-95.

**ET-719: Kitchen maid, marked
"DAVAR ORIGINALS, Japan."
Measuring Spoons and 3 minute
timer. $60-80.**

ET-720: Welsh woman, plastic. $25-35.
ET-721: Geisha woman, marked "Germany." $85-95.

ET-722: "Tillie the Timer," cast iron. This timer is still in production. $15-25.

ET-723: Lady in cap, sticker reads "Josef Originals, Japan," composition. $25-45.

Right: Gift & Art Buyer, January 1956. This trade magazine reflects wholesale prices.

ET-724: Colonial lady, marked "Made in Japan." $65-85.

ET-725: Unusual lady in blue, "Germany" etched on glass tube, metal. $65-85.

ET-726: Girl with large bow in hair. $75-95. ET-727: Lady with large bow in front of dress and yellow hat, marked "Germany." $65-85. ET-728: Serving maid with tray marked "Germany 8895" on bottom. $65-85.

ET-733: Girl with green hat and dog. $65-85.

ET-729: Welsh lady by wheel, stamped "Foreign." The sand timer is only 5/8". $55-65. ET-730: Whimsical woman on telephone, 6", with foil sticker that reads "CMI Inc., Chadwick, Japan." $45-55.

ET-731: Lady with shawl. $60-80. ET-732: Victorian lady, marked "Germany." $65-85.

❖ Hanging Egg Timers

ET-800: Windmill with advertising for Keystone coffee, metal. $25-35. ET-801: Birdhouse, wood. $20-30. ET-802: Chef's head on plaque, wood. $25-35.

ET-803: Chef on plaque, Germany. $45-75. ET-804: Chick on plaque, Germany. $45-75. ET-805: Woman chef on plaque, Germany. $45-75.

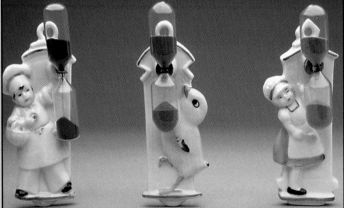

ET-806: Buccaneer, Germany. $100-150.

ET-807: Frying pan with chef, Japan. $25-45.

ET-808: Man under umbrella with basket of eggs, Germany, wood. $35-45. ET-809: Maid, Germany, wood. $35-45.

ET-810: Duck on egg, marked "Germany," wood. $25-45.

ET-811: Indian Josephine, plastic. $30-40.

The Gift & Art Buyer, April 1952. This trade magazine reflects wholesale prices.

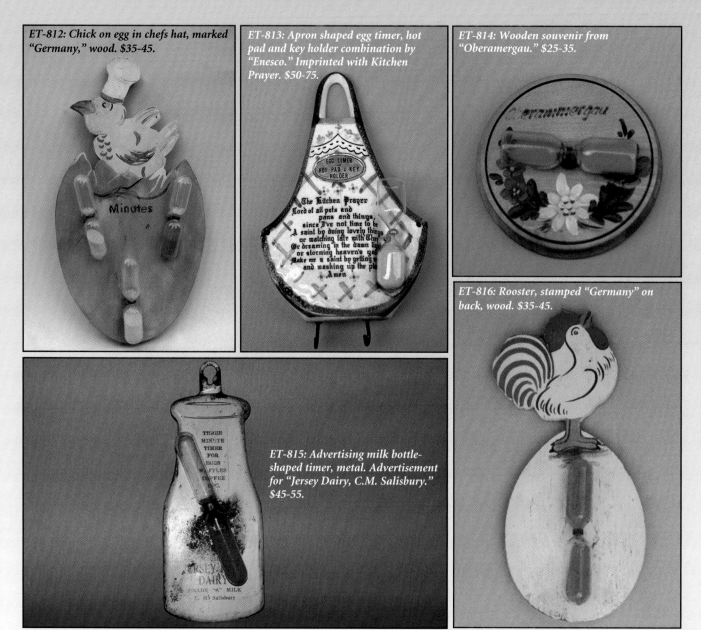

ET-812: Chick on egg in chefs hat, marked "Germany," wood. $35-45.

ET-813: Apron shaped egg timer, hot pad and key holder combination by "Enesco." Imprinted with Kitchen Prayer. $50-75.

ET-814: Wooden souvenir from "Oberamergau." $25-35.

ET-816: Rooster, stamped "Germany" on back, wood. $35-45.

ET-815: Advertising milk bottle-shaped timer, metal. Advertisement for "Jersey Dairy, C.M. Salisbury." $45-55.

❖ Goebel Egg Timers

The various Goebel animals featured here were made in a range of colors.

ET-900: Double Mr. Pickwick, modeled by Helmut Wehite in 1952. $125-175.

ET-901: These double rabbits were modeled by Helmut Wehite in 1932 and discontinued in 1984. The suggested retail price in 1984 was $9.50. Also found in red. $100-125.

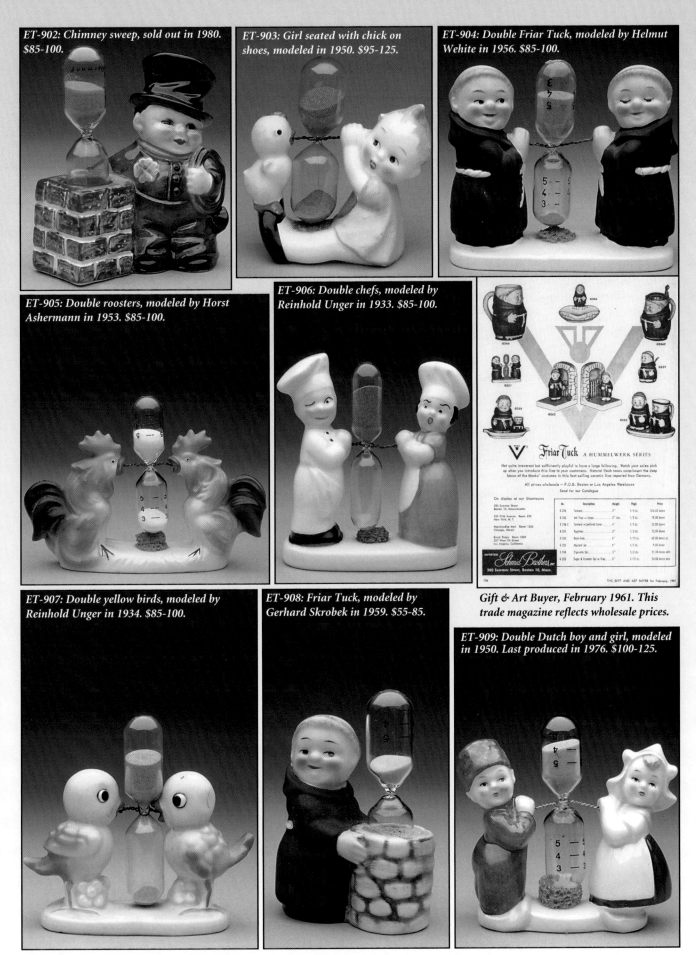

ET-902: Chimney sweep, sold out in 1980. $85-100.

ET-903: Girl seated with chick on shoes, modeled in 1950. $95-125.

ET-904: Double Friar Tuck, modeled by Helmut Wehite in 1956. $85-100.

ET-905: Double roosters, modeled by Horst Ashermann in 1953. $85-100.

ET-906: Double chefs, modeled by Reinhold Unger in 1933. $85-100.

Gift & Art Buyer, February 1961. This trade magazine reflects wholesale prices.

ET-907: Double yellow birds, modeled by Reinhold Unger in 1934. $85-100.

ET-908: Friar Tuck, modeled by Gerhard Skrobek in 1959. $55-85.

ET-909: Double Dutch boy and girl, modeled in 1950. Last produced in 1976. $100-125.

ET-910: Double chicks, modeled by Reinhold Unger in 1934. Found in other colors. $85-100.

ET-911: Double bears. $85-100.

ET-912: Little Girl Chef. $75-95.

ET-913: Rare Goebel Owl. $100-125.

ET-914: Double children, with full bee mark and sticker that reads "Vondendrisch & Heiligen, Aachen." Stamp next to the Goebel logo reads "Import d'allemagen." $100-125.

❖ Miscellaneous Egg Timers

ET-1000: Lighthouse with luster finish, Germany. $85-100. ET-1001: Lighthouse, marked "Manorware, England," glazed chalkware. $55-75.

ET-1002: Double-headed man with pipe, wood. $15-25. ET-1003: Double-headed fruit, wood. $15-25.

ET-1004: Angel. $45-65.

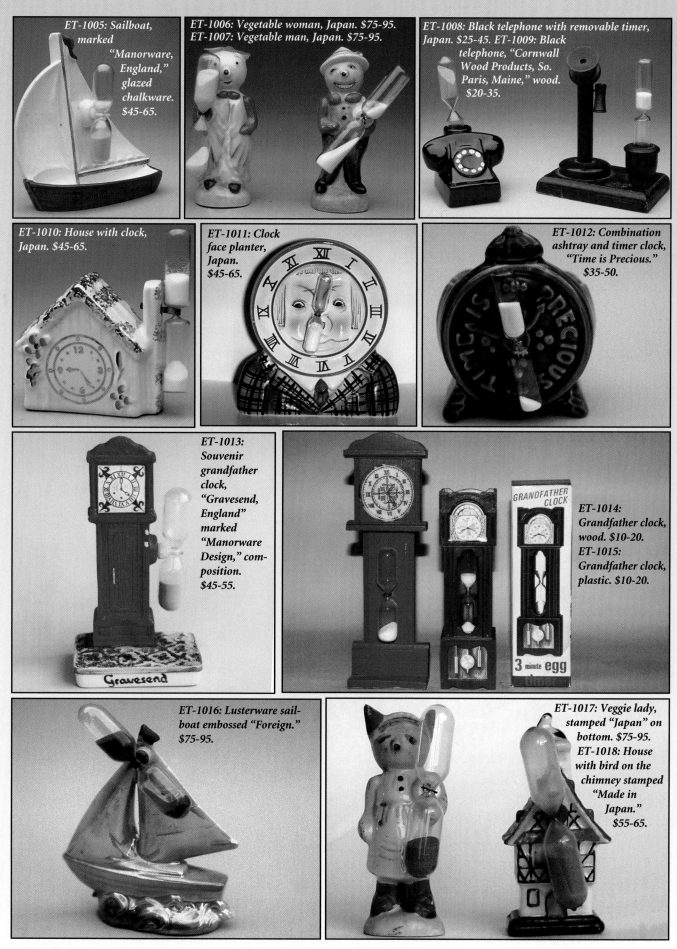

ET-1005: Sailboat, marked "Manorware, England," glazed chalkware. $45-65.

ET-1006: Vegetable woman, Japan. $75-95. ET-1007: Vegetable man, Japan. $75-95.

ET-1008: Black telephone with removable timer, Japan. $25-45. ET-1009: Black telephone, "Cornwall Wood Products, So. Paris, Maine," wood. $20-35.

ET-1010: House with clock, Japan. $45-65.

ET-1011: Clock face planter, Japan. $45-65.

ET-1012: Combination ashtray and timer clock, "Time is Precious." $35-50.

ET-1013: Souvenir grandfather clock, "Gravesend, England" marked "Manorware Design," composition. $45-55.

ET-1014: Grandfather clock, wood. $10-20. ET-1015: Grandfather clock, plastic. $10-20.

ET-1016: Lusterware sailboat embossed "Foreign." $75-95.

ET-1017: Veggie lady, stamped "Japan" on bottom. $75-95. ET-1018: House with bird on the chimney stamped "Made in Japan." $55-65.

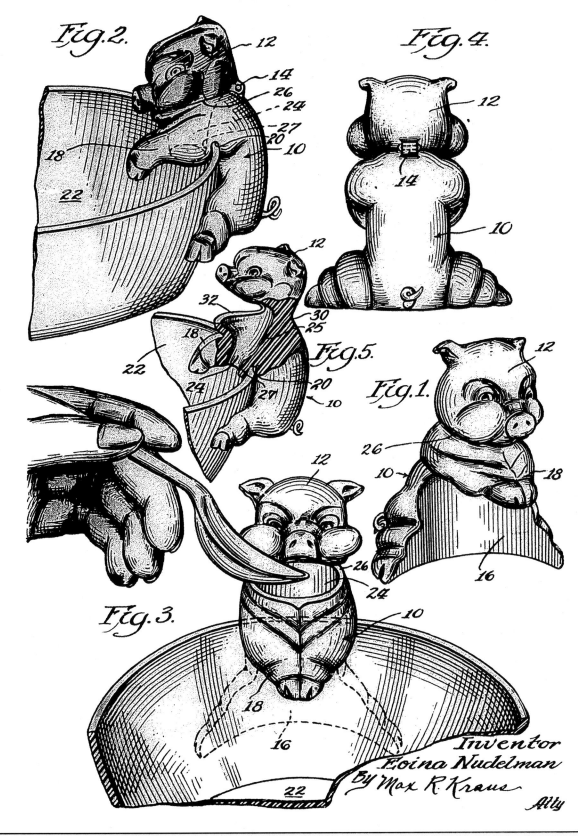

Fig.2.

Fig.4.

Fig.5.

Fig.1.

Fig.3.

Inventor
Eoina Nudelman
By Max R. Kraus
Atty

Whimsical Children's Cups and Baby Feeder Dishes

No matter how you flavor the milk or disguise the food, getting some kids to eat or drink can be a daily frustration. Long before the catchy "Got Milk" ad campaign made drinking the healthy, white stuff trendy, parents were devising ways to coax the kiddies to drink up. In the 1950s, kitschy designs conquered this challenge with whimsical children's cups. The baby feeder dishes, also featured from the same time period, made eating a fun event.

The tradition of whistling mugs was born centuries ago in Europe where they were used as toys to ward off evil spirits; some were unearthed in children's graves. The French used whistle cups to imitate nightingales in competitions. In the United States these Japanese imports were merely popular mealtime accessories. You could purchase these pieces through mail order ads in publications such as *Redbook* and *House Beautiful*, from department store catalogs like Alden's and in the popular five and dime stores—one cup was found with the W.T. Grant backstamp. The souvenir cups were probably sold in gift shops of the various attractions. Almost all the cups are Japanese imports, except for a few English examples. Unless otherwise noted, the cups measure approximately 3-1/2" high.

Our first book created a new cache of collectors who were delighted to discover these items from their childhoods. The cups with whistles and the straw/whistle combination continue to be more desirable than those with plain or figural handles. And just when we thought we've seen them all, a new piece will surface either in an online auction or an individual's private collection. We're delighted to include more than forty new cups and ten feeder dishes. Even as this book goes to press, undoubtedly another wonderful example will magically appear.

Before purchasing a whistle cup, carefully check any protrusions and whistles for damage. While you can expect that overall crazing effect, we advise steering clear of cups that are chipped or cracked, unless of course it's a rare example. Conversely, collectors of the feeder dishes are more tolerant of minor flaws, probably because they're so difficult to find in any condition. In the event you get lucky enough to find the sitter part of the feeding dish set separately, make sure the slotted base is intact so it can one day be perched on the matching bowl.

Online auctions have become an excellent retail source. Thrift shops, flea markets and antique shows also continue to be a steady outlet for cups. The feeder dishes, however, are few and far between so count yourself lucky if you add even one great set in a twelve-month period. Despite our efforts to educate dealers and collectors, the bowl sitters are still being misidentified as pie birds and plant waterers. The only time we were happy about such confusion was the recent find of a Wunfer bird, labeled as a pie bird, for a mere $30.

In the past three years, pricing for the cups hasn't fluctuated too much. Feeder dish values (whether sold as a set or each piece individually), however, have soared. Until more of these feeders enter the collecting market, you can probably expect to pay a pretty penny to own one. Puppy Tu (FD-117) and the wonderful Royal Winton dish (FD-209) are two of the exciting new finds.

Although we baby boomers seemed to have survived using ceramic dishes and cups, today's kids live in a plastic, safety conscious world. They will never have the same experience unless they, too, grow up to collect these wonderful relics of yesterday's youth. If you're looking for a collection that will feed on your passions, these cups and dishes will surely quench your thirst.

❖ *Whimsical Children's Cup and Baby Feeder Dishes*
Whistle Milk Cups

Each exmaple has a whistle attached to either the handle or cup itself.

WC-100: "Whistle For Your Milk." This is the most common cup found on the market and is found in both pink and blue. The bottom is marked "Ross Products Hand Decorated." It has a sticker that reads, "Chase Hand Painted." $15-25.

"Whistle for your milk" say the birdies on this ceramic mug, and the little warbler on the handle really tweets! Hand-decorated and trimmed in pink or blue, 7-ounce kiln-fired cup is personalized with any first name. A good idea for milk-shy youngsters! $1 ppd. Personal Gifts, Dept. R, 100 W. 61st St., New York 23, N. Y.

Right: Family Circle, November 1953. Although this ad shows the cup could be personalized, we've never found one with a name.

WC-101: On this "Whistle For Milk" variation, the birds face each other. 3-1/4" h. Pink and blue versions. A space on the bottom allowed the cup to be personalized. $20-25.

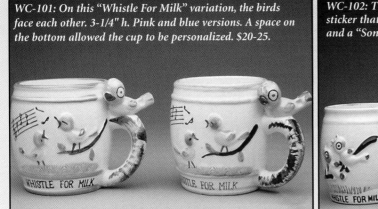

WC-102: This smaller model is only 3". The cup on the right has a sticker that reads, "Souvenir of Sugar Maple, New York" on the front and a "Sonsco" sticker on the bottom. $15-25.

WC-103: The quotation marks around the phrase "Tweet Like A Bird For Your Milk" are musical notes. A bird tail whistle protrudes from the cup. Marked "All Gone" on inside bottom. $30-40.

Variations of bird with top hat, "Sing For Your Milk."

WC-104: Bird sits on handle, whistle tail. $25-35.
WC-105: Bird tail is whistle that protrudes from cup. $30-40. WC-105 was sold with WC-103 in a 1955 Alden's Department Store Catalog at two for $1.00.
WC-106: Whistle is stem on handle. $25-35.

WC-107: "Sing For Your Milk," with bird tail whistle protruding from the cup, and cat handle. $30-40.

Empty nest "Whistle For Your Milk."
WC-108: Whistle stem on handle. $25-35. WC-109: Smaller 3" cup with no writing or whistle. $15-20. WC-110: Although this cup reads, "Whistle For Your Milk," it has no whistle. $20-25. ($25-35 with whistle.)

"Whistle For Your Milk"
WC-111: A whistle bird tail protrudes from this cup. $30-40.
WC-112: Similar to WC-111, with a deer handle. The inside bottom reads, "All Gone." $35-45.

WC-113A/B/C: "Whistle for Milk" 3" cups with birds facing each other. The bottoms are marked "Grantcrest hand painted Japan." Found in other color combinations. $25-35.

WC-114: "Sing a Song of Sixpence." This English cup is marked, "Genuine Staffordshire Hand Painted Shorter & Sons Ltd., England Patent Applied For." May pre-date Japanese cups. $40-50.

WC-115: "Let's All Sing Like The Birdies Sing For Milk." Cup with bird tail whistle. The bottom is marked "Pioneer Mdse Co., NY." $30-40.

Whimsical Children's Cups and Baby Feeder Dishes 161

WC-116A/B: "Tweet Like A Birdie For Your Milk." With whistle stem on handle. $25-35. WC-116B has a rabbit handle and a "Sonsco" sticker on the bottom along with a price of 49 cents. $35-45.

WC-117: "Sing For Your Milk." Singing chickens with chicken whistle tail on handle. The bottom is marked, "Pioneer Mdse. Co., N.Y." $30-40.

WC-118: "Whistling For Milk." Bird in cage on cup, bird tail whistle on handle. $30-40.

WC-119: "Whistle For Milk." Birds on cup facing handle. Bird whistle sits on handle that resembles a tuba. $30-40.

WC-120: "Drink Milk and Whistle." Stamped "Made in Japan" on the bottom. The bird on cup faces the handle. Whistle is separate piece. $25-35.

WC-121: The front reads, "Today I Am A Little Dear," and the back, "Today I Am A Little Stinker." $45-55.

162 Whimsical Children's Cups and Baby Feeder Dishes

WC-122A/B: "Sip N' Whistle Milk Mug For A Little Dear." The bird tail is a whistle, and the stem is a built-in straw. A poem on the back of both reads, "Whistle Whistle in my cup, when I blow Mom fills it up." $45-55.

WC-123: "Donuts & Milk For A Little Dear." This cup has an extra handle on the left. The back reads, "As you ramble on thru life brother . . . Whatever be your goal . . . Keep your eye upon the doughnut . . . And not upon the hole. The Mayflower Optimist Creed." $50-60.

WC-124/125: "I'm A Little Dear." The deer tail is a whistle. "I'm A Little Stinker" cup has a skunk tail whistle. $45-55.

WC-126: "Whistle For Milk." Puppy with frog on front, dog bow whistle. Frog on inside bottom $45-55.
WC-127: "Whistle For Milk." Kitty and mouse on front, kitty bow whistle. Kitty on inside bottom. Also found with bird on front, handle, and in bottom of cup. $45-55.

Whimsical Children's Cups and Baby Feeder Dishes 163

WC-128A/B: "Whistle For More Milk." Whistle protrudes from cow's neck. $35-45.

WC-129: "Drink Milk and Whistle." With romping bears on front, little bear sits next to whistle on handle. $45-55.

WC-130: The Hawthorn Melody Farms "Always Drink Milk" cup was a dairy promotion. $45-55.
WC-131: The "Lani Moo Says Whistle For More" cup promoted Dairymen's Milk. Lani Moo was the trademark figure for Meadow Gold (formerly known as Dairymen's dairy products) in Hawaii. The inside of the bottom is marked. "All Pau"-Hawaiian for "All Done" or "All Gone." $50-60.

WC-132A/B: "Whistle For Your Milk" cup with little dog on front and on handle next to the whistle. Found with painted eyes (WC-132A) and "wiggly" eyes (WC-132B, center). $45-55.

WC-133A/B: "Whistle For Your Milk" lion cup with bird on handle next to the whistle. Found with "wiggly"eyes and painted eyes. Sticker on bottom of WC-133B reads, "World Creations by Orimico - Japan." $45-55.

WC-134: *Cat face with "wiggly" eyes on cup, bird on handle next to whistle. The bottom is stamped "Elpro Hand Decorated - Japan." $45-55.*
WC-135: *Bear face with "wiggly" eyes on cup, bear on handle next to the whistle. The sticker on the bottom reads, "Gold Castle Made in Japan." $45-55.*

WC-136: *"Whistle For Your Milk."Owl face with "wiggly" eyes, bird on handle. $45-55.*

WC-137: *"Souvenir of Canada." Rabbit face with "wiggly"eyes, rabbit on handle. $45-55.*
WC-138: *"Whistle For Your Milk." Pig face with "wiggly""eyes, bird on handle. $45-55.*

WC-139: *"Whistle For Your Milk" waving bear with wiggly eyes, bear on handle. $45-55.*

WC-140: *"Whistle For Your Milk." Ugly cat with "wiggly"eyes on the front, bird on handle. $45-55.*

Whimsical Children's Cups and Baby Feeder Dishes 165

WC-141: "Drink More Milk." Football player running with ball. Man's hat on handle is a whistle. $45-55.

WC-142: "I Like Milk." Begging poodle. Squirrel on the handle is a whistle. $40-50.

WC-143: "Drink Milk and Whistle." Train on front. Handle looks like track, with whistle sticking out of the train top. $50-60.

WC-144: Found in Holland, this Japanese cup is in two languages. The front shows Dutch couple near windmill and reads, "Drink Je Melk En Fluit." The back shows a cow and reads, "Drink Your Milk and Whistle." $50-60.

WC-145: Cup with deer face on front and whistle on handle, 3". $30-40.
WC-146: Poodle face on front with whistle and bird on handle, "Lefton." $30-40

WC-147: *Train-shaped cup, handle is whistle. The bottom is embossed "Parksmith Corp." $25-35.*

WC-148: *Elephant head "Whistle For Your Milk" cup. Trunk is whistle, ears are handles. $35-45.*

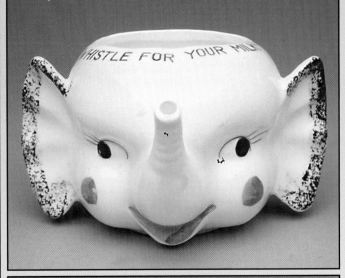

WC-149: *"Count Down Blast Off" space theme cup. Rocket ship handle is whistle. $25-35. The bottom of the cup allowed it to be personalized.*

WC-150: *"Drink Milk & Hoot" with owl whistle on branch handle. Marked "C-30" on bottom. $50-60.*

"Whistling For Your Milk Cups."
WC-151: *Clown with balloons, plastic, 3-1/4". $10-20.*
WC-152: *Ceramic marked, "Spencer Gifts, Inc. 1976." $15-20.*

WC-153: Deer cup with bird on handle marked "Lefton." $30-40.
WC-154: Steer cup with pistol handle, marked "Lefton." $30-40

WC-155: Cow cup with bird on handle, tail is whistle. $25-35. A similar cup in the shape of a hippopotamus has also been found.

WC-156: Goose on the front of the cup and clown handle with whistle in the hat, $30-40.

WC-157: Cute bluebird and squirrel with yellow bird on the handle. Companion to WC-126 and 127. Sometimes found with a little bird in the bottom. $45-55.

WC-158: Three little pigs dance on the front of this cup while a pig on the handle looks on. Companion cup to WC-150. $50-60.

WC-159: Waving Teddy Bear with bear on the handle, $45-55.

WC-160: Rare tug boat cup with tug boat whistle on the handle. Companion to cup WC-143. $50-60.

WC-163: Baby blue bird in bonnet. Bird on handle is the whistle, marked "Japan." $45-55.

Both cups are stamped "Made in Japan" on the bottom.
WC-161: Frog with wiggly eyes and bird on handle. "Whistle for your Milk." $45-55.
WC-162: Cat with wiggly eyes, cat on the handle. $45-55.

WC-164: Spotted Dog with wiggly eyes, $45-55.
WC-165: Hippo with wiggly eyes, stamped "Made in Japan." $45-55.

WC-166: Bear, with wiggly eyes, "Souvenir of Canada." $45-55.

Whimsical Children's Cups and Baby Feeder Dishes 169

WC-167: Cow with wiggly eyes, bird on handle and separate whistle. "Whistle For Your Milk." $45-55.

WC-168A/B: Birds feeding chicks in nest. Tail of one bird is the whistle. All of the cups come from Canada and most are found without writing. With writing: $30-40. Without writing: $25-35.

WC-170: "Whistling For Your Milk," depicts a bird on a swing, $35-45.

WC-169: "Whistle Like a Mocking Bird For Your Milk." This cup has a courting couple on the front and a little bird in a top hat on the handle. Sticker on the bottom reads "Sonsco." $35-45.

WC-171: "Little Boy Blue" is companion to WC-114. Notice the horn on the handle is a whistle. Bottom is stamped "Genuine Staffordshire Hand Painted Shorter and Sons Ltd. England, Patent Applied For." $40-50.

WC-172: One side shows a smiling girl, "I am a little Eskimo who drinks milk." The crying girl on the other side says "I am a little Eskimo who doesn't drink milk." Polar bear on the handle with whistle on his neck. $45-55.

❖ Souvenir Cups

These cups were probably sold in gift shops at various tourist attractions.

WC-200: Palm trees on cup with bird whistle on handle. $35-45.
WC-201: "Sip N' Whistle Milk Mug For A Little Dear" cup features flamingo, with whistle and straw on handle. The poem on the back reads, "Whistle, whistle on my cup, when I blow mom fills it up." $40-50.

WC-202: "Washington, D.C." with relief of the Capitol. $40-50.

WC-203: "Ariel Tramway, Franconia Notch, NH" sticker on the bottom, "_G Nov Co. Made in Japan." $40-50. WC-204: "Old Man Of The Mountains, Franconia Notch, NH." $40-50

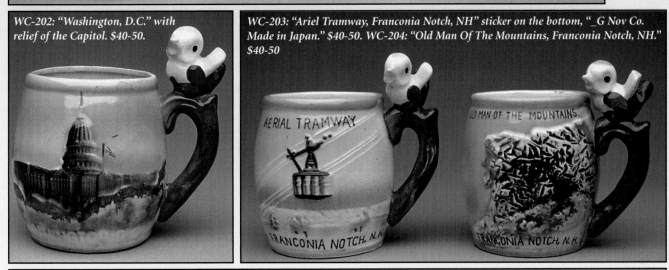

WC-205: "Sip N' Whistle Milk Mug For A Little Dear." From an unidentified amusement park. Straw on this cup was never opened. Same poem as on WC-201. $40-50. WC-206: "Whistle For Your Milk." Yellowstone Park. Same poem as on WC-201. $40-50.

WC-207: Seattle Space Needle cup says "Whistle For Your Milk" on the handle. The back reads, "A gift from the Seattle World's Fair, For the Personal Use Of _____." $20-40.

WC-208: Whistle stein with Seattle Space Needle. The back says "A Gift From the Seattle World's Fair." This cup could also be personalized. 5-1/2" h. $20-40.
WC-209: Colorado Centennial, "Rush To The Rockies," whistle cup. 1859-1959, produced by Holt Howard, 1958. $20-40.

WC-210: "Souvenir Whistle Milk Mug, New York City," features the Empire State Building and the Statue of Liberty. $40-50.

WC-211: This rare Knott's Berry Farm mug is from the famed attraction in Anaheim, California that was popular in the 1950s to the 1970s. Berries on the front and says "Drink Milk and Whistle" The back is embossed "Knotts Berry Farm California." $50-60.

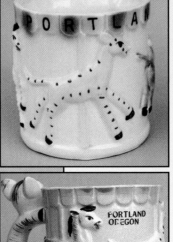

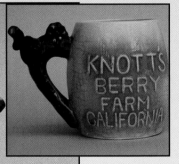

WC-212A: "Portland Oregon Children's Zoo," resembles WC-305, has "All Gone" written on the inside bottom. This version has the words "Portland Zoo" embossed on the rim. $40-50. WC-212B (lower right): This version is stamped on the top of the mug, "Portland Oregon" on one side and "Children's Zoo" on the other. $40-50.

WC-213: "New Jersey Turnpike/Make Birdie Whistle for Milk." Just when we thought we had seen all the cups this last minute addition turned up. $50-60.

❖ Miscellaneous Milk Cups

Each of these has its own endearing quality.

WC-300A: *Mystery mugs and fairy tale mystery mugs by Nasco, NY & LA, were marketed in different series, 3". "What's At The Bottom Of The Well?" with fish in bottom. $30-40.*

WC-300B: *"Guess Who Is In The Bottom Of Your Mug?" Boy with guitar in bottom. (Fairy Tale Mug.) $30-40.*

House and Garden, October 1956.

AROUND

A shy feeder will take a keen interest in finishing his milk if you serve it in the Mystery Mug. Permanently attached to the bottom of the white ceramic cup is a china animal: a colorful squirrel, a chipmunk, a kitten. This is a feeding aid which will help to stimulate a child's appetite. $2.95 the set of 6 ppd. Prestige Products, 3450 Wilshire, Los Angeles.

❖ Straw-handled Cups

WC-301A: *Mother cat serving milk to kittens. The original tag reads, "Milk Time Mug, The mug with the built-in straw handle, Item No. 5257, Our Own Import." The cup reads, "There's time for everything in an average day. There's time for Milk and time to play. So drink your milk from this mug so gay, and when you are finished Back to Play." "Back to Play" is also marked on the inside bottom. $15-25.* **WC-301B:** *Milk Time, girl on swing. $15-25.*

WC-301C: *Milk Time, boy with cork gun. $15-25*

WC-302: *Elephant handle, trunk is straw. Bear inside bottom, marked "That's A Good Boy." $20-30.* **WC-303:** *Giraffe straw handle. Bunny inside bottom, marked "That's A Good Girl." $20-30.*

WC-304: Stick children with straw handle clown. "All Gone" inside bottom. Pink and blue versions. $20-30.

WC-305: Carousel cup with deer handle. "All Gone" inside bottom. Pink and blue versions, 2-3/4". $20-25. Also found in 3-1/4" (not shown). $25-30.

WC-306: Elephant design with straw handle clown. "All Gone" inside bottom. $20-30.

WC-307: Clown circus cup with clown handle. Inside bottom reads, "Summer, Winter, Spring, Autumn, Drink Milk." 3-1/2". $25-35.

WC-308: Clown circus cup with clown handle, 3". The bottom is marked "Grantcrest, hand painted, Japan." $25-35.

WC-309: Ducks and chicks circle the outside, bird on handle. "All Gone" inside bottom. $30-40. **WC-310:** Circus animals circle the outside, puppy is the handle, "All Gone" inside bottom. $30-40.

WC-311: Smokey The Bear "I Like Milk" Cups. Each back reads, "F is for forests, keep fire away." Smokey, holding right hand up, on handle. $35-45. WC-312: Small bear without hat, facing foward, on handle, hole in head is whistle. Made by WCKay, this is the most difficult-to-find Smokey cup. $65-75. WC-313: Smokey with both hands at his side on handle. Made by WCKay, face on the front is the same as WC-312. $35-45.

WC-314: "Always Drink Milk." Clown on cup doing handstand, full-figured clown handle. Marked "Chase hand decorated" on the bottom. $30-40.
WC-315: "Always Drink Milk." Cow on cup with cow handle. $30-40.

WC-316: "Always Drink Milk." Colonial-style couple on cup with boy handle. $30-40. WC-317: "Always Drink Milk." Common cup with Dutch couple, woman holding bucket, on front, and boy handle. Figure on handle varies. $20-30. WC-318: "Always Drink Milk." Similar to WC-317, but the woman is on left and appears to be holding a loaf of bread, and boy on handle differs. $30-40.

WC-319: "Always Drink Milk." Pixie face, pixie handle. $35-45.

WC-320: "Always Drink Milk." Duck family with full-figured duck in overalls handle, $30-40. WC-321: "Always Drink Milk." Three bears on front, bear handle. Design on cup matches WC-129. $30-40.

WC-322: "Always Drink Milk." Lambs on front, lamb handle. $30-40. WC-323: "Always Drink Milk." Rabbit on front, floppy-eared rabbit handle. $30-40.

WC-324A: Right: "Always Drink Milk." Common deer cup, deer handle. The sticker on the bottom reads, "Chase, hand painted." $15-20
WC-324B: Left: Harder to find, reads "Drink More Milk." $25-35.

WC-325: Deer near branch with bird on front. Handle resembles a mouse more than a deer. $30-40. WC-326: Deer lying in grass on front, deer handle. $30-40.

WC-327: "Always Drink Milk." Mother and baby deer featured on cup with deer handle. $30-40.

WC-328: (left and right): Mother holds the hand of little girl bear on cup with a bear handle. Bottom marked "© Hand Decorated." Pink and blue versions. $30-40. WC-329: (center): This cup, featuring a baby bear holding a honey pot, with bear handle, was probably a promotional item. The bottom is marked "Honey Bear Farm hand decorated." $40-50.

WC-330A: "Always Drink Milk." Child milking cow on cup with little girl handle. $30-40.
WC-330B: "Drink More Milk." Child milking cow on front, little boy handle. $30-40.

WC-331: Cows on cup with cow handle. $30-40. WC-332: Sheep on the front, deer handle. The sticker on the bottom reads, "Hand painted, Royal, Japan." $30-40.

WC-333A: "Drink Milk Every Day." Rabbits on cup with rabbit handle. $30-40.
WC-334: Deer on cup, deer handle. $30-40. See coordinating juice cups WC-402 and WC-403 on p. 182.

WC-333B: "I Drink Milk Everyday" with rabbit on front and handle. $30-40.

WC-335A: "Drink Milk Every Day." Father and mother duck on front, duck head handle. $35-45. WC-336: "Duckie Likes Milk Too." This version has baby ducks on front, duck head handle. $35-45.

WC-335B: *"Duckie Likes Milk Too"* also features the duck parents, marked *"Shafford"* on the bottom. $35-45.

WC-337: *"Always Drink Milk."* Baby duck on cup, duck head with hat handle. $35-45.

WC-338: *"Always Drink Milk."* Jack and Jill. Little boy handle. $35-45. WC-339: *"Always Drink Milk."* Humpty Dumpty with soldier handle. Pink and blue versions. $35-45.

WC-340: *"Always Drink Milk."* Santa in sleigh with reindeer on front, holly handle. $40-50.

WC-341: *"Always Drink Milk."* Little Boy Blue on cup, boy with straw hat handle. $35-45.

WC-342: Baker on cup, bobby handle. $35-45. WC-343: Baby in cradle on front, bobby handle. $35-45.

These "I Like Milk" cups appear to be made by the same manufacturer as WC-342 and WC-343.
WC-344: Hen and chicks on cup, clown handle. $35-45. WC-345: Lamb and schoolhouse on cup, little girl handle. $35-45.

WC-346: "I Like Milk." Horse head inside horseshoe, cowboy handle. Pink and blue versions. $35-45.

180 Whimsical Children's Cups and Baby Feeder Dishes

WC-347: "I Like Milk" transferware. Bears, penguin, and giraffe playing on a teeter-totter on cup, clown head handle. $20-30.

WC-348: "Monkey See, Monkey Do, Monkey Having a Drink, How About You?" Cup pictures monkey milking cow and squirting milk at second monkey. Lithopane with monkey in the bottom when held up to light. $40-50.

WC-349: "Milk The Cow While You Drink The Milk." Inside the cup, milk flows through the udders. $30-40.

WC-350: "Milk." Fish on cup with coral-shaped handle. $20-30.

WC-351: "Drink Milk Every Day" has elephants on the front and a clown handle. This cup is a companion to WC-401 juice cup. $35-45.

WC-352: "All Good Indians Drink Their Milk" with toma-hawk handle. "Japan" stamped on the bottom, $30-40.

WC-353A: "Where has my horse gone?" with horse in the bottom of the cup. $30-40. WC-353B: "Where has my blooming cactus gone?" with cactus in the bottom of the cup. $30-40.

WC-354: "Good Morning Mama," 3" cup with matching cereal dish. Cup only: $35-45. Bowl only: $40-50. Set $75-100.

❖ Whimsical Juice Cups

These small cups were designed for juice.

WC-400: "I Drink My Orange Juice Every Day." Cows on cup with deer handle. $40-50.
WC-401: Elephants on cup with clown handle. $40-50.

WC-402A/B: "Juice For Good Teeth." Rabbit on front, rabbit handle, 2-1/2". Pink and blue versions. Companion to WC-333. $25-35. WC-403: "Drink More Juice." Deer, deer handle, 2-1/2", matches WC-334. $25-35.

"Drink Orange Juice," 3-1/4".
WC-404: Orange on front and branch for handle. $10-15. WC-405: Orange with cute face on front, branch-style handle. $10-20.

"Drink Orange Juice," 3-1/2".
WC-406: Orange on cup with plain handle. $10-15. WC-407: Orange, *"Florida,"* on cup. Marked *"Ross Products Inc. Hand Decorated,"* under glaze. $10-15.

WC-408: Half an orange on front, marked *"Ross Products hand decorated."* $10-15. WC-409: Double orange on front. $10-15.
WC-410: Single orange on front, marked *"Ross Products hand decorated."* $10-15.

WC-411: "Pineapple Juice is Good," 3". $15-20.

WC-412: "Drink Your Juice and Whistle A Merry Tune" cup has yellow fruit. A piper on the back plays his flute; handle is whistle. $25-35.

WC-413A: "Tomato Juice is Good," 3". $10-15.
WC-413B: "Drink Tomato Juice," 3". $10-15.

WC-414: "I Drink My Orange Juice Every Day." 3-1/2" cup with cows. Companion to WC-331 milk cup. $40-50.

WC-415: Basket of Fruit, "Always Drink Juice," 3". $25-35.

WC-416: "Drink Pineapple Juice," 3". $25-35.
WC-417: "Drink Apple Juice," 3". $25-35.

WC-418A/B: 3" cup with pineapple on front. $35-45.

❖ Other Whimsical Cups

These cute cups from the same era seem to fit into a category of their own.

WC-500: "For A Good Little Lamb." $20-30.

WC-501: Baby toys decorate front, baby rattle handle, 2-1/2". $10-20.

WC-502A: Baby Face with bead handle. Little girl, "All Gone" inside bottom. $20-30. WC-502B: Little boy, "All Gone" inside bottom. $20-30.

WC-503: Raised relief of Jack and Jill falling down the hill on front. One of a nursery rhyme series. $20-30.

WC-504A: This "Drink Me Dry and The Kitty Will Cry" cup came with a crying mechanism in the bottom. Two cats singing. $25-35.
WC-504B: Cat in beret singing with mice. $25-35.

WC-505: Two cats on cup with cat handle. $20-30. Also found with a matching cereal bowl.

WC-506: Santa in sleigh on front, Rudolph handle. (Found in Australia.) $20-30.

WC-507: Santa with rhinestone eyes on cup, red and white handle. Bottom marked "Kreiss & Co." $10-20.

WC-508A: Reindeer on the front, Santa handle. $10-20.
WC-508B: Bells on the front, Santa handle. $10-20.
WC-508C: Santa on the front, Santa handle. $10-20.

WC-509: Santa waving with Santa handle. $10-20.

WC-510: "Paul Bunyan Mug" is embossed, "1955 Georg. Lefton." $30-40.

WC-511: This Humpty Dumpty mug has the words "Humpty Dumpty Sat on a Wall" stamped on the backside. $20-30.

WC-512: Little girl with lamb on the front; back is stamped "Mary Had a Little Lamb." $20-30. WC-513: "There was an Old Woman who lived in a shoe" is stamped on the back of this mug. $20-30.

WC-514: "Old King Cole" is stamped on the back of the mug. $20-30.

WC-515: Cup with rabbit head on the front and a rabbit handle, "Japan." $20-30. WC-516: Cup with rabbit playing the fiddle, and a blue rabbit on the handle. $20-30.

WC-517: Cup with rabbits on the front and a rabbit handle; sticker on the back reads, "Souvenir of Atlantic City, NJ." $20-30.

WC-518: Cup with duck head in a green hat on the front and duck in a top hat on the handle. "J-358" on the bottom. $20-30.

WC-519: Cup from England has a windmill on the front and a bear on the handle. Inside reads "All Gone Good Girl." $25-35.

WC-520: Baby Rattle handle and train on the front. Sticker on the bottom reads "Rubens Originals, Los Angeles, Made in Japan." $20-30.

WC-521: Little Boy with a bear or fox on the handle. $15-25.

WC-522: Straight Shooter Milk Mug. Tag reads "Western style mug for boys and girls, Chase Import" and the other side of the tag reads "Yippee Milk Mug, Fast on the Trigger, Japan." Backside reads "REWARD WELLS, FARGO & CO.'S EXPRESS BOX on SONORA AND MILTON STAGE ROUTE, was ROBBED this morning, near Reynolds' Ferry, by one man, masked and armed with sixteen shooter and double-barreled shot gun. We will pay $250 for ARREST and CONVICTION of the Robber. JNO. J. VALENTINE, Gen. Supt., San Francisco, July 26, 1875." $35-45.

❖ Baby Feeder Dishes

While baby feeder dishes are often popular with collectors, those featured in this chapter are more unusual than most. These dishes cleverly enticed the baby to eat by also feeding the cute figure on the bowl; e.g.: "One for the baby, one for the clown." All of these attachments funnel the food back into the dish.

The First feeder dish, FD-100, was found complete with the duck. That made it easy to identify the feeder duck in FD-101, which was found separately from the dish at a large flea market but it was marked as a pie bird. These detachable figures represent at least seventy to eighty percent of a two-part dish's value, and will be harder to locate and more costly than their one-piece counter-parts.

Due to their rarity and desirability to collectors, prices on the feeders have escalated more than the cups.

❖ Two-Piece Feeder Dishes

FD-100: Bowl, 6" dia., marked "Ross Products Hand Decorated." The paper sticker reads, "Chase Hand Painted, Japan." The duck is 5" h. and also has a "Chase" sticker. Set: $100-125. Feeder only: $65-75. Bowl only: $40-50.

FD-101: Feeder, 5" h., on 6" dia. bowl, resembles Donald Duck. Set: $120-150. Feeder only: $75-95. Bowl only: $40-50.

These feeders are often mistaken for pie birds, but it's easy to distinguish them as feeders by the slot on the bottom, which is designed to slip over the bowl's edge.

FD-102: This boxed set includes dish, feeder, cup, towel, and bib. The sticker on the bottom of the bowl and cup reads, "Wales" and "Made in Japan" with a crown. The sticker on the box reads, "Bouquet Linens." Bowl, 5" dia.; Bird, 3-1/2". Set: $150-200. Feeder only: $75-95. Bowl only: $40-50.

FD-103: *This 4-3/4" Cardinal China Wunfer Bird has now been found with its original bowl. The side of the box reads, "Wunfer Bird & Bowl a product of the Cardinal China Company, Carteret, N.J." $1.25 is also written in pencil. Set: $80-110. Feeder only: $60-80. Bowl only: $20-30. (Add $20 for original box.)*

meet the **wunfer** BIRD

*a great help when feeding the kiddies —
one for the bird- and
one for the tot . . .
a spoonful for each!*

#1196 Wunfer Bird & Dish

Meet the Wunfer Bird. He sits on the edge of the baby's cereal dish and helps you feed the tot. Wunfer the baby and Wunfer the bird. Not too much help as far as junior's concerned because the birdie lets his share go back into the dish again. Bird and dish complete, gift boxed.

$7.20 *per dozen — 2 doz. minimum*

1954 Cardinal China Catalog.

Thrifty Gifts from Mac the Canny Scot!

WUNFER BIRD FOR BABY

Meet the Wunfer Bird. He sits on the edge of baby's cereal dish and helps you feed the tot. Wunfer the baby and Wunfer the bird. Not too much help as far as junior's concerned because the birdie lets his share go back into the dish again. Ceramic bird and dish, gift boxed.

$1.25 per set postpaid

2 Sets for **2.25** postpaid

SUNFLOWER THERMOMETER

You'll be able to view the temperature with a sunny disposition when you look at this lovely wall decoration. Excellent for kitchen, foyer or playroom, it is guaranteed accurate and has an unbreakable crystal. 5 x 6" deep. Gift boxed. Green and yellow or yellow and red.

$1.50 each postpaid

2 for **2.75** postpaid

EGG CADDY

For boiled eggs in or out of the shell. The bowl section holds the contents of two jumbo eggs and besides there are two built-in egg cups. Hand decorated.

$1.25 postpaid

2 for **$2.25** postpaid

Write for New Spring Catalog.
Dept. HB-5

Highland Gifts
4 Chester Circle · New Brunswick, New Jersey

House Beautiful, May 1954.

FD-104: *This dish resembles FD-101 and FD-102, 6" dia. $40-50. (May be bowl for feeder FD-106 but has not been found together.)*

ONE FOR THE BABY

ONE FOR THE CHICK

FD-107: *Cowboy, 4-3/4". $95-125.*

FD-105: *Green and yellow bird similar to the Wunfer Bird, 4-3/8". $75-95.*

FD-106: *Chick with scarf, 4-1/4". $75-95.*

FD-108: Duck with bib, 5-1/2", Italian earthenware. Originally came with matching bowl, plate, and cup. Set: $100-125. Feeder only: $75-95.

FEED THE DUCK a spoonful of pablum or whatever before you feed one to Buster. The duck's open mouth tunnels the grub right back into the dish but your baby won't know the difference. He will be so fascinated by the whole routine, that he'll bang the high chair for his turn. Italian earthenware feeding dish with matching cup and plate. $6.95 ppd. LeWitt Jewelers, 299 Main St., New Britain, Connecticut.

House Beautiful, October 1956.

FD-110: Clown head, 3", with matching bowl, 5-1/2" dia. Found in different colors. Set: $75-95. Feeder only: $45-55. Bowl only: $30-40.

FD-109: Polka-dot cat, 4-1/4". Appears to be a companion to FD-115. $75-95.

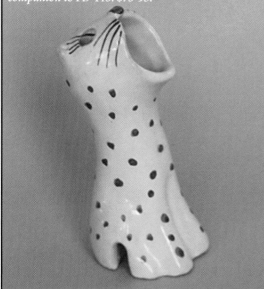

FD-111B: This clown with the "+" eyes is marked "Italy." The size is the same as FD-111A. $50-60.

FD-111A: This clown head has been found in several colors, 2-1/2" x 4". Bowl, believed to be the original, 6-1/4" dia. Set: $90-125. Feeder only: $50-60. Bowl only: $40-50.

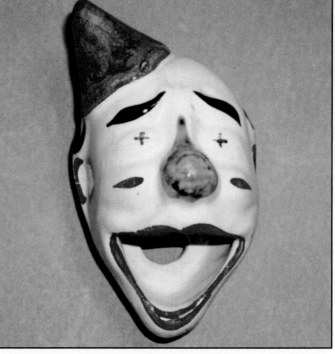

FD-112: *The plastic clown bear snaps off the bowl. Bowl, 6" dia., bear, 4-3/4". The bowl is marked "1990 Catena International, All rights reserved, Made in China." Set: $35-45.*

FD-113: *This colorful clown was found with its original box and spoon. The box reads "One For You, One For Me" Circus Feeding Set. Although unmarked, the period graphics date it as being from the late 1940s to the early 1950s. Bowl, 6" dia., clown, 4" h. Set: $125-150. Feeder only: $80-100. Bowl only: $40-50. (Add $20-25 for original box.)*

FD-114: *"Hungry Piggy" pink plastic pig clips on the side of matching, plastic bowl. The smiling pig in the bottom declares "All Gone." The mouth is hinged to insert food. Bowl, 4-3/4" dia., pig 3". Marked "Topic Toys, Made in the USA, US Patents Pending, Copyright 1948." Set was also sold with matching silverware in the shape of pigs or rabbits. $55-75. (Add $15-25 for original box.)*

HUNGRY PIGGY A UTILITY-TOY WHICH SOLVES THE FEEDING PROBLEM

HUNGRY PIGGY is a radically new conception in the baby field which provides a definite solution to the ever present feeding problem. Combining the practicality of a utility and the appeal of a toy, Piggy encourages baby to imitate Piggy's happy, healthy appetite. HUNGRY PIGGY clamps over the edge of the bowl, opening his mouth wide when a spoonful of food is inserted. He gives the appearance of actually swallowing with unflagging enthusiasm. However, he is so constructed that the food returns right back into the bowl and baby isn't denied a single morsel. Piggy comes in a pleasant tone of pink Lustrex—a plastic that withstands hot water without distortion or change in color. He is accompanied by a companion 'Piggy Bowl' comprising a two piece set with the further addition of a novel spoon, fork and stand in a five piece ensemble. Accessories are in complementary colors of heat-resisting Lustrex. Based on the psychological mechanism of mimicry ("One for the baby and one for piggy") HUNGRY PIGGY easily persuades baby to eat where all of mother's commands and wiles may fail.

Hungry Piggy
SOLVES FEEDING PROBLEM

Piggy opens his mouth when spoon is inserted. Food returns to bowl.

A loveable Table Pal for Baby

House Beautiful, May 1949.

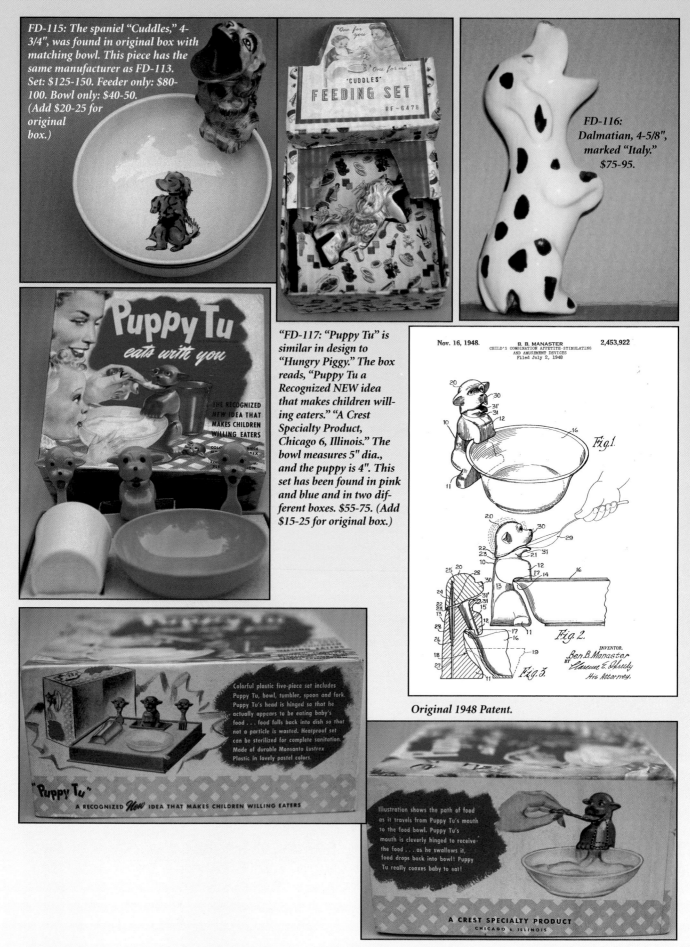

FD-115: The spaniel "Cuddles," 4-3/4", was found in original box with matching bowl. This piece has the same manufacturer as FD-113. Set: $125-150. Feeder only: $80-100. Bowl only: $40-50. (Add $20-25 for original box.)

"One for you" "One for me" 'CUDDLES' FEEDING SET RF-6478

FD-116: Dalmatian, 4-5/8", marked "Italy." $75-95.

Puppy Tu eats with you
THE RECOGNIZED NEW IDEA THAT MAKES CHILDREN WILLING EATERS

"FD-117: "Puppy Tu" is similar in design to "Hungry Piggy." The box reads, "Puppy Tu a Recognized NEW idea that makes children willing eaters." "A Crest Specialty Product, Chicago 6, Illinois." The bowl measures 5" dia., and the puppy is 4". This set has been found in pink and blue and in two different boxes. $55-75. (Add $15-25 for original box.)

Nov. 16, 1948. B. B. MANASTER 2,453,922
CHILD'S COMBINATION APPETITE-STIMULATING AND AMUSEMENT DEVICES
Filed July 2, 1948

INVENTOR.
Ben B. Manaster
BY Clarence E. Ohridy
His Attorney.

Original 1948 Patent.

Colorful plastic five-piece set includes Puppy Tu, bowl, tumbler, spoon and fork. Puppy Tu's head is hinged so that he actually appears to be eating baby's food . . . food falls back into dish so that not a particle is wasted. Heatproof set can be sterilized for complete sanitation. Made of durable Monsanto Lustrex Plastic in lovely pastel colors.

"Puppy Tu"
A RECOGNIZED New IDEA THAT MAKES CHILDREN WILLING EATERS

Illustration shows the path of food as it travels from Puppy Tu's mouth to the food bowl. Puppy Tu's mouth is cleverly hinged to receive the food . . . as he swallows it, food drops back into bowl! Puppy Tu really coaxes baby to eat!

A CREST SPECIALTY PRODUCT
CHICAGO 6, ILLINOIS

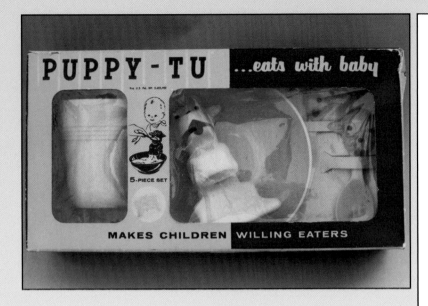

Meals are a Game with PUPPY TU

Let this wistful, hungry little puppy make your childs feeding time a more enjoyable experience for him. Puppy Tu's cleverly hinged jaws gladly gobble up all the food you may offer him. The food then falls back into the dish so that not a particle is wasted. Puppy Tu's appetite sets a good example. Made of non-breakable, beautiful plastic that may be sterilized.

Five piece set, only **$1.25** postpaid
Write for free, illustrated, gift catalogue.

The LEMAC Co.
Dept. HG-11, 154 W. Tremont Ave., N. Y. 53, N. Y.

257

Better Homes and Gardens, November 1949.

❖ *One-Piece Feeder Dishes*

FD-200/201: "One For Baby, One For The Clown." "This Little Pig Went To Market," 6" dia. Although unmarked, it matches the paint and writing style of FD-100. $100-125 each.

FD-202: Clown feeder, 6" dia. $50-60.
FD-203: Clown feeder, sticker on bottom reads, "Made in Taiwan," 5" dia. $50-60.

FD-204: Newer bear, marked "HIC Japan 1985," 6"dia. Found in brown, blue, pink, and yellow. $35-45. Matching cup (not shown). $5-8.

FD-205: Similar to FD-204, this bear holds a spoon and fork. The original box reads, "Teddy Bear Baby Feeding Cereal Bowl, A spoonful for baby, a spoonful for bear - watch them share. Copyright JSNY, Taiwan." Bowl, 6" dia. $35-45.

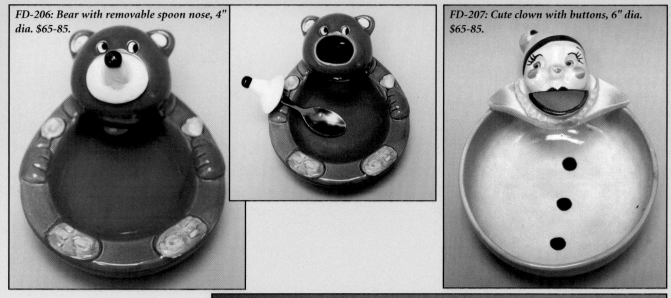

FD-206: Bear with removable spoon nose, 4"
dia. $65-85.

FD-207: Cute clown with buttons, 6" dia.
$65-85.

FD-208: This Cleminson clown feeder recently surfaced. Notice the distinct differences from the Japanese clown FD-200 pictured at (right). Since this piece is made by an American pottery company, it is considered more rare and valued higher than the Japanese piece, 6" dia. $125-175.

One for the clown and one for Baby makes feeding time fun for pokey Pablum eaters. Food spooned into clown's open, laughing mouth returns to bottom of bowl, and Baby's none the wiser. Gaily-painted ceramic dish, 6″ in diameter, is only $2.95 ppd. Collector's Corner, Dept. R, 527 W. 7th St., Los Angeles 14, Calif.

Redbook, January 1955.

FD-209: Rare English Royal Winton feeder dish, 6-3/4" dia. The bottom is marked "Royal Winton, Grimwades, Made in England." $150-200.

What to do with

YOUR OLD RAZOR BLADES

*Man's
Most Baffling Problem
Is Discussed by the
One Who Created It—*

KING C. GILLETTE

(Interpolations by
Franklin Fargo, who can
skin himself daily with
any safety razor ever made)

[EDITOR'S NOTE: King C. Gillette possesses the best known face in the world. His portrait is printed almost 1,000,000,000 times a year. It is seen in every inhabited place of the known globe. Not even Lydia Pinkham's picture is so well known as his. Compared with him, the Smith Brothers are unknown. The man himself is little known outside of his organization. He is modest. The fact that Arabs in a Sahara oasis recognized him on sight and went through the motion of shaving terrorized rather than pleased him. Mr. Fargo tried to extract this article from him. The only way he could do it was to prompt him and to interpolate, because Mr. Gillette usually avoids telling the most interesting things, due to his desire to credit everyone else with something. Mr. Fargo went to Boston to find out what we should do with our old razor blades, and discovered that, instead of being a joke, this is a problem the best of minds of the organization have struggled with, and that it is so big that anyone finding the proper solution for re-using blades can have a fortune almost as great as that of the inventor.]

WHAT to do with your used razor blades is not entirely a jesting subject. Considering the fact the Gillette Company will turn out almost 700,000,000 blades this year, which, if laid side by side and end to end, would cover a space 1,600 miles long by 900 miles wide, it is a real problem.

Disposing of one thin bit of bright steel may seem simple, but when you consider that we are turning out about 2,600,000 of these blades each day, and using about 800 tons of the finest steel a year to make them, the problem becomes more complicated.

In fact, it is one of the most interesting of the problems connected with the making of safety-razor blades, and nothing I know of so well shows the ingenuity of the American people.

We have had literally hundreds of sugges-

WHILE I was groaning over the prospect of shaving with a dull razor, the idea of the Gillette popped into my head.

Pictures by R. B. FULLER

tions of how to re-use old blades, many of them valuable, and it is probable no American product is used in so many different ways. The person fortunate enough to hit upon a practical idea for re-using blades might have a fortune at his command.

Seriously, one of the best ways of solving the blade problem in the household is to keep a jar of strong salt solution at hand and drop the blades into it until they corrode and may be thrown out without danger to anyone. Another suggestion is that each blade-user shall replace the blades in the original package, take them to be resharpened, and then never call for them.

We have had suggestions, models of scores of different handles and other devices for holding blades. The commonest use of old blades is by the women for ripping cloth, although it is probable that almost as many are used for cutting corns and calluses. They are used largely by typists for erasing. One genius produced a shield inclosing one old

blade which he used as a cigar-cutter. Many women who have gardens solve the problem by burying blades at the roots of shrubs or rose bushes to supply the iron.

The really simple method of disposing of blades is to replace them in the container provided, and, when it is full, to place it with refuse, to be carted away or burned. The furnace disposes of millions of blades.

THE problem of disposal has become so pressing that the Pullman Company has a special slot in washrooms into which they may be dropped, and many hotels provide special containers.

A Cleveland newspaper conducted a contest, last year, offering prizes to readers who furnished the best ideas. It received thousands of replies, and the prize went to a woman whose idea was to drop them into a

[CONTINUED ON PAGE THIRTY-NINE]

Liberty Magazine, January 15, 1927

Razor Blade Banks

If you've ever nicked yourself while shaving you can appreciate the expression "razor sharp." Thanks to the ingenuity of King C. Gillette in the early twentieth century, straight razors were replaced with safety razors and their disposable blades. However, the question soon arose, where does one dispose of these blades? This was a household concern that remained unsolved for more than twenty years.

In a 1927 article in *Liberty Magazine*, Franklin Fargo interviewed Mr. Gillette and focused the first part of the story on the disposal of used blades. According to Fargo, "… this is a problem the best minds of the Gillette organization have struggled with and that it is so big that anyone finding the proper solution for reusing blades can have a fortune almost as great as that of the inventor." This entertaining story went on to describe how others were addressing this problem.

The Pullman Company recognized the importance of safe disposal and had already installed a special slot in the washrooms of their trains—see BB-107 and BB-108. Hotels, too, were concerned for their guests and supplied a special container for this purpose (BB-222 A and B). According to the *Liberty Magazine* article, in 1926, a Cleveland newspaper actually conducted a contest and offered prizes to readers for the best solution for this used blade disposal dilemma.

From the 1930s through the 1950s, many homes were equipped with a slot in the medicine cabinet to allow the blades to be discarded between the walls. Other concerned shavers used a separate receptacle (known as blade banks, vaults or safes) that could be filled with the used blades, then discarded. If you look at BB-227 or BB-231, you can see how blade manufacturers built their own disposal container into the packages of new blades. Other companies soon saw the value in offering this service to their customers and provided blade banks as a premium with purchase. The BB-200 series offers some wonderful advertising examples.

The earlier banks in the BB-100 category were merely functional with little regard given to their appearance. Following World War II and the resumption of trade with Japan, inexpensive, decorative imports were much in demand, and the razor blade bank was no exception. We've enhanced the BB-300s from our first book with some exciting pieces.

The questionable class still raises a few eyebrows and causes debates among collectors. Since the publication of Book I, we've been able to confirm that the BB-402 pig is definitely a blade bank and has been reclassified as BB-363 in the figural group. At the risk of offending the individuals who include a few of these pieces in their own collections (and we all seem to have one or two), we'll continue to keep any doubtful bank in this group.

Despite our efforts with the first edition of *Collectibles for the Kitchen, Bath and Beyond* to educate the collecting community, "Wannabes" still abound. We've seen a rise in the number of piggy banks described as blade banks in the online auctions, which seems to justify charging astronomical prices. Some sellers still believe that if there is no opening to remove coins, any figurine with a slot is automatically a blade bank. While these characteristics are often helpful hints, they are not absolute qualifications.

So far, blade banks have escaped the reproduction craze. Perhaps, unlike stringholders, pie birds and many other items in this book, the disposal problem of the ever-sharp razor blade is a thing of the past. Blade bank collectors—be thankful!

❖ Early Razor Blade Banks

Although King Gillette started marketing his disposable blades in the early 1900s, we have been unable to find blade safes that date before 1920. The following are examples of some of these early razor blade banks. Since so little information has been uncovered regarding their origins or manufacturers, we've estimated that they date from the 1920s to the early 1940s.

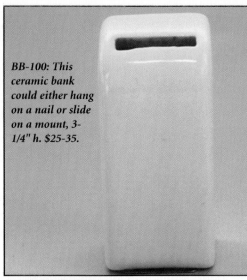

BB-100: This ceramic bank could either hang on a nail or slide on a mount, 3-1/4" h. $25-35.

BB-101: Countertop ceramic model embossed "Razor" and "Blades" on either side of the slit, 1-3/4" h. x 2-3/4" w. $40-60.

Left: BB-102: Very early wooden bank with a faded paper insert on one end which reads, "Dog House" and "Old Razor Blades," 2-1/2" h. x 2" w. x 1-3/4" dia. $50-65.

BB-103: Unusual Australian aluminum bank, 5" h. $50-60.

JH
THE SILVERCREST

Old Razor Blade Disposer has been manufactured to fill a long-standing want in every home.

Each container will hold approximately 500 odd razor blades and will last the careful blade user up to five years.

When your container is full, throw the whole unit in the rubbish tin and buy a replacement.

Take down every six months and tap the bottom firmly to ensure closer packing inside.

Manufactured by
AUSTRAL CASTINGS PTY. LTD.
64 Little Bourke Street, Melbourne
Patent applied for No.

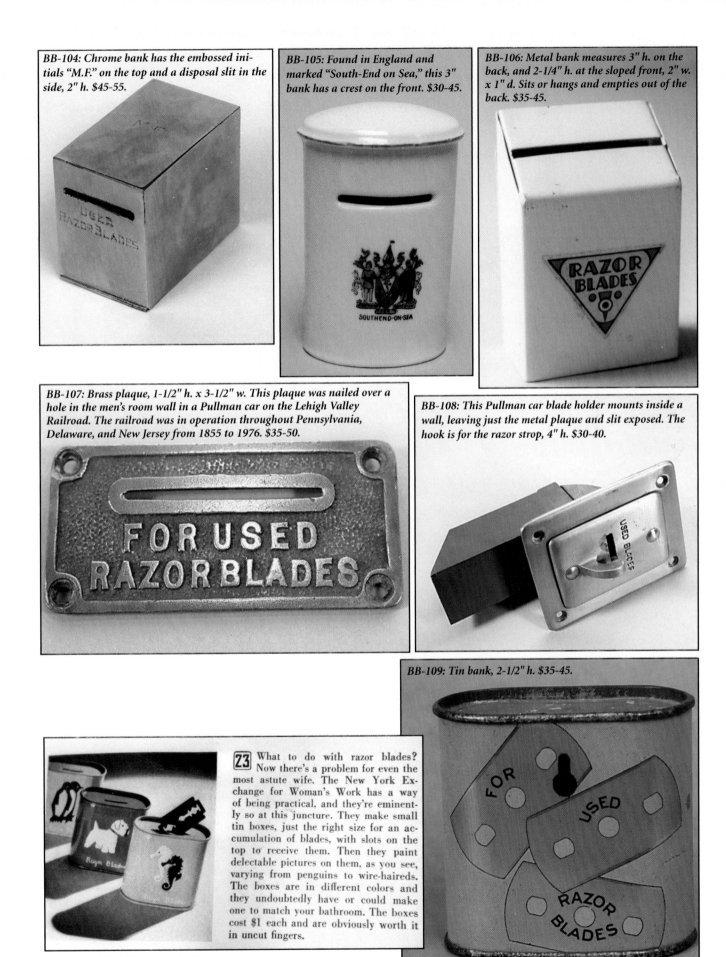

BB-104: Chrome bank has the embossed initials "M.F." on the top and a disposal slit in the side, 2" h. $45-55.

BB-105: Found in England and marked "South-End on Sea," this 3" bank has a crest on the front. $30-45.

BB-106: Metal bank measures 3" h. on the back, and 2-1/4" h. at the sloped front, 2" w. x 1" d. Sits or hangs and empties out of the back. $35-45.

BB-107: Brass plaque, 1-1/2" h. x 3-1/2" w. This plaque was nailed over a hole in the men's room wall in a Pullman car on the Lehigh Valley Railroad. The railroad was in operation throughout Pennsylvania, Delaware, and New Jersey from 1855 to 1976. $35-50.

BB-108: This Pullman car blade holder mounts inside a wall, leaving just the metal plaque and slit exposed. The hook is for the razor strop, 4" h. $30-40.

BB-109: Tin bank, 2-1/2" h. $35-45.

23 What to do with razor blades? Now there's a problem for even the most astute wife. The New York Exchange for Woman's Work has a way of being practical, and they're eminently so at this juncture. They make small tin boxes, just the right size for an accumulation of blades, with slots on the top to receive them. Then they paint delectable pictures on them, as you see, varying from penguins to wire-haireds. The boxes are in different colors and they undoubtedly have or could make one to match your bathroom. The boxes cost $1 each and are obviously worth it in uncut fingers.

House Beautiful, November 1935.

BB-110: Bakelite razor holder has a spot for new blades in the front and used blades in the top. 2-1/2" h. $35-45.

BB-111: Pullman blade cover, with hook for a strop, from a B&O railroad car. Marked "Pat.91." The U.S. Patent Office has lost the records on this patent, 1-1/2" h. x 3" w. $40-45.

BB-112: Red and Gold metal tin, reads "Discarded Blades," 2-5/8" h. $40-45.

BB-113: Wall-hanging tin bank with a decal of a fox terrier, 2-1/4" h. $30-40.

BB-114: Green metal chest marked "For Used Razor Blades," 2" h. x 3-1/2" w. $35-45.

BB-115: Wall-hanging ceramic bank, possibly English, 3" h. $40-45.

❖ Advertising Razor Blade Banks

Blade banks were often advertising premiums given away by manufacturers of razor blades, shaving cream, and related sundries. Whether referred to as safes, vaults or banks, they all had the same purpose: to safely dispose of used razor blades.

BB-200: Metal Gem Blades bank resembles a ledger, 1-7/8" h. The top reads, "File Old Blades Here." The bottom reads, "Patented Made in the USA. Discard when filled. New books free with package of 10 Gem blades at dealer." $30-40.

BB-201: Top lifts up and new blades are removed from this Williams Shaving Cream Bank, 2-1/4" h. x 1-1/4" w. $35-45.

Store display for the Williams Shaving Cream Bank.

BB-202/203: These 2-1/2" h. Williams Shaving Cream's banks resemble safes, with combinations and a slot for the blades. The back of BB-201 reads, "Used Razor Blades should not be left lying around. This box provides a convenient place to keep them. When filled, it may be discarded with other waste. Williams Shaving Cream and Aqua Velva for The Perfect Shave." The side reads, "The J.B. Williams Co. Glastonbury, Conn. USA and (Canada) Ltd. Montreal." The back of SB-202 reads, "Loose razor blades are dangerous. When this box is filled, it can be discarded with other waste. William's Shaving Cream and Aqua Velva for the perfect shave." $30-40.

BB-204: Burma Shave, known for its famous road signs, produced a 2-1/4" h. jar of shaving cream that could be turned into a bank when emptied. The top gives instructions on the use of the product, and the writing above the slot indicates it is "For Used Blades" or a "Coin Bank." $25-35. (Add $10-20 for box.)

BB-205/206: The top on the treasure chest on the left reads, "For Old Blades," 1-3/4" h. The back reads, "Insist on Genuine Ever-Ready Blades Keenest Edges In The World. Patented." The chest on the right has a removable top, and it came filled with new blades. The top reads, "For Old Blades," and the bottom, "When filled with old blades throw away secure. Another FREE from your dealer with package of 10 Ever-Ready Blades." $35-40 (Add $10-20 for box.)

free!

Treasure Chest
for old blades .. *free!*
with 10 Ever-Ready Blades—

IT'S HERE—solved at last—a *practical* container for used blades—the Ever-Ready Treasure Chest—cleverly designed —metal—handy size—ornamental as well as useful. Your dealer will present it to you *free* with a package of 10 Ever-Ready Blades for 69c. This super-keen new blade sings through the toughest whiskers so smoothly you hardly know they're off!

No flimsy wafer is the new Ever-Ready—but a sturdy, substantial blade—rugged, rigid, with a backbone of solid steel. It stands up to the most obstinate beard and stands in with the most tender skin. You don't know how keen a blade can be, until you have watched Ever-Ready waltz off with your whiskers—until you have revelled in the smooth comfort of a Singing Shave!

Get your free Treasure Chest! Treat yourself to 10 super-keen Ever-Ready Blades! Dealers everywhere are ready to supply Treasure Chests, free.

AMERICAN SAFETY RAZOR CORPORATION
BROOKLYN, NEW YORK

Ever-Ready Blades

This rare paper box served as the over-wrap to the BB-205 Ever-Ready Safety Razor Blade treasure chest, accompanied by two packages of blades. The box advertises a package of Ever-Ready Safety Razor Blades. $15-25.

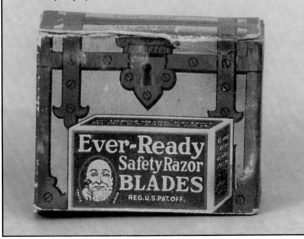

Right: Liberty Magazine, March 3, 1928.

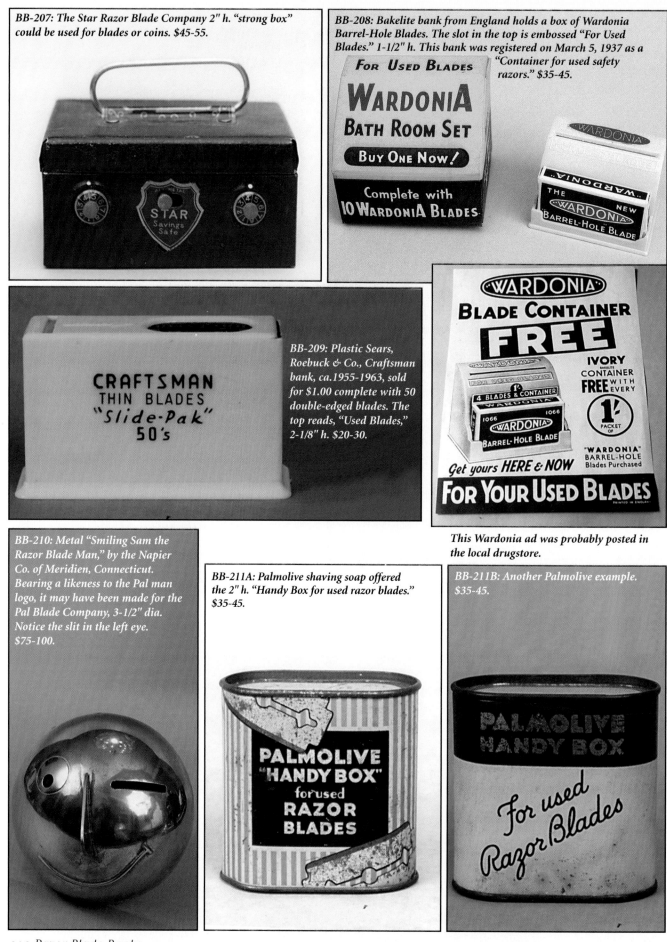

BB-207: The Star Razor Blade Company 2" h. "strong box" could be used for blades or coins. $45-55.

BB-208: Bakelite bank from England holds a box of Wardonia Barrel-Hole Blades. The slot in the top is embossed "For Used Blades." 1-1/2" h. This bank was registered on March 5, 1937 as a "Container for used safety razors." $35-45.

FOR USED BLADES
WARDONIA
BATH ROOM SET
BUY ONE NOW!
Complete with
10 WARDONIA BLADES

BB-209: Plastic Sears, Roebuck & Co., Craftsman bank, ca.1955-1963, sold for $1.00 complete with 50 double-edged blades. The top reads, "Used Blades," 2-1/8" h. $20-30.

CRAFTSMAN
THIN BLADES
"Slide-Pak"
50's

"WARDONIA"
BLADE CONTAINER
FREE
IVORY CONTAINER FREE WITH EVERY 1 PACKET OF "WARDONIA" BARREL-HOLE Blades Purchased
Get yours HERE & NOW
FOR YOUR USED BLADES

This Wardonia ad was probably posted in the local drugstore.

BB-210: Metal "Smiling Sam the Razor Blade Man," by the Napier Co. of Meridien, Connecticut. Bearing a likeness to the Pal man logo, it may have been made for the Pal Blade Company, 3-1/2" dia. Notice the slit in the left eye. $75-100.

BB-211A: Palmolive shaving soap offered the 2" h. "Handy Box for used razor blades." $35-45.

PALMOLIVE "HANDY BOX" for used RAZOR BLADES

BB-211B: Another Palmolive example. $35-45.

PALMOLIVE HANDY BOX
For used Razor Blades

BB-212: Patrons of Skin Bracer, Talc, or Skin Balm got this 2" bank from Mennen. Disposal slot is in the top. $45-55.

BB-213: This Mennen bank came with a styptic pencil for the sloppy shaver, 1-3/4" h. $45-55.

BB-214: Langlois Lavender Shaving Cream by Liggetts produced this 2" h. tin. The side reads, "For Old Razor Blades," and "When this box is filled it can be discarded with other waste with entire safety." $45-55.

BB-215A/215B/215C: B.T. Babbitt Lye banks advertised their use for "Daily Savings or old Safety Razor blades." $25-40.

BB-216: Twinplex Stroppers produced this wonderful tin litho bank, 2-1/4" h. x 2-1/2" w. $125-150.

BB-217: U.S. Deck Paint sample tin, 2-1/4" h. $40-50.

BB-218: Dual purpose Ocean Spray Cranberry Sauce bank. According to Ocean Spray Cranberries officials, this bank dates to 1940; 2-5/8" h. $35-45.

BB-219: National Can Corporation premium bank, 2-3/4" h. $40-50.

BB-220: "1st National Bank of Kansas City 10th and Baltimore" 3-1/4" h. bank with a black background (1954) and cream background (1955). Below the rim it reads, "For your used razor blades." One side reads, "Put your savings account under the protection of 1st," and the other side, "More than half a century for protection of your savings account 1886 to 1955." $30-40.

BB-221: This 2-1/4" h. plastic receptacle has a screw-off cap and was available to travelers staying at the Manger Hotel and Motor Inns. $30-40.

BB-222: This bank is typical of the ceramic countertop models found with different hotel names and cities. The tops are embossed "Razor Blades." 2-1/8" h. x 3" w. x 1-3/4" d. $75-95.

BB-223: Sheraton Hotels 4-1/4" h. paper envelope bank protected the maid's fingers. $10-15.

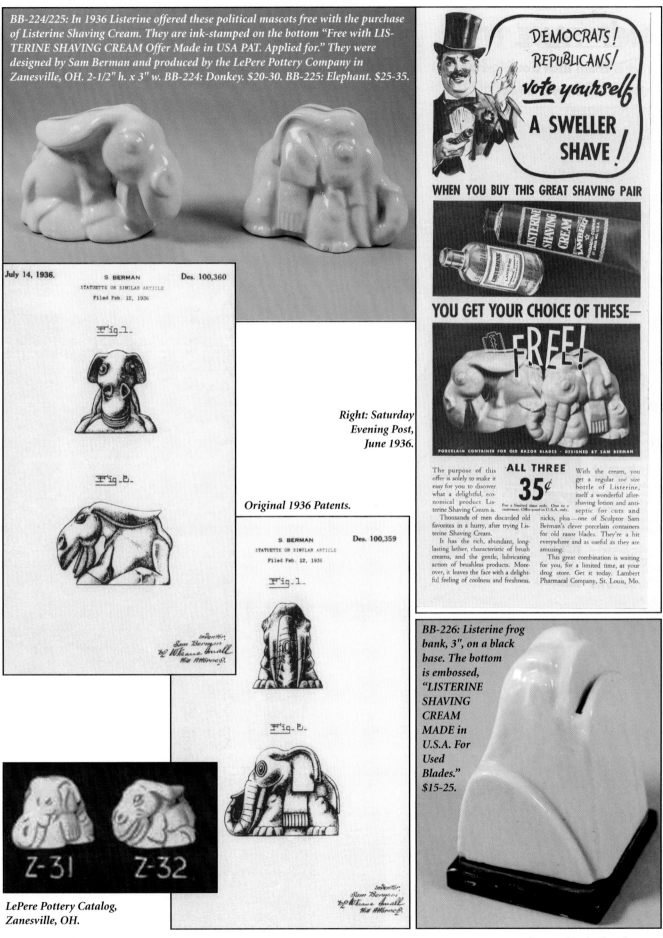

BB-224/225: *In 1936 Listerine offered these political mascots free with the purchase of Listerine Shaving Cream. They are ink-stamped on the bottom "Free with LISTERINE SHAVING CREAM Offer Made in USA PAT. Applied for." They were designed by Sam Berman and produced by the LePere Pottery Company in Zanesville, OH. 2-1/2" h. x 3" w. BB-224: Donkey. $20-30. BB-225: Elephant. $25-35.*

July 14, 1936.

S. BERMAN

Des. 100,360

STATUETTE OR SIMILAR ARTICLE

Filed Feb. 12, 1936

Fig. 1.

Fig. 2.

Inventor
Sam Berman
by W. Keane Small
His Attorney.

Right: Saturday Evening Post, June 1936.

Original 1936 Patents.

S. BERMAN

Des. 100,359

STATUETTE OR SIMILAR ARTICLE

Filed Feb. 12, 1936

Fig. 1.

Fig. 2.

Inventor
Sam Berman
by W. Keane Small
His Attorney.

Z-31 Z-32

LePere Pottery Catalog, Zanesville, OH.

DEMOCRATS! REPUBLICANS! *vote yourself* A SWELLER SHAVE!

WHEN YOU BUY THIS GREAT SHAVING PAIR

YOU GET YOUR CHOICE OF THESE—

FREE!

PORCELAIN CONTAINER FOR OLD RAZOR BLADES · DESIGNED BY SAM BERMAN

The purpose of this offer is solely to make it easy for you to discover what a delightful, economical product Listerine Shaving Cream is.

Thousands of men discarded old favorites in a hurry, after trying Listerine Shaving Cream.

It has the rich, abundant, long-lasting lather, characteristic of brush creams, and the gentle, lubricating action of brushless products. Moreover, it leaves the face with a delightful feeling of coolness and freshness.

ALL THREE 35¢
For a limited time only. One to a customer. Offer good in U.S.A. only.

With the cream, you get a regular 10¢ size bottle of Listerine, itself a wonderful after-shaving lotion and antiseptic for cuts and nicks, plus—one of Sculptor Sam Berman's clever porcelain containers for old razor blades. They're a hit everywhere and as useful as they are amusing.

This great combination is waiting for you, for a limited time, at your drug store. Get it today. Lambert Pharmacal Company, St. Louis, Mo.

BB-226: *Listerine frog bank, 3", on a black base. The bottom is embossed, "LISTERINE SHAVING CREAM MADE in U.S.A. For Used Blades." $15-25.*

BB-227: *A box of new Gibson's Blades came complete with a place for used blades, 1-1/8" h. x 2-1/8" w. $20-30.*

BB-228: *Fitches Powder for Men, Des Moines, Iowa, offered this 4-1/4" h. Found in both tin and cardboard. $25-35.*

BB-229: *When emptied, this Watkins Blades box, 2" h., served as a receptacle for used blades. $20-30.*

BB-230: *This 3-5/8" h. tin resided at the Book Cadillac Hotel in Detroit, Michigan. $50-60.*

BB-231: *Marlin Blades cardboard box, 1-1/8" h. x 2-1/8" w. $20-30.*

BB-232: *Red Cap Blades, distributed by F.W. Woolworth Stores, New York, New York, included a bank with new blades, 2" h. x 2-7/8" w. $20-30.*

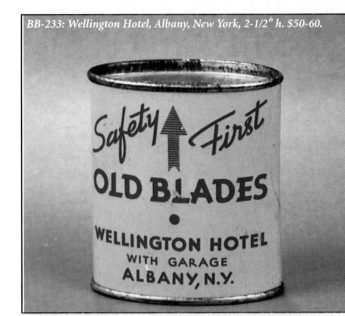

BB-233: *Wellington Hotel, Albany, New York, 2-1/2" h. $50-60.*

Safety First
OLD BLADES
WELLINGTON HOTEL
WITH GARAGE
ALBANY, N.Y.

BB-234: *After including the Personna ad below in the first book, we launched a search for this small pig. We were surprised to find that he was actually 5" tall. $40-50.*

BB-235: *Matador Razor Blades tin, 3-1/2" h. $45-55.*

A gay blade, Porky the Pig accompanies 50 sharp Personna blades which, in themselves, are a wonderful present for a man. He'll use Porky for blade disposal if Junior doesn't appropriate him for a penny bank. The price for the set is $5 from John Wanamaker, New York and Philadelphia.

House & Garden, December 1947.

BB-237: *Click Razor Blade Holder, 2-3/16" h., marked "Lyon & Lyon, Chicago, Ill." $35-45.*

Click!
HOLDER
FOR
USED
BLADES

BB-236: *Colgate blade bank, 2-1/2" h. $35-45.*

COLGATE'S
"HANDY-BOX"
FOR USED
RAZOR
BLADES

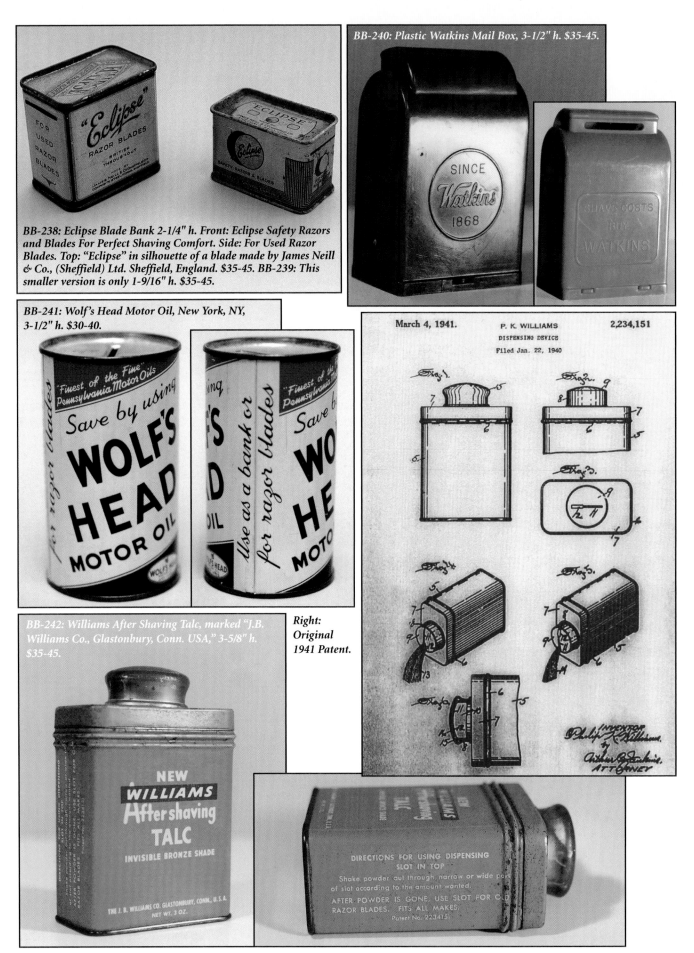

BB-240: *Plastic Watkins Mail Box, 3-1/2" h. $35-45.*

BB-238: *Eclipse Blade Bank 2-1/4" h. Front: Eclipse Safety Razors and Blades For Perfect Shaving Comfort. Side: For Used Razor Blades. Top: "Eclipse" in silhouette of a blade made by James Neill & Co., (Sheffield) Ltd. Sheffield, England. $35-45.* **BB-239:** *This smaller version is only 1-9/16" h. $35-45.*

BB-241: *Wolf's Head Motor Oil, New York, NY, 3-1/2" h. $30-40.*

BB-242: *Williams After Shaving Talc, marked "J.B. Williams Co., Glastonbury, Conn. USA," 3-5/8" h. $35-45.*

Right: Original 1941 Patent.

March 4, 1941.   P. K. WILLIAMS   2,234,151
DISPENSING DEVICE
Filed Jan. 22, 1940

BB-243: Anchor Chemical Co., 3" h. $35-45.

ANCHOR

SAVE WITH
ANCHOR CHEMICALS
FOR MORE PROFITS AND SAFETY

FOR SAFETY SAKE DEPOSIT
YOUR OLD RAZOR BLADES AND
AVOID UNNECESSARY CUTS
AND FIRST AID.

Bank on Anchor to provide safe chemicals to meet today's technology and in compliance with O.S.H.A. Since 1937 we have done much research and development of products that are safe replacements for all hazardous and toxic materials found in print shops. Anchor Chemical continues this program to meet the new challenges of the new technology with its new hazards.

ANCHOR CHEMICAL CO., INC.
HICKSVILLE, NEW YORK (1801)

BB-244: Schick "Old Blades Home," 2-3/8" h. Notice that the small slit can only accommodate the narrow Schick injector blades. $75-95.

SCHICK "OLD BLADES" HOME

FOR USED SCHICK INJECTOR BLADES

When through your beard I've ceased to roam Just drop me in The Old Blades Home

The Bathroom shelf at last is clear All used SCHICK BLADES "are Parked" in here

BB-245: Wm. Beckman Garage, Ossian, IA, 6" h. $50-60.

Barbasol Blades

Here is the Place for
The Razor and Blades
WM. BECKMAN GARAGE
General Automobile Service
--- Phone 54 ---
Ossian, - - Iowa
SAMPLE NO. 998

TO EMPTY, push this box about one-half inch, then pull box down.

BB-246: Midland Safe-Way Blade Disposer, Midland Mfg. Co., Toledo, OH. Pat. Pend., 4-1/2" h. $25-35. (Add $10-15 for the box.)

MIDLAND
SAFE-WAY BLADE DISPOSER

MIDLAND MFG. CO.
TOLEDO 3, OHIO
PAT. PEND.

MIDLAND
ONE NO. 105

INSTRUCTIONS
FOR MOUNTING

MOUNT ALUMINUM WALL PLATE
SPRING DOWN FACING OUT. USE
SCREWS OR ANY SUITABLE MASTIC.
ASSEMBLE DISPOSER TO WALL
PLATE BY INSERTING EAR INTO
FORMED TOP OF THE WALL PLATE.
PRESS IN UNTIL THE SPRING CLIP
SNAPS INTO PLACE. TO OPEN:
INSERT BOBBY PIN OR SIMILAR
ARTICLE IN "T" SLOT AT THE BOTTOM
OF DISPOSER RELEASING SPRING
CLIP AT THE SAME TIME RELEASE
DISPOSER.

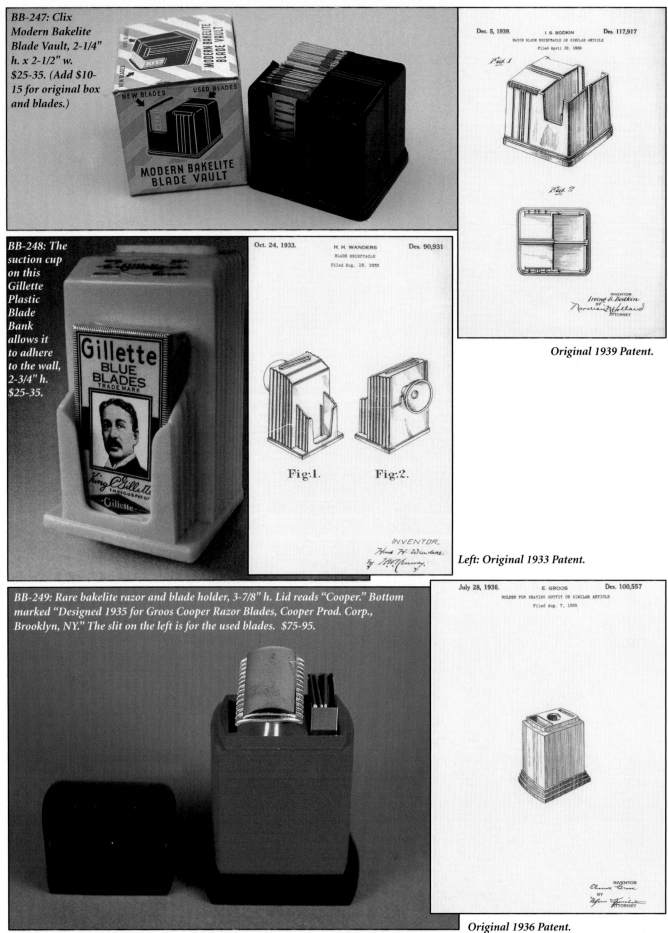

BB-247: Clix *Modern Bakelite Blade Vault,* 2-1/4" h. x 2-1/2" w. $25-35. (Add $10-15 for original box and blades.)

BB-248: The suction cup on this *Gillette Plastic Blade Bank* allows it to adhere to the wall, 2-3/4" h. $25-35.

Dec. 5, 1939.   I. S. BODKIN   Des. 117,917
RAZOR BLADE RECEPTACLE OR SIMILAR ARTICLE
Filed April 19, 1939

Original 1939 Patent.

Oct. 24, 1933.   H. H. WANDERS   Des. 90,931
BLADE RECEPTACLE
Filed Aug. 19, 1933

Fig:1.   Fig:2.

Left: Original 1933 Patent.

BB-249: Rare bakelite razor and blade holder, 3-7/8" h. Lid reads "Cooper." Bottom marked "Designed 1935 for Groos Cooper Razor Blades, Cooper Prod. Corp., Brooklyn, NY." The slit on the left is for the used blades. $75-95.

July 28, 1936.   E. GROOS   Des. 100,557
HOLDER FOR SHAVING OUTFIT OR SIMILAR ARTICLE
Filed Aug. 7, 1935

Original 1936 Patent.

BB-250: Metal giveaway from Monark Gasoline & Oil Company, Kansas City, MO. 2-1/2" h. $35-45.

BB-251: Bakelite with razor holder in center and three used blade slots across the top. It's marked "Gillette" below the center slot, 2-1/8" h. $45-55.

BB-252: Fabulous cast iron Gem bank. Marked "Gem" in the center and "Pat'd" on the crown, 3-3/8" h. $125-175.

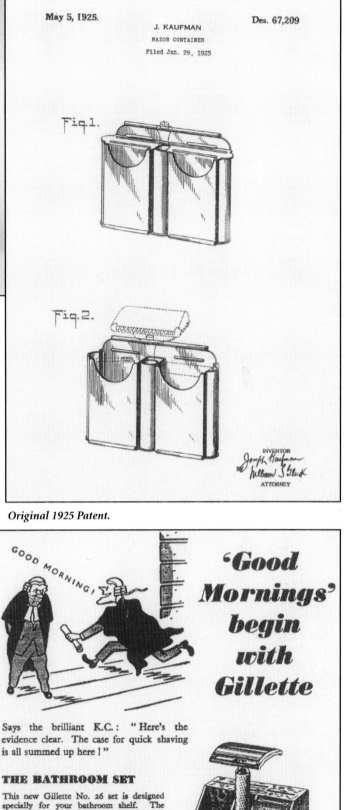

May 5, 1925.

J. KAUFMAN

RAZOR CONTAINER

Filed Jan. 29, 1925

Des. 67,209

Fig.1.

Fig.2.

INVENTOR
Joseph Kaufman
William J. Gluck
ATTORNEY

Original 1925 Patent.

'Good Mornings' begin with Gillette

GOOD MORNING!

Says the brilliant K.C.: "Here's the evidence clear. The case for quick shaving is all summed up here!"

THE BATHROOM SET

This new Gillette No. 26 set is designed specially for your bathroom shelf. The Gillette razor is bright nickel plated, with a telescopic handle, extending to full length when screwed together. There are two Blue Gillette Blades. All fit conveniently into a plastic container which combines razor stand with special compartment for used blades.

3/8d INCLUDING PURCHASE TAX

BB-251 Insert, November 1946.

❖ Figural Razor Blade Banks

From the 1940s to the early 1960s, figural banks were popular gifts. These examples are among the most desirable.

BB-300: Barber head by Ceramic Arts Studio, Madison, Wisconsin. Slot in the top of head, no opening on the bottom, 4-3/4" h. $90-100.

BB-301A/B: Occupied Japan barber, slot in top of head, "drain hole" in bottom, 4" h. Barber with black hair has the word "Blades" on his back. Brown hair: $50-60. Black hair: $65-75.

BB-302: Roly-poly barber has a slot in the top of his head and a "drain hole" in the bottom, 5" h. One example was recently found with the Cleminson stamp on the bottom. $65-75.

SHAVINGS BANK keeps used blades in its account, and accumulates interest by keeping them away from unwary fingers! The only bank that no one tries to rob, it's black and white ceramic styled like a chubby 5½"-high old-fashioned barber complete with mustache. Have one made with Dad's name for Father's Day giving! $1.50. Crown Craft, 246-AM Fifth Avenue, New York 1, N. Y.

Above: American Home, June 1959. This bank could be personalized at the time of purchase.

BB-303A: "Tony the Blademan," 5-7/8" h., has a slot in his head and "drain hole" in bottom. Hole on back for hanging. $65-85.

BB-303B: Unusual handmade Tony, 5-7/8" h. $50-60.

Right: Gift & Art Buyer, April 1951. This trade magazine reflects wholesale prices.

BB-304: "The Old Blade" wooden barber, 5-1/4" h. Marked on the back below the slot, "For Old Razor Blades." On the base "Copyright 1950 by Woodcroftlry Shops Inc." Also made in Canada. The bottom of the bank unscrews to remove blades. $65-75.

BB-305: Dapper man with handlebar mustache, 4-1/2" h., has been found in several colors. Has a slit in the back top of head and an opening in the bottom to remove the blades. $50-70.

BB-306: Bank, 5-1/2" h., has hole in the head to accommodate a shaving brush and disposal slit in rear of shoulders. Found in different colors, he's often advertised as a head vase. Bottom marked "Copr. 1950 Lipper & Mann, New England Ceramics." $75-95.

BB-307: The dandy razor bank on the right has a mustache, bow tie, and wavy hair. Shown with matching brush or razor holder, 4" h. Bank: $65-85. Brush holder: $45-55.

BB-308: Looie, 7" h., was made by different companies. He holds a razor in his right hand. He sold for $1.00 in the 1964 Montgomery Ward Christmas Catalog. $85-100. BB-309 (c.): This slightly shorter Looie, 6-1/2" h., is marked "Kreiss & Co." $95-110.

BB-310: Looie look-alike grips a razor holder/pole. Blades drop in the center part of hair. Marked "Blakeramics Reg. Pat Pending," 6" h. $85-110.

BB-311A: Looie cousin has a tray in front for shaving soap or razor, a slot in its head for blades, and back opening for a brush, 7-1/2" h. $85-100.

BB-311B: This other Looie look-alike is holding a tray in one hand, 7-1/2". $85-100.

BB-312: Two-part bank by Tilso of Japan found with original box. The bottom is a shaving cup; the top is the blade bank, 7-1/2" h. $100-125. Top only: $50-60. (Add $20-30 for box.)

BB-313: "Razor Bum," 8" h., sign reads, "I'm a rough, tough guy-As you can see, No fancy sharp razor blades for me, I shave with blades dull and abused, So gimme the ones You've already used." Sign is also the blade receptacle. Some of these banks have surfaced with the saying on a foil sticker rather than directly imprinted on the bank. $85-100.

BB-314: "The Gay Blades" barber shop quartet, 4-1/4" h. x 5-1/4" w., with blade slot in top and felt over the hole in the bottom. $75-100.
BB-316: Colorful barber shop quartet, 4-1/2" h. x 5" w. with disposal slot in top. $100-125.

Right: Family Circle, November 1953.

GAY BLADE CATCHER will safely house those used razor blades that are so dangerous to leave around. Merry faces of the quartet will help father start the day with a smile; 5¼"x2¼"x4¼". Ceramic, in bright and cheerful colors. $1.25 postpaid. Merrill Ann, Dept. FC, 102 Warren St., New York 7, N. Y.

BB-315: "The Gay Blades" duo appears to have Oriental features, marked "E. Murran, E.M. Pottery." Slot is located between the two men, 4" h. x 4-1/8" w., with hole in the bottom to remove blades. $85-100.

BB-317: Nicknamed "The Matador" by collectors, this 6" h. bank is shown both painted and undecorated. Dwight Morris of East Palestine, OH designed it. It has a large opening in the bottom. Painted: $55-65. Unpainted: $30-40.

BB-318: Wooden English box reads "I'm for safety first" on front, below the long narrow slit. Top can be removed to empty container. 4" h. $50-60.

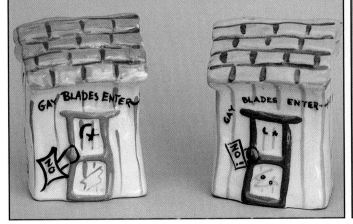

BB-319: Wood-burned souvenir bank has been found marked with the names of different cities and states, 5-1/2" h. $35-45.

BB-320: Ceramic outhouse with slot in roof. The bottom is embossed "Specialist in Used Razor Blades," 3" h. $75-90.

BB-321: Outhouse stop sign on the front door reads, "Gay Blades Enter." Turn the bank clockwise and the side reads, "->at rear ->" with an arrow pointing to slit in the back. $150-175.

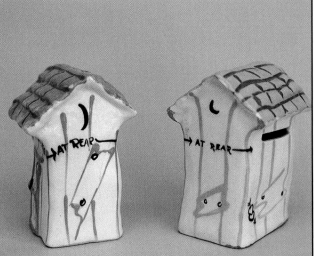

These ceramic banks hang on the wall, 2" h. in the sloped front and 2-1/2" at the back.

BB-322A /322B: The bank on the left was made in Japan. The bank on the right reads "Made for Abercrombie and Fitch Co. by The Trent Company Pottery." $55-75.

BB-322C: Man shaving, marked "Abercrombie and Fitch." $55-75.

BB-322D: English rider, "Old Blades," marked "Abercrombie and Fitch." $55-75.

BB-322E: Englishman with top hat, marked "Abercrombie and Fitch." $55-75.

BB-322F: Man in riding clothes drinking from a flask, marked "Abercrombie and Fitch." $55-75.

BB-322G: Man with mutton chops, marked "Abercrombie and Fitch." $55-75.

BB-323: Bowling ball and pin set on base, 5" h. x 5" w. The pin has a slot in the front for blades, and the bowling ball has a hole for a razor stem. The poem on the pin is the same as the one on the Razor Bum (BB- 313). "Dabs Japan" sticker on bottom. $90-110.

I'M A ROUGH, TOUGH GUY
AS YOU CAN SEE
NO FANCY, SHARP RAZOR
BLADES FOR ME
I SHAVE WITH BLADES,
DULL AND ABUSED
SO, GIMME THE ONES
YOU'VE ALREADY USED

BB-324: Square ceramic safes, 2-1/2" h., with slot on top can either sit or hang. No hole in bottom. $40-60.

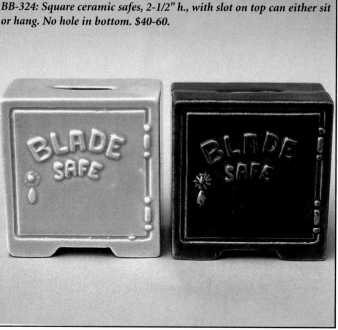

BB-325: Embossed "Safe for Blades" on top of 3" h. square ceramic safe. $40-60.

SAFE FOR BLADES

BB-326: Grinding stone with slot on top of wheel. Marked "Made by Decora Ceramics Inc., Hand Painted, California #3501," 2-3/4" h. x 4-1/2" w. $80-100.

FOR DULL ONES

BB-327A: Bell-shaped bank is marked, "California Cleminsons, Hand Painted," 3-1/2" h. $25-35.

Consider Men's plight, both distressing and SAD, To dispose of old Blades is driving them MAD!

GAY GADGETS, ALL FOR BOTH SHORT AND TALL
from the
California
CLEMINSONS

AND FOR THE MEN! — RAZOR BANK — $7.50 doz.

RAZOR BANK

BB-327B: A personalized version could be ordered. $45-55.

Put-er there
Bill!

The insert to the right came inside BB-327 when it was purchased new.

Gift & Art Buyer, February 1947. This trade magazine reflects wholesale prices.

House Beautiful, June 1947

BB-328: Handmade knockoffs of the Cleminsons banks are slightly smaller, 3" h. This version says "Daddy's Razor Bank" on the top. $35-45.

Daddy's Razor Bank

BB-329: California Cleminsons heads are found with burgundy, green, and blue collars, 4" h. It's pictured here with the original insert which is usually missing. $30-40. (Add $15-25 for insert.)

For OLD BLADES safety, Folks all THANK, the User of a "GAY" BLADE bank!

"GAY BLADE" RAZOR BANK

For old blades safety

Folks all thank
The User of
A "Gay Blade"
bank

Hand painted ivory ceramic—4" high (hat is a paper gift tag)

$1.25 each

add 15c for delivery
Please, no COD's

HOUSE of HAMILTON
1208 N. Field Ave.

Inglewood 2   California

House Beautiful, June 1949.

BB-330: Shaving brush examples are fairly common. Original "Blades" paper label is sometimes missing. Sticker on the bottom reads, "Gustin Company, Van Nuys, Calif.," 5" h. $45-65.

BLADES

BB-331A: This handmade brush was sold as a souvenir, marked "Eureka Springs, Ark." 4-3/4" h. $65-85.

BLADES

Eureka Springs Ark.

FOR THAT "Wonderful Guy"

"SHAVING BRUSH BLADE BANK" Give him the newest, gayest blade bank in town and he'll bristle with pleasure. Guaranteed to keep old blades from becoming a menace around the house. Brightly colored ceramic, 5" high, blades can be removed from bottom and container re-used. Holds just scads of discarded blades. Only $1.25 postpaid.

BLADES

THE **"PUTT-PAK"** A Golfer's Delight . . . holds cigarettes, matches and tees—two loops securely attaches to "HIS" or "HER" belt . . . always handy and always out of the way. Finest quality fM-

PORTED ENGLISH hazel pigskin, expertly hand-sewed by skilled craftsmen. Zippered compartment holds cigarettes, pocket: matches, with the 4 tees included. Packed in Gift Box. **$3.95** postpaid.

Small collection fee on C.O.D. orders.

Send for new gift catalog.
Money refunded if not pleased.

Frances-Morris Dept. I, 1016 Carroll St. Brooklyn 25, N. Y.

House Beautiful, May 1950.

BB-331B: *This piece shows three fellows singing on the front and the word "Gay" on one side and "Blades" on the other, 4-3/4" h. $65-85.*

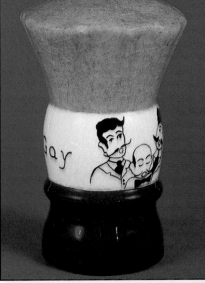

BB-332: *Cream and tan brush, 6" h., made by the APCO division of the American Bisque Company, Marietta, Ohio, is marked "U.S.A." Slot in top, opening in bottom. Found in various colors. $50-60.*

BB-333: *Brush with red trim on hexagonal base, 5-1/2" h. $50-60.*

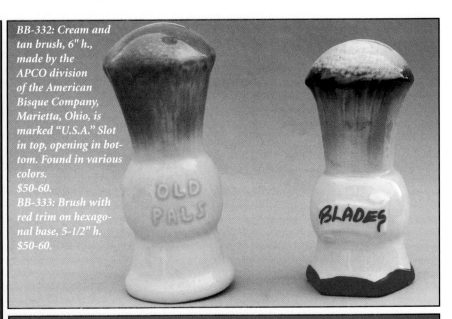

BB-334: *Unusual metal hanging bank features an English bobby and warning sign. Bottom is marked, "Made in Austria," 3-3/4" h. $75-100.*

BB-335/336: *This barber chair comes in two sizes, 5" h. and 5-3/4" h. Rubber plug in bottom. According to the original tag, the bank could be used for blades or coins. The front reads, "Barber Chair Bank for the Little Shaver." Small: $100-125. Large: $125-150.*

BB-337: *Mailbox appears handmade, 3" h. $55-65.*

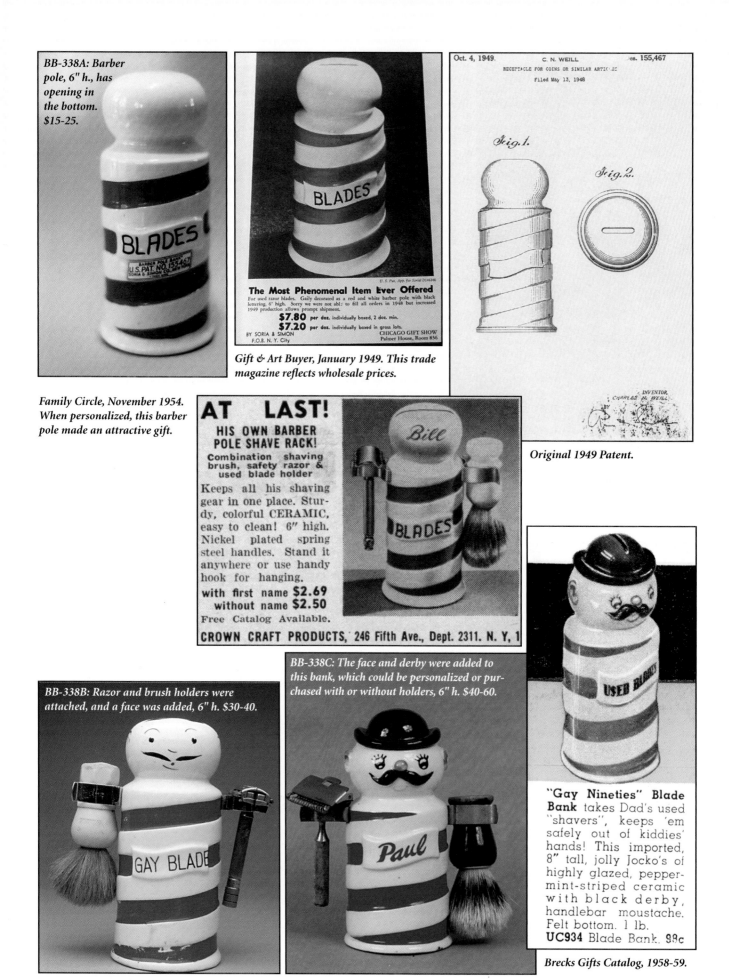

BB-338A: Barber pole, 6" h., has opening in the bottom. $15-25.

BLADES

BARBER POLE BANK
U.S. PAT. NO. 155467
SORIA & SIMON CO., NEW YORK

BLADES

The Most Phenomenal Item Ever Offered

For used razor blades. Gaily decorated as a red and white barber pole with black lettering, 6" high. Sorry we were not able to fill all orders in 1948 but increased 1949 production allows prompt shipment.

$7.80 per doz. individually boxed, 2 doz. min.
$7.20 per doz. individually boxed in gross lots.

BY SORIA & SIMON   CHICAGO GIFT SHOW
F.O.B. N. Y. City   Palmer House, Room 836

U. S. Pat. App. for Serial D146346

Gift & Art Buyer, January 1949. This trade magazine reflects wholesale prices.

Oct. 4, 1949.   C. N. WEILL   es. 155,467
RECEPTACLE FOR COINS OR SIMILAR ARTICLES
Filed May 13, 1948

Fig.1.   Fig.2.

INVENTOR.
CHARLES N. WEILL
BY

Original 1949 Patent.

Family Circle, November 1954. When personalized, this barber pole made an attractive gift.

AT LAST!

HIS OWN BARBER POLE SHAVE RACK!

Combination shaving brush, safety razor & used blade holder

Keeps all his shaving gear in one place. Sturdy, colorful CERAMIC, easy to clean! 6" high. Nickel plated spring steel handles. Stand it anywhere or use handy hook for hanging.

with first name **$2.69**
without name **$2.50**

Free Catalog Available.

Bill

BLADES

CROWN CRAFT PRODUCTS, 246 Fifth Ave., Dept. 2311. N. Y. 1

BB-338C: The face and derby were added to this bank, which could be personalized or purchased with or without holders, 6" h. $40-60.

USED BLADES

BB-338B: Razor and brush holders were attached, and a face was added, 6" h. $30-40.

GAY BLADE

Paul

"Gay Nineties" Blade Bank takes Dad's used "shavers", keeps 'em safely out of kiddies' hands! This imported, 8" tall, jolly Jocko's of highly glazed, peppermint-striped ceramic with black derby, handlebar moustache. Felt bottom. 1 lb.
UC934 Blade Bank. 98c

Brecks Gifts Catalog, 1958-59.

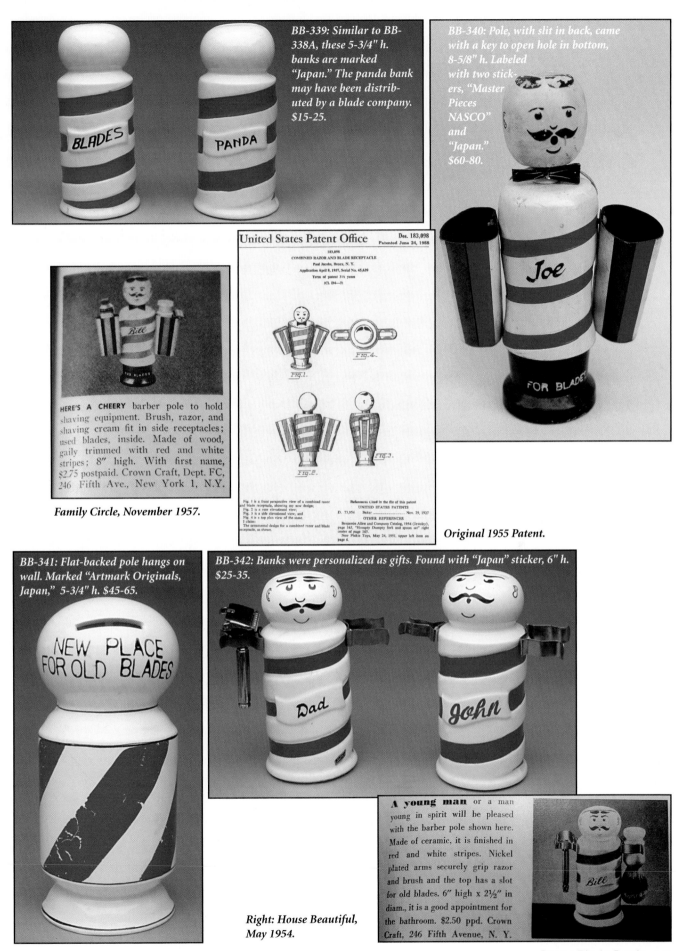

BB-339: Similar to BB-338A, these 5-3/4" h. banks are marked "Japan." The panda bank may have been distributed by a blade company. $15-25.

BB-340: Pole, with slit in back, came with a key to open hole in bottom, 8-5/8" h. Labeled with two stickers, "Master Pieces NASCO" and "Japan." $60-80.

BLADES

PANDA

Joe

FOR BLADES

HERE'S A CHEERY barber pole to hold shaving equipment. Brush, razor, and shaving cream fit in side receptacles; used blades, inside. Made of wood, gaily trimmed with red and white stripes; 8" high. With first name, $2.75 postpaid. Crown Craft, Dept. FC, 246 Fifth Ave., New York 1, N.Y.

Family Circle, November 1957.

United States Patent Office — Des. 183,098 — Patented June 24, 1958

Original 1955 Patent.

BB-341: Flat-backed pole hangs on wall. Marked "Artmark Originals, Japan," 5-3/4" h. $45-65.

NEW PLACE FOR OLD BLADES

BB-342: Banks were personalized as gifts. Found with "Japan" sticker, 6" h. $25-35.

Dad

John

Right: House Beautiful, May 1954.

A young man or a man young in spirit will be pleased with the barber pole shown here. Made of ceramic, it is finished in red and white stripes. Nickel plated arms securely grip razor and brush and the top has a slot for old blades. 6" high x 2½" in diam., it is a good appointment for the bathroom. $2.50 ppd. Crown Craft, 246 Fifth Avenue, N. Y.

Bill

BB-343A/343B: Common plastic "Dandy Dan." The one on the left has holders all around and was used as a brush display; the one on the right has just two holders. The black plastic top with the slot screws off for removal of blades. The bottom piece also screws off but is solid underneath. The bottom is marked "M-R Products Co., Pat. Pending, Made in U.S.A." Side of box reads, "Holds Shaving Brush and Razor, Container for Used Blades, Rigid Unbreakable Polyethylene." $25-35. (Add $35-45 for box.)

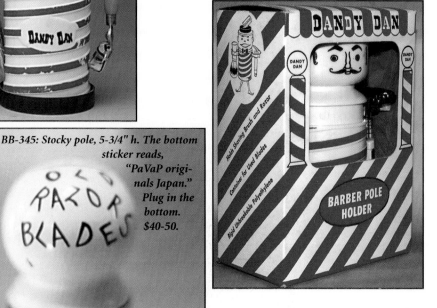

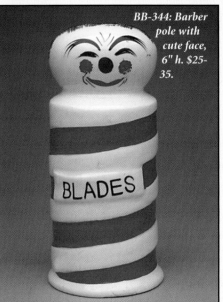

BB-344: Barber pole with cute face, 6" h. $25-35.

BB-345: Stocky pole, 5-3/4" h. The bottom sticker reads, "PaVaP originals Japan." Plug in the bottom. $40-50.

BB-346: Artistic gentleman with beret, 6-1/4" h. $60-70.

BB-347: Goebel ceramic pole marked "Used Blades," 4", is stamped "Germany" on the bottom. It also has an "X88" mold mark and Goebel logo. This was created by master sculptor Arthur Moeller in 1951 and discontinued in 1962. Both the molds and models were destroyed. Sticker reads, "IRICE Import" (Irving W. Rice & Co. NYC). Shown with matching cotton ball dispenser. Bank only: $150-200.

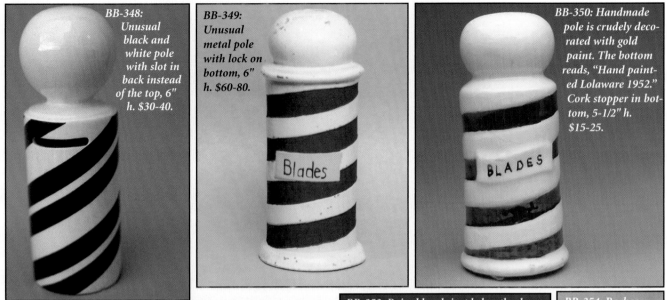

BB-348: Unusual black and white pole with slot in back instead of the top, 6" h. $30-40.

BB-349: Unusual metal pole with lock on bottom, 6" h. $60-80.

BB-350: Handmade pole is crudely decorated with gold paint. The bottom reads, "Hand painted Lolaware 1952." Cork stopper in bottom, 5-1/2" h. $15-25.

BB-351: Charlie's 5" h. pole has a flat back and hole for hanging. The bottom has a paper label that reads "Murray Kreiss and Co. Copyright 1950." The back has a red copyright mark and the initials "M.K." $40-60. BB-352: The paint job on this bank is similar to Cleminsons pieces, 5-1/4" h. $40-60.

BB-353: Raised beads just below the dome distinguish this Royal Copley pole. Some examples have been found with original Royal Copley sticker. Those with the gold dome are more difficult to find, 6" h. White dome $45-55; Gold dome $60-70.

BB-354: Barber head, which sits on top of a pole, is marked "I Take Old Blades" on the base, 7" h. $55-65.

Left: House Beautiful, May 1949.

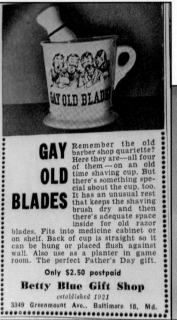

BB-355A: Ceramic shaving mug, 4" h., holds brush and blades. The bottom is marked "Goms of Ca., Pat. Pending." Flat back and hole for hanging. $65-75.
BB-355B: This floral decorated version is harder to find, 4" h. $75-100.

BB-356: Metal mustache cup has slot for blades in front, and the back holds soap or a razor, 3-3/4" h. x 6" w. Removable bottom. $75-100.

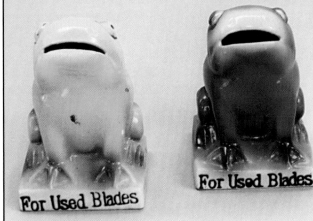

House Beautiful, November 1949.

BB-357: Frogs, 3" h., are marked "Made in Japan" on bottom. $60-70.

For Used Blades

For Used Blades

BB-358: Singing barbers with pole have slot in top, 6-1/2" h. Free standing or wall mount. $125-150.

BB-359: Handmade hanging wood bank, 7" h. $ 30-40.

OLD BLADES

BB-360: Pig with flowers has blade outline embossed and painted on its back. Recently found with a "Gayet Pottery of California" label, 2-1/2" h. x 4" w. $55-65.

RAZOR
BACK HOG

BB-361: This bank marked "Chuckline Ceramics Calif. 1961," looks very similar to the banks by California Cleminsons, 4-1/4" h. $125-150.

BB-362: Rare Goebel Friar Tuck razor blade holder is Goebel Mold Number X-103, 4-1/2" h. It is often confused with the Goebel's coin bank, Mold Number SD 29. From the front they look alike. X-103, however, is distinguished by the words "Razorblade Holder" in raised white letters molded into the piece on the back under the slot. There is a small "drain hole" in the bottom of the blade bank. The X-103 Friar also has exposed toes. The X on the razor blade holder represents Verschiedenes, or Miscellaneous, and is found on the Miscellaneous page of the Goebel catalog. It was first produced in 1956, but it is not known how long production continued. According to Goebel collectors, very few of these banks are known to exist, making it very desirable to both blade bank and Goebel Friar Tuck collectors. $500+.

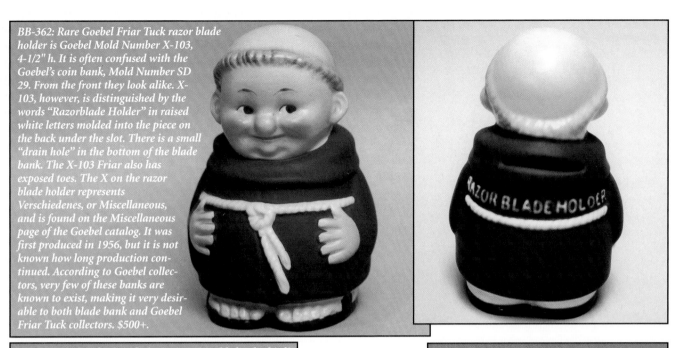

BB-363: Previously classified as a questionable bank, this little pig marked "Made in Occupied Japan" has since been found with a decal near the slot on his bottom that reads "Put used blades in pig's_____," 2-1/2" h. x 4" l. $65-85. (Previously BB-402.)

BB-364: Pig with gold strip that reads "Used Razor Blades." 3-1/4" h. x 4-3/4" l. $65-85.

BB-365: This boar, standing in grass, has the words "Razor Blades" embossed in the base, 3" h. x 4-1/4" l. $75-95.

BB-366: Ornate shaving half-cup with gold trim, marked "Four Blades," by LePere Pottery. $95-125.

BB-367: *Ceramic shaving half-cup features a man with a mustache that reads "Old Blades." This piece looks very similar to the style of painting on Cleminsons pieces. 2-7/16" h. $65-85.*

BB-368/369: *Wood "Gay Blades" mug-shaped banks. The one on the left is taller and thicker, 3-1/4" h. x 1-3/4" d. $35-45. The one on the right is 3" h. x 7/8" d. $30-40.*

BB-371: *Barber Pole, marked "Carl," has a flat back that allows it to hang on the wall, 6" h. $50-60.*

BB-370: *Brush blade bank resembles BB-330; this bank, however, has a flat back allowing it to be hung on the wall, 5-1/4" h. $75-90.*

BB-372: *Dome-shaped bank with a blue decoration, 5" h. $45-55.*

BB-373: *Red and white bank with initials on front, 4" h. $40-50.*

BB-374: *Pole with barber head, 7" h. $125-150.*

BB-375: Pole with singing barber, embossed "1952 Robert Zeidman," 6" h. $150-175.

BB-376: Barber blade bank hangs on the wall or stands, and has holders for razor and brush, and slot in the front for blades, 7-1/4" h. $75-95.

BB-377: Man with shaving brush, has a stopper in the bottom and an "Enesco" sticker, 6-1/2" h. $50-60.

BB-378: Italian three-piece set. Two piece holder "Dull Old Blades," 3-1/3", marked "FA-147/D203 Italy" on the bottom. Found with tall container "Things" and glass marked "Tumbler." Set: $175-200. Bank only: $100-125.

BB-379: Wood outhouse bank "For Old Blades and Young Shavers," 4-1/4" h. $45-65.

BB-380: Horse head trophy bank decorated with colored rhinestones; has a "Japan" sticker on the bottom, 6-1/2" h. $85-95.

BB-381: Jester sitting on ball, blades are inserted into the mouth, composition. Decal reads "For Used Razor Blades" and "Japan" is written on the back, 4-1/2" h. $75-95.

BB-382: Dog house by California Cleminsons, marked "HIS," 2-1/2" h. Also found marked "DAD." $45-55. (Formerly BB-413.)

BB-383: Top hat, 3" h. $20-25.

ABOVE:
MINIATURE CERAMIC HAT BANKS for coins or old razor blades. Baseball caps will be decorated on order with the name and colors of major league baseball teams. Priced at $7.80 a dozen by the N. S. Gustin Co., 712 South Olive St., Los Angeles 14.

Gift & Art Buyer, October 1947. This trade magazine reflects wholesale prices.

❖ Questionable Razor Blade Banks

These examples inhabit every blade bank collector's inventory. Whether these were actually produced for the disposal of used blades has not been confirmed. However, as pointed out earlier, some banks had dual purposes. Small holes in the bottom of some could be "drain" or "slag" holes. Many have been purchased from dealers who claim they are blade banks since they have no way to be emptied. As noted in the introduction, many coin banks have also been produced without openings and, in turn, some blade banks actually have stoppers to remove the blades. We've also featured banks on which the writing appears to have been added after the piece was manufactured. Until we find an advertisement or catalog listing to confirm the purpose of these banks, you be the judge.

BB-400: Indian, 4" h., was listed as a blade bank in another collectibles book, probably because of the small "drain holes" on the bottom. $15-25. BB-401: Dog, 4-1/2" h. $25-35.

BB-402 reclassified as BB-363

BB-403: Although this 3-1/2" h. pig is marked "Razor Back," we're unsure if that is a reference to the wild hog or its purpose as a used blade bank. $50-75.

BB-404: Ceramic fish bank sits on a counter, 3-1/2" h. $20-30.

BB-405: This Mexican man with sombrero and serape is often mistaken for a barber, 6-1/2" h. Slot in back of head. $30-45.

BB-406: Owl with flat back and "drain hole," 2-1/2" h. $15-25.

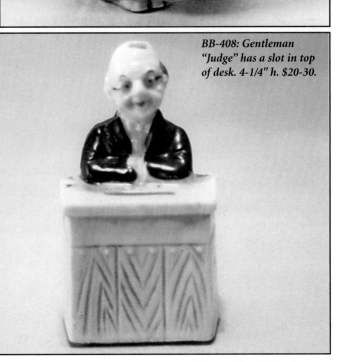

BB-407: Flat on one side to hang on the wall, this iron has been identified as a possible blade bank. Marked, "Made in Japan," 5-3/4" h. $25-35.

BB-408: Gentleman "Judge" has a slot in top of desk. 4-1/4" h. $20-30.

BB-409: *Wooden man with key was found with used blades inside, 3-1/2" h. $30-40.*

BB-410: *Bird in cage, with slot in top, has a flat back to hang on the wall, 6-1/4" h. $25-35.*

BB-411: *Hound dog, 5" h., with a "drain hole." The narrow slot is not wide enough for coins and barely takes a blade. $15-20.*

BB-412: *Frog, 3-1/2" h., with drain hole. $15-25.*

BB-413 reclassified as BB-382

BB-414: *Prisoner with ball and chain marked "Making $3.00 bills seemed like a good idea" on front. The bottom is marked "Jail Bird ca. 1961, F. Wilkinson No. 5101." Japan sticker, 4-1/4" h. $25-35.*

BB-415: *Pig in tuxedo marked "Made in Occupied Japan," 4-1/2" h. $25-35.*

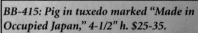

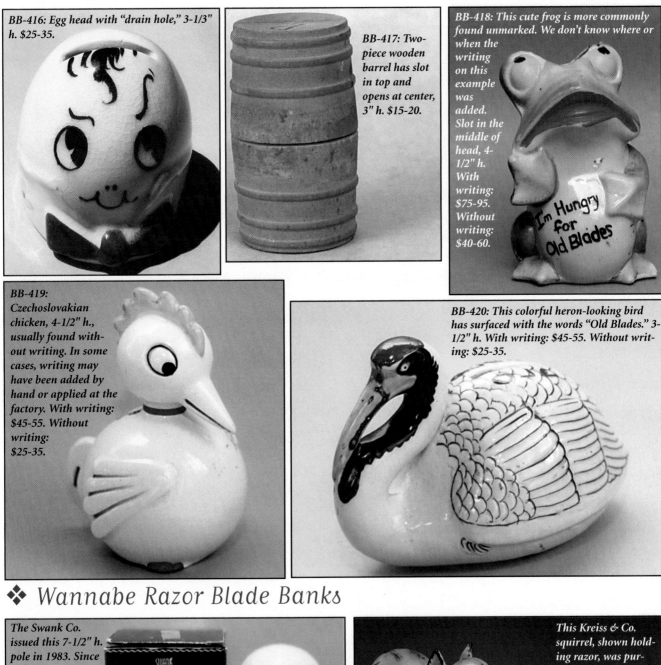

BB-416: Egg head with "drain hole," 3-1/3" h. $25-35.

BB-417: Two-piece wooden barrel has slot in top and opens at center, 3" h. $15-20.

BB-418: This cute frog is more commonly found unmarked. We don't know where or when the writing on this example was added. Slot in the middle of head, 4-1/2" h. With writing: $75-95. Without writing: $40-60.

BB-419: Czechoslovakian chicken, 4-1/2" h., usually found without writing. In some cases, writing may have been added by hand or applied at the factory. With writing: $45-55. Without writing: $25-35.

BB-420: This colorful heron-looking bird has surfaced with the words "Old Blades." 3-1/2" h. With writing: $45-55. Without writing: $25-35.

❖ Wannabe Razor Blade Banks

The Swank Co. issued this 7-1/2" h. pole in 1983. Since it shows a dollar bill and some change, it was probably marketed as a coin bank. The box is marked "98-6320 1992 Swank, Inc. Made in Taiwan."

This Kreiss & Co. squirrel, shown holding razor, was purchased as a blade bank. Other similar banks by Kreiss & Co. have been identified as gentlemen's dresser caddies. Tray for cufflinks, slot for coins, paws can hold a watch.

Gift & Art Buyer, June 1952.

And Beyond ....

Chapter 8

Who would have guessed that a number of the items featured in this chapter would be among the most popular in the entire book? However, some collectors felt "cheated"—for many it was their first glimpse at a figural tea ball, egg separator, or lipstick lady. The general consensus was— "We want to know more!"

When revisiting the format for the "Beyond" chapter we decided in this case that less would definitely be more. So we're featuring fewer items, with expanded coverage of each selection. We hope the additional photos will entice collectors to start searching for plant waterers, condiment jars and measuring spoon holders.

Take a look at these adorable additions to our own collections. You might be tempted to squeeze together that shelf of napkin dolls, or rearrange your countertop of pie birds, because "enough" is *never* enough when it comes to collectibles!

❖ Egg Separators

Anyone who's ever made a lemon meringue pie will tell you that the secret to a stiff meringue is in separating the eggs ... even the smallest hint of yolk can spell failure.

Today we seemed to have eliminated this challenge—visit your local grocery store and you'll find liquid egg whites in the dairy section and cans of powdered whites in the baking aisle. But the bakers of days gone by had to rely on skill when carefully juggling yolks and whites.

Egg separators, those handy devices that capture the yolk while letting the whites cleanly escape, have been around for years. The early examples were simple metal or tin devices, many of which were used as advertising premiums by merchants such as flour producers, bakeries and stove manufacturers. Some of us are still relying on the plastic Tupperware piece given away at home parties. But none of these utilitarian household helpers can compare to the cute egg separators featured in this chapter.

Once an unknown in collecting circles, egg separators have recently developed a following. We're delighted to feature some of the more interesting pieces from such popular companies as Enesco, Josef Originals and England's Sylvac Pottery.

We hope we've egged you on to start a new collection that you won't ever want to be separated from.

ES-100A: Egg-shaped separator with embossed flowers has the original "Made in Japan" sticker, 2-1/2". $12-15.
ES-100B: This Josef Originals egg-shaped separator with decaled flowers is marked "Lorrie Designs Japan," 2-1/4". $12-15.

ES-101: Egg-shaped separator with face is embossed "Spectrum" on the bottom, 2-1/4". $15-18.
ES-102: Floral egg separator, marked "Toni Raymond Pottery Hand Painted England," 1-1/2". $18-20.

ES-103: This chicken is embossed "Japan" on the bottom, 3-1/2"
from top of comb. $12-15.
ES-104: Chicken has an "Enesco" sticker on the bottom, 2-1/2" from
top of comb. $12-15.

ES-105: This chicken is smaller than the others and measures
3-1/4" from top of comb. $12-15.
ES-106: Josef Originals chicken marked "Lorrie Design,"
3-1/2" from top of comb. $12-15.

ES-107: Josef Originals owl, 3-1/4". $18-20.

ES-108: Josef Originals frog, 3". $15-18.
ES-109: Homemade frog with a misspelling of the word "seperator,"
2-3/4". $12-15.

ES-110: Josef Originals turtle, 2-1/2". $22-25.

ES-111: Chick in egg wearing
scarf, 3-1/4", Josef Originals.
$22-25.

ES-112: Flat yellow chicken marked "Made in
Japan," 3-3/4". $12-15.

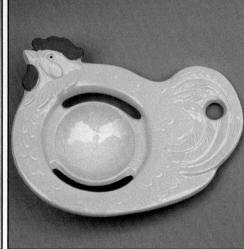

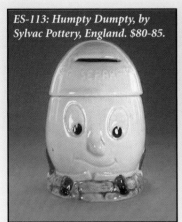

ES-113: Humpty Dumpty, by Sylvac Pottery, England. $80-85.

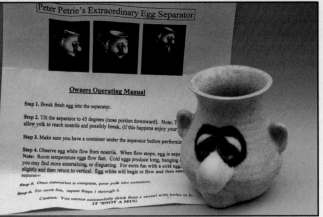

ES-114: This 3-1/2" pottery piece is new, but we couldn't resist including it in this section. "Peter Petrie's Extraordinary Egg Separator" is accompanied by an owner's operating manual. Egg whites pour out of the nostrils and the instructions end with "It 'snot a mug." $20-25.

❖ Garlic and Onion Condiment Jars

When we saw this cute collection it brought "tears" to our eyes. The rage in the 1950s, whimsical containers were designed for condiments like ketchup, mustard, jam, jelly, relish, onion, garlic and olives, as well as hard-to-find food stuff like cherries, nuts and saccharine. Since there are so many condiment sets out there, we thought a sampling of garlic and onion jars was the perfect fit for this chapter.

The pieces shown here run the gamut in value, with highly collectible items from companies like Holt Howard and DeForrest Pottery being the priciest. Jars from lesser-known manufacturers are still affordable, and a display can be amassed with a little patience. The biggest obstacle in putting together this collection is finding the pieces with both top and bottom intact. Those with attached spoons (referred to as "spoofy" spoons) present an even bigger challenge since they apparently broke easily; be sure to check the neck of these spoons for repairs.

If you're looking for something to spice up your collections, these onion anmd condiment jars will satisfy your appetite.

CJ-100: This unmarked, 5-1/2" garlic jar has 3-3/4" matching salt and pepper shakers (which are marked "52/714"). Set: $70-85; Jar only: $45-55; Shakers only: $25-30.

CJ-101: Red, white and blue-stripped garlic jar sits on an attached underplate and is marked "Hand Painted," 5". $65-75.

CJ-102/103: This DeForest onion pot comes in two sizes, 6" and 4-3/4". The small one is marked "DeForest-California Hand Painted" on bottom. $35-45.

CJ-104: This unique clown onion container doesn't seem too happy. 5-3/4". $65-75.

CJ-105: *The reverse side on the first of this teary trio is marked "Handle with Care;" the other side is marked "K2967" and has a "Japan NAPCO" foil sticker, 5-1/2". $35-45.*
CJ-106: *The flat-topped onion is 4". $25-35.*
CJ-107: *This "Onion Salt" shaker is a mere 3". $12-20.*

Above: 1957 Helen Gallagher-Foster House Spring & Summer Gifts For Casual Living.

CJ-108: *This DeForest onion jar is wearing a bowler-style hat, 4-3/4". The bottom is marked "DeForest Calif.-Hand Painted" and incised on one side "© 1956." $40-50.*
CJ-109: *The Fedora hat on this garlic condiment makes it unique. The bottom is marked "DeForest-California Hand Painted," 5-1/2". $40-50.*

Clothespin noses are the unique features on these two pots.

CJ-110: *"Mr. Garlic Pot," 4-3/4", is marked "Westwares, Pasadena, Calif., Handpainted ©." $65-75.*
CJ-111: *This unmarked red-topped garlic jar is 3". $12-20.*

CJ-112: *"Gertie" Garlic is 5". $25-35.*
CJ-113: *Here's a cute clove, 3-1/2". $8-12.*

CJ-114: *This 4-1/4" garlic container has 3-1/2" matching salt and pepper shakers. Set: $70-80; Jar only: $40-50; Shakers only: $20-30.*

The American Home, September 1953.

Holt Howard's "Pixieware" line is one of the hottest 1950-1960s condiments set categories, and these two pieces are no exception. Both have the trademark "spoofy spoon" (attached hidden spoon) with a drain hole for the onion juice. As with all the Pixieware jars, the face and nose design refelects their contents. The bottoms are marked "1958 Holt Howard."

CJ-115A: Cocktail Onions, 5-1/2". $95-125.
CJ-115B: Onions, 5-1/2". $65-85.

CJ-116: The bottom of this 5" jar is marked "516 Sylvac England." $40-60.
CJ-117: Twin Winton's onion pot is one of the few smiling faces in this group, 5-1/4". $85-125.

CJ-118: We're not sure if this fellow is turning the other cheek, or if he's just two-faced, 5-1/4". $75-85.
CJ-119: He's put on a happy face, 5". $35-45.

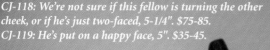

CJ-120: You could almost reach out and pull on his tongue, 7". $45-55.
CJ-121: Green onion, 5". $25-35.
CJ-122: This teary-eyed clove has a separate underplate, 5". $15-25.

❖ *Lipstick Ladies*

Do you remember when a woman's vanity—a skirted, kidney-shaped table with its trifold mirror—was the sacred centerpiece of her bedroom? Growing up, we spent hours sitting there, dreaming over the bright blue Evening in Paris perfume bottles, the round plastic containers of face powder and eye make-up, and the brightly colored tubes of lipstick neatly arranged in a pretty lady lipstick holder. If only we could be magically transported back to that time so we could safely tuck away that lipstick lady until we grew up to be collectors.

Lipstick ladies are hot, hot, hot. And like many of the other items in this book, the different styles seem to be endless. In addition to the multitude of Japanese imports, we've included some homemade examples and a few that were designed to accomplish a number of tasks. For example, LL-141 to LL-145 do double duty as head vases and lipstick holders. Since the openings on most of these heads never appear to have been used, we assume that women were more inclined to store their make-up brushes and other accessories, rather than plants. LL-144 is also a boudoir lamp and we believe LL-133 is a perfume lamp.

The details on some of these figures are exquisite, from the finely chiseled facial features to the manicured hands, jeweled accessories and dress decorations. Designs are equally elaborate; one finely coifed matron gazes at her image in the vanity mirror (LL-127) while LL-125 reflects crossing the threshold from tomboy to young lady.

Although most of these ladies probably date back to the 1950s and 1960s, a new issue based on the designs of Josef Originals is being marketed today under the Dakin label.

After viewing this small sampling of ladies, we have no doubt that you'll be licking your lips to start a collection of your own.

LL-100: *The skirt of this two-piece, 6" lipstick holder hides the lipstick tubes when not in use. It's marked "Shafford." $85.*

LL-101: *This lady carrying two baskets is fairly common, 6". $50.*
LL-102: *Decorated with gold trim and rhinestones, this beautiful lady has two baskets and holds a fan. She is quite unique, 6". $85.*
LL-103: *The lipstick tube holders are in the skirt of this 6" lady. $50.*

LL-104: *A large skirt holds lipstick on this lady, 5". She is found in various colors and with her hand in different positions; marked "Wales." $50.*
LL-105: *Lipsticks are easy to store in the baskets of this Enesco lady. She's marked "Milady's Valet," 5-1/2". $65.*

LL-106: *This cute 6" brunette seems to be ready to curtsy. There are three holders in the front and two in the back. The bottom is marked "Enesco." $65.*
LL-107: *Blonde holding skirt, 5". $65.*

LL-108: *Commodore produced this very common lipstick lady in various colors, 6-1/4". $55-60.*
LL-109: *Dressed in an unusual bronze colored dress, this 6" lady is quite striking. $65.*
LL-110: *"Miss Pretty Face" is 6". $55-60.*

Helen Gallagher-Foster House Classic Gifts Catalog, 1966-67.

LL-111: Cute lady in white holding a bouquet by "Essay," 4-1/4". $65.
LL-112: This homemade lady is marked "Hansen" on the bottom, 3".
$35. LL-113: Sweet lady in pink sports a gold purse, 5-1/4". $55.

LL-114: This 4" brunette is marked "Norcrest." $55.
LL-115: "Daisy Dorable" is marked "Holt Howard 1959,"
3-1/4". $75.
LL-116: Cute brunette in yellow, 4-1/". $55.

LL-117: This Josef Originals blonde is holding a fan, 5-1/4".
$75. LL-118: Here's another Josef Originals lady but this one is
holding a mirror, 4-1/4". $75. LL-119: This Josef Originals
blonde is holding glasses, 4". $75.

Each of these ladies are Josef Originals.
LL-120: This blonde has a big heart, 4" $75.
LL-121: Cute 4" brunette with blue dress. $55.
LL-122: Pretty in pink, this sweet blonde is 4". $55.

LL-123: These Duncan mold
ladies were made in a ceramic craft class, 3-1/2". $15-20.

LL-124: Fairy on a
bowl, Josef
Originals, 5-1/4".
$75.

LL-125:
This lip-
stick hold-
er depicts a
young lady
changing
from
tomboy
to young
miss, 6".
$85.

LL-126: Little girl
with powder puff sit-
ting at vanity marked
"Pandora Products,
Japan," 4-1/2". $75.

LL-127: Lady by mirror with bronze Dresden style skirt, 6". $50-65. LL-128: Lady by mirror (mirror missing) with green Dresden style skirt, 6". $50-65. LL-129: Lady by mirror with yellow Dresden style skirt, 5-1/2". $50-65.

LL-130: This 5" lady, gazing in a mirror is marked "I Rice Imports." $50-65. LL-131: Japanese Geisha standing by mirror, 5". $50-65. LL-132: Little girl is applying her lipstick, 5-1/2". $50-65.

LL-133: This large lady is a combination lipstick holder and perfume lamp. The lady sits on the base, which has a tulip to hold perfume, 9-1/2". $125.

LL-134: These ladies with flower heads hide the lipstick holders. The mirror is missing. 4". $40-45.

LL-138: This unmarked blonde is 6-1/2". $100-125.
LL-139: The foil sticker on this beauty reads "INARCO Japan," 6-1/2". $100-125.

LL-135: This blonde looks like she stepped right out of the 1960s, 5-1/4". $75. LL-136: Josef Originals blonde is wearing a flowered hat, 7". $75. LL-137: Mod looking 1960s lady is marked "Our Own Imports," 5-1/4". $55.

LL-140: The lipstick tubes were displayed in the hat of this demure miss, 4-3/4", the sticker on the bottom says "© Lefton - 3591." $75-85.

LL-141: This coifed brunette, 5-1/2", has an "Imported Enesco Japan" sticker on the bottom. $110-135. LL-142: The pearl necklace and earrings on this Japanese lady make her special, 6-1/4". $100-115.
LL-143: This example is marked "Imported Enesco," 5-1/2". $100-135.

LL-144A/B: Talk about multi-purpose ... these little ladies are also lamps, 7-1/4". The sticker on the bottom reads, "Alladin Giftware, Los Angeles, Calif., Portable Lamp, Underwriters Laboratories, Issue #65, 092." $125-150.

LL-145: Based on her appearance, we assume this lady is from the 1960s. She is ink-stamped on the bottom, "Coop. Crf. Art. QUADRIFUGLIO Florence, Hand Painted in Italy," 6-3/4". The original price tag is $3.50. $75-95.

❖ Measuring Spoon Holders

How do your collections measure up? For some, their cup runneth over if their hobby is collecting vintage measuring spoon holders.

Decorative measuring spoon holders seemed to have enjoyed a period of popularity from the late 1940s to the 1960s, at the same time that other colorful post-WW II accessories found their way into the American home. These cute, whimsical and definitely functional figures run the gamut in size and theme from animals, plants and people, to souvenir icons representing a region or local attraction. Regardless of form (some hang on the wall while others were designed to sit on the kitchen counter) and composition (ceramic, plastic or chalkware), the common feature is four slots to hold the colorful plastic measuring spoons. Don't be discouraged if you find a nifty piece without the spoons; the spoons are still turning up at flea markets and garage sales.

Occasionally there is some confusion between a measuring spoon holder and the highly collectible and pricier toothbrush holder (see these examples at the end of this chapter). If the object in question has four holes or slots (one for each spoon) and the piece is made of a lightweight material, chances are your item is not a toothbrush holder.

Check out some of these terrific pieces and you'll know why one ad in a 1947 magazine called the measuring spoon holder an "asset to any kitchen."

MS-100: Cardinal China's "Measure Boy" is part of an entire line of accessories, 5". $28-35.

MS-101: The Cardinal China potted plant measuring spoon holder, 6", is probably the most common example on today's market. $15-20.
MS-102: This window box/planter is quite unique, 4-1/2" w. $22-28.
MS-103: This planter (also pictured with the Measure Boy) is marked "Cardinal China Co.," 5-3/4". $12-18.

The Gift & Art Buyer, January 1950. This trade magazine reflects wholesale prices.

Kitchen Companions by CARDINAL

Cardinal packaged and marketed the potted plant spoon holder and the accompanying spoon rest as a set.

Miller Studios produced this wonderful chalkware flowerpot. Notice it only has three measuring spoons. The Gift & Art Buyer, October 1949. This trade magazine reflects wholesale prices.

MS-104A: This plastic red rooster seems to be strutting his stuff, 7". Some examples have been found embossed with an ad for chicken feed. $35-45.

MS-104B: This version of the rooster has potholder hooks, 7-1/2". $35-45.

MS-105: Chalkware measuring spoon holders in good condition are hard-to-find, and this colorful rooster is a wonderful example, 7-1/4". $55-75.

MS-106: There's no clowning around with this 6" guy! The colored measuring spoons make it appear as if he is holding balloons. $45-55. MS-107: The chicken motif was a popular form and this 4" California souvenir is no exception. $12-18. MS-108: The square spoons in this 6" ceramic duck make it an unusual piece. $15-25.

House and Garden, November 1949.

MS-109: Plastic banana with fruit spoons, 6-1/2" w. $24-30.

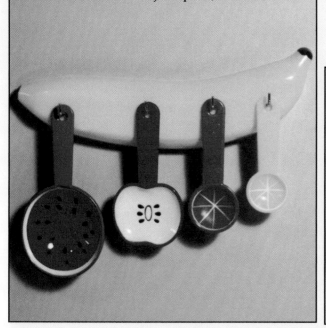

MS-110: A souvenir of Colorado, this smiling frog is 4-1/2". The bottom has a "Japan" paper label. $40-50. MS-111: This Hawaiian frog is only 4-1/4". The paper label on the bottom says "RB Made in Japan." $20-30.

MS-112: Ceramic Florida Pelican and lighthouse, 7". $35-45. MS-113: We don't think this ceramic 5" flamingo is very old, but it's still a nice addition for a collection. $26-32.

MS-114: Chalkware apple, 5", only has three spoons. $18-25.

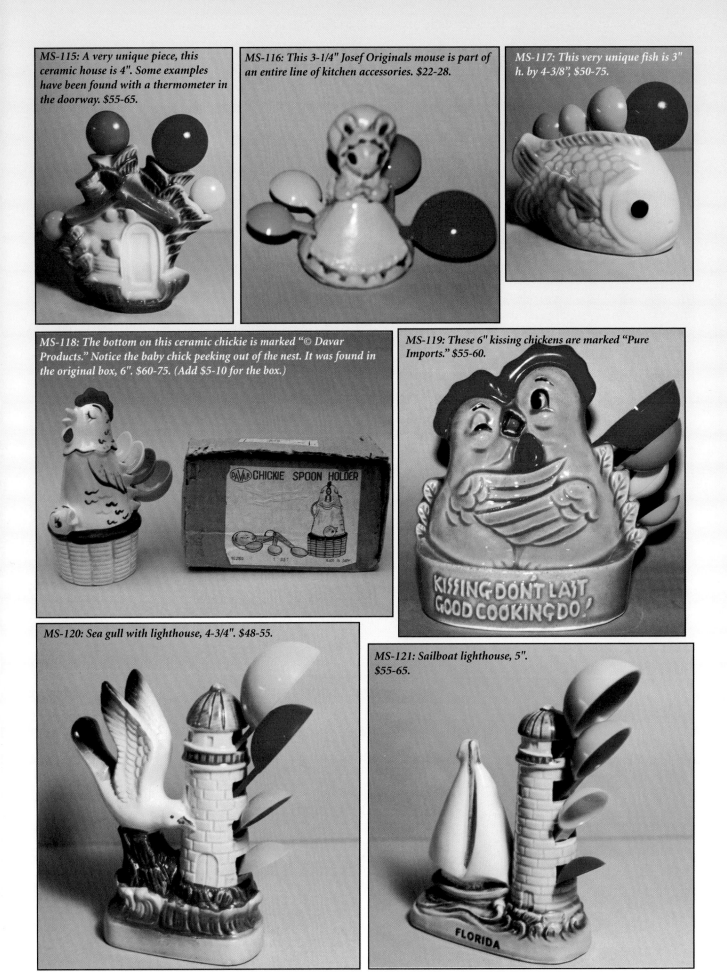

MS-115: A very unique piece, this ceramic house is 4". Some examples have been found with a thermometer in the doorway. $55-65.

MS-116: This 3-1/4" Josef Originals mouse is part of an entire line of kitchen accessories. $22-28.

MS-117: This very unique fish is 3" h. by 4-3/8", $50-75.

MS-118: The bottom on this ceramic chickie is marked "© Davar Products." Notice the baby chick peeking out of the nest. It was found in the original box, 6". $60-75. (Add $5-10 for the box.)

MS-119: These 6" kissing chickens are marked "Pure Imports." $55-60.

MS-120: Sea gull with lighthouse, 4-3/4". $48-55.

MS-121: Sailboat lighthouse, 5". $55-65.

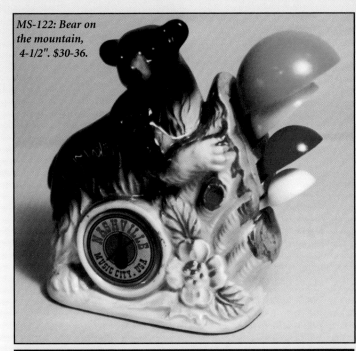

MS-122: Bear on the mountain, 4-1/2". $30-36.

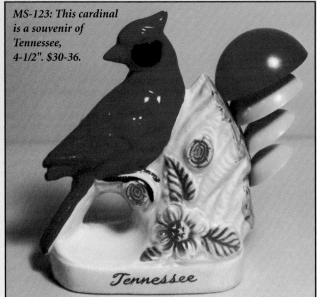

MS-123: This cardinal is a souvenir of Tennessee, 4-1/2". $30-36.

Tennessee

These ceramic souvenir owls are usually found with the names of different cities, states or regions. $40-20.

MS-124: Obviously Virginia Beach was touting its reputation for fresh seafood with the lobster souvenir, 3". $55-75.
MS-125: This Roadrunner and cactus, 3-1/2", is a souvenir from Tombstone, Arizona. $44-50.

MS-126: "The Ozarks" owl has a nice, pretty pink flower on the base, 4-5/8". MS-127: This 4-1/2" owl hails from Nashville.

The trays on the front of these ceramic chickens were used to hold rings.

MS-128: Earth tones give you a warm feeling about this little guy, 4". $12-18.
MS-129: "Spooning for You" is a recurrent theme on many measuring spoon holders. The word "Rings" is stamped in the tray of this 4-1/4" chicken. $12-18.
MS-130: The design on this piece is a bit more elaborate than the others, 4-1/4". $16-22.

Right: 1966-1967 Helen Gallagher-Foster House Classic Gifts Catalog, Peoria, IL.

SPOON REST SET
Rooster's tail is of 4 measuring spoons. Baskety base forms trays for drippy cooking spoons. 5½" hi, all-ceramic. Colorful! (1 lb.) X2480 5-pc. set $1

❖ Plant Waterers

Here's a collectible that's finally coming in to its own. Plant waterers were designed in a variety of shapes, usually ranging from 4-1/2" to 6". The top has a hole that is filled with water, which seeps through the pointy, porous stem into the planter or flowerpot. This ingenuous invention allowed the homeowner to leave town without fear that their plants would die of thirst.

Many of the older (1950s and 1960s) pieces found today may have some erosion and paint loss caused by the water, as well as the usual glaze crackling effect we see on the ceramics of this era. The plastic models of the period are also pretty nifty. Plant waterers are still being made today, although the different look and feel of these newer versions is pretty obvious. Unless you encounter a hard-to-find example, we suggest you pass on any waterer that is chipped, cracked or missing paint.

Talk about an identity crisis—these functional feeders are constantly mislabeled as pie birds; maybe that's how some people rationalize the ridiculously high prices we've seen lately. In order to clear up this confusion once and for all, we've pictured two pie birds next to a plant waterer. While plant waterers are still affordable, don't wait too long to start collecting: We predict that as their popularity rises, so will the prices!

PW-100: Holt Howard's "Weekend Willie" is a cross-collectible, coveted by both HH and plant waterer collectors, 6". $18-25. (Add $8-10 for the box.)

Right: Gift & Art Buyer, August 1952. This trade magazine reflects wholesale prices.

WEEK-END WILLIE. Gaily decorated ceramic bird with porous clay stem. Filled with water, he keeps plants moist for days. 6" long. **$7.20** dz.
$6.60 dz. in gross lots.

THIRSTY BIRD, named Willie, keeps plants healthy and moist—even if you forget them for week end. Willie's wide-open mouth holds water, his porous stem feeds it to plants as needed. Painted ceramic 6½" high, Willie is an early bird, bright, decorative, useful. $1 ppd. May Birn, 79 W. Grand St., FC, Mt. Vernon, N.Y.

Family Circle, September, 1952.

PW-101: These black and white cats, 4-3/4", appear to be homemade. $6-12. PW-102: This green deer has two spikes that form legs. The original box top reads, "THE WATER DEARS. Water your plants with the Water Dear. The bisque legs inserted in the plant will allow slow seepage so as to keep your plants properly watered while you are away from home. One filling of the Water Dear should keep the plants watered approximately one week." The box is marked, "Victoria Ceramics, Made In Japan." $12-18 (Add $5 for the box.)

PW-103: Watering cans are obviously a popular motif. This same design is found in different color combinations, 4-1/8". $8-15.
PW-104: The spike on this 3-5/8" watering can is incised "Japan." $8-15.

Right: Household, December 1952.

Miniature watering can plant tenders designed to hold a week's supply of water which seeps through porous bisque tip as plant needs it. In green, yellow, or red. 69 cents each, 2 for $1.25, 4 for $2.40, all ppd. Black & Co., 99-20 Metropolitan Ave., Forest Hills, N. Y.

PW-105: Wide-mouthed frog, 6-1/8". $8-12. PW-106: This worm with removable head is 6-1/8". $15-22. PW-107: The flowers decorating this 4-1/8" frog make it unusual. $8-12. PW-108: This brown snail has green and blue highlights, 4-1/2". $8-12. PW-109: Dark green turtle, 4". $6-10.

PW-110: Bird sitting on the birdbath, 4", still has the original "Josef's Original" foil sticker. $22-30.
PW-111: This 4-1/2" waterer depicts a frog sitting on the edge of a lily pad. The sticker says "Korea." $15-25.

PW-112: This 4-1/2" double mushroom is fairly common. $6-10.
PW-113: Avon Products mouse in a mushroom house is ca. 1985, 4-3/4". $8-14.

PW-114: Josef Originals adorable 6" girl is highly desirable to both plant waterer and Josef's collectors. $55-75.

PW-117: The windmill design on this tulip gives it a delft-look, 6". This piece appears to be of newer vintage. $20-25.

PW-115: Maroon tulip, 4-1/2". $15-18. PW-116: Notice the leaves on the bottom of this 5" pottery tulip. $15-20.

The variety of owl plant waterers seems endless.
PW-118: White rimmed eyes on this owl make him a standout, 4". $8-12. PW-119: This 4" owl has a more abstract look. $8-12.
PW-120: Traditional looking owl, 3-3/8". $8-12.

PW-121: Homemade scarecrow, 6", holds a crow on his extended arm. $10-15. PW-122: Figure in flowing robes is marked, "© INARCO Cleve-Ohio, E-192," 2". $18-24. PW-123: Most likely a craft class project, this young girl, 5-1/4", was signed by her maker. $20-25. PW-124: This Dutch maid is 6". $8-12.

A collector in Canada sent these three plant waterers. Not much is known about their origin or age.

PW-125: Adorable chick peeks out of its shell. $15-25.

PW-126: This little guy seems to have big feet. $15-25.

PW-127: Pink pelican, $20-30.

PW-128: This 6" pelican actually has body rests. $15-20.

PW-129: Chubby chick, 5-3/4", still has the "Enesco" sticker. $18-25. PW-130: This bird seems to be waiting to be fed, 4-1/2". $8-10. PW-131: Graceful swan is 4". $8-12.

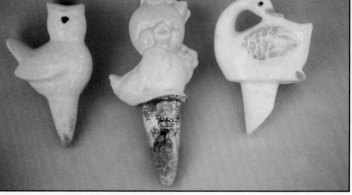

❖ Plant Waterer Wannabes

This birthday candle circus train has shown up on online auctions at least twice in the last year, selling as an "unusual" plant waterer. One auction ended with the high bidder paying over $100! This example cost $7 in the original box.

Plant waterers are often mismarked as pie birds. Notice the difference in the base. The pie bird arches are designed to allow steam to escape from the pie up through the opening in the top. To further confuse the issue, the baby feeders that sit on the edge of the bowl are also often confused with pie birds and plant waterers.

This 4-1/2" teapot whistler has been wrongly identified as both a pie bird and a plant waterer. It is marked "Made in Czech."

❖ *Figural Tea Balls*

These fabulous ceramic tea balls give new meaning to the phrase "getting into hot water." Imagine submerging one of them into a cup of boiling liquid!

Today we think nothing of putting a mug of water and a pre-packaged bag of tea into the microwave for a quick cup. But there was a time in the not-too-distant past when loose tea was the common method for brewing one of the world's most popular beverages. Any true tea connoisseur will tell you there is a method to their madness, from boiling the water, to the precise amount of tea and the proper steeping time per cup.

Sterling silver (later stainless steel) tea balls have always been a popular collectible. But until the last few years, little was known about these ceramic whimsies. While the seated, kneeling or standing Asian man seems to be the most common, other popular forms have now emerged, attracting collector interest. There is a lot of confusion between the Asian men and the similar eggcup with its matching salt shaker, so we've shown you a close-up for comparison. If the "egg" has only holes on the crown, it's a salt shaker. Conversely, the tea ball has a small hook for the chain on the top, and tiny holes on both the top and back of the "egg" to allow the tea to steep.

Here are a variety of the wonderful examples we've found.

TB-100: Colors vary on these two-piece kneeling "egg-head" style tea balls. The example on the right is unmarked; the piece on the left is stamped "Germany" on the bottom and incised "Germany, D.R.C.M." on the screw-off top of the head. $85-125.

We found listings for TB-100, 108 and 112 in the 1934 catalog from Adolf Röhring Porzellan-Atelier, Bavaria. Notice the fabulous German sprinkler bottle on the left.

TB-101: The top cover of this 4" cross-legged Asian man is marked "Germany." Notice how the eyes differ from TB-100. $85-125. TB-102: Full-figured Asian man is 3-3/4". The top cover is marked "Germany, D.R.C.M." $85-125.

BELOW: *Illustrated here are China dolls whose heads, filled with loose tea, are used as tea-balls, and whose bodies are made to catch the drips after the tea-ball has been used. They are priced at $3.60 a dozen. The jugs of green glazed pottery, 8 inches tall, are filled with Ming syrup of maple, which is blended with Ming sugar crystals. This item is also priced at $3.60 a dozen by the Stephen Leeman Products Corp., 215 Fourth Ave., New York.*

The Gift & Art Shop, August 1933. This trade magazine reflects wholesale prices.

TB-103: *The screw cap on this large kneeling Asian man has a luster head. The top is stamped "Goldcastle, Handpainted Chikusa, Made in Japan," with a Pagoda logo. It's more unusual than TB-100-102. $85-125.* **TB-104:** *This 3" hard-to-find tea ball bears a close resemblance to TB-103. He's marked "Made in Japan." $100-125.*

This combination egg cup and salt shaker (right) is often mistaken for a tea ball. It's easy to distinguish between the two if you look closely. Notice that the holes on the shaker are only located on the egg's crown. The tea ball, however, has holes on the top and back of the head to allow the tea to steep. Although it's not uncommon for the chain to be missing, the hook is usually still attached at the top.

TB-105: *This 3-1/2" mouse has a "Sigma" label and is marked "Made in Japan." Rather than a hook, it hangs over the cup from a plastic anchor. This tea ball actually unscrews to be filled. $75-95.*

The same manufacturer apparently made both of these examples. They bear a gold "Quality Product Japan" sticker.

TB-106: Pig, 3", $55-65.
TB-107: Cat, 3", $55-65.

TB-108: *This 3" German fish is marked, "DRGM" on the bottom and "8899" on the side. $95-125.* **TB-109:** *"Tillie the Tea Strainer" is a mere 2". $25-35. (Add $10-15 if complete with tray.)*

Feeling that nothing could be done to improve the well known Ming teas the Stephen Leeman Products Corp. 215 Fourth Ave. New York decided to improve the manner of serving. The Priscilla teapot rests on the Epi Curio tea warmer which keeps the tea hot right at the table. The tea warmers are obtainable in various models at $7.20, $9 and $12 a dozen complete. At the upper left are drip catchers that fasten on the teapot spout and which come in assorted styles at $1.80 a dozen. At the lower left is a tea brewer in which you place the tea leaves to brew. Assorted styles at $3.00 a dozen, with an individual tray.

The Gift & Art Shop, July, 1932. This trade magazine reflects wholesale prices.

Coy little ceramic fish has a cork bottom, so you can stuff her with tea leaves and immerse her in the pot by a chain. When you pull her up, there's a shell saucer for her to drain and dry off on. White with painted decorations. *Tillie the Tea Strainer*, $1.50, ppd. Edith Chapman, 50 Piermont Ave., Nyack, N.Y.

Better Homes & Gardens, May, 1952.

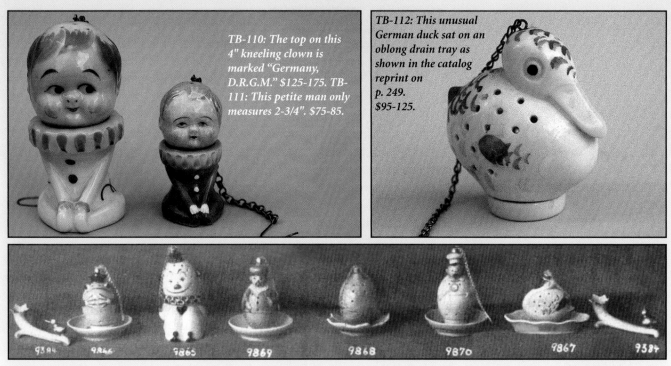

TB-110: The top on this 4" kneeling clown is marked "Germany, D.R.G.M." $125-175. TB-111: This petite man only measures 2-3/4". $75-85.

TB-112: This unusual German duck sat on an oblong drain tray as shown in the catalog reprint on p. 249. $95-125.

9394   9846   9865   9869   9868   9870   9867   9384

We were very excited to see these fabulous tea balls in the 1934 catalog from Adolf Röhring Porzellan-Atelier, Bavaria. The hunt is now on!

❖ Toothbrush Holders

"Brusha, brusha, brusha … with the new Ipana," sang Bucky Beaver. If you grew up in the 1950s like we did, this Ipana Toothpaste commercial will stand out as one of the era's most memorable television advertisements. Many a parent mimicked this catchy jingle to kids all over the country to get them to brush their teeth before going to bed.

And from the 1930s to the 1950s, another motivation for children to practice good dental hygiene was the decorative toothbrush holder. Available in a wide variety of sizes, shapes and forms, these holders were cute yet functional. Whether they were hanging on the bathroom wall or perched on the edge of the sink, they were a neat way to keep junior's toothbrush (and in some cases toothpaste) close at hand for this nightly ritual.

While the majority of toothbrush holders seem to be made in some form of ceramic material (china, pottery or bisque), older versions were also made from celluloid, chalkware, wood, and metal. Subject matter is just as diverse, ranging from nursery rhymes, comic strip characters, animals, small children in colorful costumes, and a wide variety of occupations.

There are various opinions on how to differentiate a toothbrush holder from a figural bud vase. Some collectors claim it's the square versus round holes, others feel that the toothpaste tray is a giveaway. Unfortunately only a fraction of these items feature a tray and there are some confirmed "TBHs" (as we refer to them in this book) that are sporting the round holes. Hint: look for the drain hole in the bottom (a vase would obviously be completely sealed). Unfortunately, not all TBHs include this drain hole. Therefore, from time to time, each collector has to make the call.

The variety is so vast we could do an entire book on this subject alone. Here are just a few of these wonderful items from days gone by.

Soldiers were always popular with little boys.

TBH-100: Soldier, marked "Made in Japan," has holders in boots, 4-3/4". $45. TBH-101: Tall soldier, marked "Made in Japan," with one holder in front and toothpaste tray. Stands or hangs. 6-1/2". $45. TBH-102: This marked soldier with a sash has holders in his boots and a tray for toothpaste; stands or hangs, 6". $55.

MAJOR BRUSH-UP dental sentinel protects your child's teeth. Major comes with child's nylon toothbrush in his hat as a plume. Child's name decorated on Drum-Drinking cup. Makes tooth care child's play. Colorful. Hang or stand. Each $1.25. Crown Craft, 246-C Fifth Ave., New York 1, N.Y.

Family Circle, November, 1958.

Nursery rhymes were a popular toothbrush holder motif. Each of these examples either stand or hang, and have drain holes in the bottom.

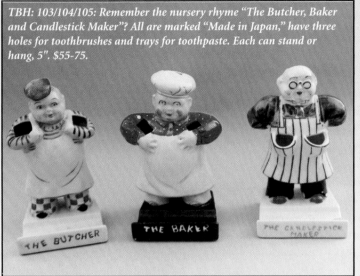

TBH: 103/104/105: Remember the nursery rhyme "The Butcher, Baker and Candlestick Maker"? All are marked "Made in Japan," have three holes for toothbrushes and trays for toothpaste. Each can stand or hang, 5". $55-75.

TBH-106: This Three Bears TBH has two holders and tray for toothpaste. Marked "Made In Japan," 5". $55-75. TBH-107: Little Red Riding Hood, marked "Made in Japan," has one holder for the toothbrush and the feet form the toothpaste tray, 5". $55-75. TBH-108: Old King Cole, marked "Made in Japan," 5-1/4". He, too, has one holder and feet that hold the toothpaste. $55-75.

These cute pieces represent only a sampling of animal toothbrush holders.

TBH-109: Plaid horse, marked "Made in Japan," has three holders with tray. It can stand or hang, 5". $85-95. TBH-110: Spotted cow with bell, marked "Made in Japan," sports two holes and a tray, 3-1/4". $95-125. TBH-111: Pink sitting elephant, marked "Made in Japan," with three holes and a tray, 5". $85-95.

Cartoon characters were also popular with the children in the 1930s and 1940s. The three examples below are all made of bisque.

There were several Disney-themed TBHs made in the late 1930s and early 1940s.

TBH-112: This is one of three bisque, Three Little Pigs designs. It's marked, "Made in Japan, Walt Disney," and there are two holes in the back and a drain hole in the bottom, 3-3/4". $100-125. TBH-113: Bisque Mickey and Minnie Mouse on a couch with Pluto at their feet. This highly collectible pair is marked, "Made in Japan, Walt Disney." There are two holders in the back, 3-1/2". $200-300. TBH-114: This ceramic pig playing the flute is a bit older than the other two, probably from the late 1940s to the early 1950s. It is marked, "Genuine Walt Disney, copyright Reg. No. 801-48, Foreign." Maws of England has made similar pieces, although this example is unmarked. It has one holder in back, 4-1/4". $125-150.

TBH-115: Moon Mullins and Kayo, marked "FAS S1553," 3-1/2", with one holder. $110-125. TBH-116: Very rare Popeye is marked, "Made in Japan." Toothbrush goes through the arm and rests on his foot. There is a drain hole in the bottom, 4-1/2". $500+. TBH-117: Little Orphan Annie and Sandy are marked, "© Famous Artists Syndicate S631", made in Japan. There are two holders in the back and a drain hole in the bottom, 3-1/2". $95-125.

These models are highly prized by both Black memorabilia and TBH collectors.

TBH-118: Standing Moor or Swami has "#2930" stamped into the bottom. This piece, with two holders in the top of his head, is most likely German, 5-1/2". $150-175. TBH-119: Black chef carrying fruit is marked, "Made in Japan, hand painted." It has two holders, a tray and a drain hole, 4-1/2". $250-350. TBH-120: Sitting Moor or Swami is marked, "Made in Japan," and has two holders in the top of his head, 3-3/4". This is a Japanese copy of a German Swami. Japanese model: $95-125; German model: $150-175.

Each of these adorable children have one holder and a tray for toothpaste.

TBH-121: Little girl, marked "6075 Foreign," 4-1/4". TBH-122: Cute Scottish lassie, marked "Foreign," 4-1/4". TBH-123: Little boy, marked "Made in Germany, 6078," 4-1/4". Although the first two are marked Foreign they are believed to be German. Since both bear what are likely registration or catalog numbers, they're probably from the same manufacturer. Each: $125-150.

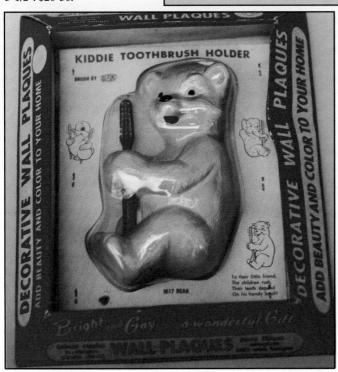

Below: TBH-124: Chalkware bear in original box from 1955, 5-1/2". $20-30.

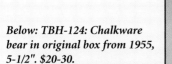

M17 Bear
6 in. high.

Courtesy of the Miller Studio Catalog archives.

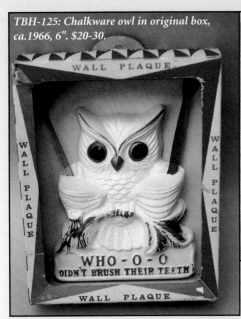

TBH-125: Chalkware owl in original box, ca.1966, 6". $20-30.

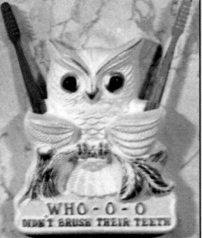

Courtesy of the Miller Studio Catalog archives.

TBH-126: Colorful fish, ca. 1965, 7-1/2". $20-30.

TBH-127: This chalkware sailor duck dates to 1968. One wing holds the toothbrush, 7". $20-30.

M24 FISH TOOTHBRUSH HOLDER

Finished in decorative bathroom colors. Measures 7½ inches high. Packaged with two nylon bristle toothbrushes. Weight per dozen: 11 lbs.

Courtesy of the Miller Studio Catalog archives.

Courtesy of the Miller Studio Catalog archives.

M26 DUCK
TOOTHBRUSH HOLDER

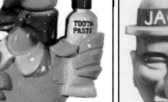
House Beautiful, November 1953. Although we don't have this funny fellow to show you, we thought this ad was worth including.

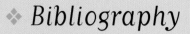
Books

Dworkin, Walter, *Price Guide to Holt Howard Collectibles and Related Ceramicwares of the 50s & 60s,* Krause Publications, Iola, WI, 1998.

Hall, Doris & Burdell, *Morton Potteries: 99 Years, Vol. II,* L-W Book Sales, Gas City, IN, 1995.

Harris, Dee and Whittaker, Jim and Kaye, *Josef Originals Charming Figurines with Price Guide,* Schiffer Publishing Ltd., Atglen, PA, 1994.

Giacomini, Mary Jane, *American Bisque Collectors Guide With Prices,* Schiffer Publishing Ltd., Atglen, PA, 1994.

Lehner, Lois, *Lehner's Encyclopedia of U.S. Marks on Pottery, Porcelain,* Collector Books, Paducah, KY, 1988.

Schneider, Mike, *Ceramic Arts Studio Identification and Price Guide,* Schiffer Publishing, Ltd., Atglen, PA, 1994.

White, Carole Bess, *Collectors Guide to Made in Japan Ceramics,* Collector Books, Paducah, KY, 1994.

Catalogs

Adolf Röhring Prozellan-Atelier, Newstadt bei Coburg, Bavaria, 1934.

Bancroft's Gifts, Chicago, IL, 1951.

Bostwick & Braun Company Wholesale Catalog No. 55, Toledo, OH, 1955.

Breck's Gifts, Boston, MA, 1958-59.

Butler Brothers, New York, NY, Spring, 1940.

Cardinal China Company, Carteret, NJ, 1954, 1956 and 1959.

Fireside Gifts, Fireside Industries, Inc., Adrian, MI, 1927-1928.

Frederick Herrschner Needlework and Specialties Co., Chicago, IL, 1937-1938.

Gebrüder Plein o.H.G.

Glasierte Luxus-Porzellan.

Helen Gallagher-Foster House, Peoria, IL, 1957, 1963, 1966-67.

Hertnig, 1932.

Holland Mold, Trenton, NJ.

Holt-Howard, Stamford, CT, 1958.

House of Ceramics, Supply Catalog No. 2, Memphis, TN.

Lugene's Inc. Wholesale Souvenir and Gifts, Branson, MO, 1966.

Mahoning Gifts, Youngstown, OH.

Mallory Ceramic Studio, Los Angeles, CA.

Marcia of California, Los Angeles, CA, 1956-1958.

Miller Studio, New Philadelphia, OH, 1955-1968.

Montgomery Ward, Chicago, IL, 1944 Christmas, and 1960 Spring/Summer.

NYMCO Wholesale Catalog, New York, NY, 1957.

Weiss, Kuhnert & Co.

Magazines

The American Home
The American Home Corporation, New York, NY
September 1953, p. 17
June 1959, p. 90

Better Homes & Gardens
Meredith Publishing, Des Moines, IA
November 1949, p. 252
May 1952, p. 326

Crockery & Glass Journal
Haire Publications, New York, NY
November 1950, p. 38
August 1952, p. 48

The Family Circle
The Family Circle, Inc., Mount Morris, IL
September 1952, p. 115
November 1953, p. 195
November 1954, p. 193
November 1957, p. 103
November 1958, p. 96

The Gift & Art Buyer
Geyer-McAllister Publishing, New York, NY
February 1937, p. 105
September 1937, p. 82, 96
February 1939, p. 108
September 1939, p. 82, 123
April 1941, p. 64
November 1943, p. 70
July 1944, p. 52
May 1945, p. 93
March 1946, p. 165
February 1947, p. 130
January 1949, p. 75
October 1949, p. 159
January 1950, pp. 37, 163
March 1950, p. 83
June 1950, p. 101
February 1952, p. 211
April 1952, p. 131
July 1952, p.67
August 1952, p. 109
July 1953, p. 111
June 1957, p. 42
February 1961, p. 106

Gift & Art Shop
Andrew Geyer, Inc., East Stroudsburg, PA
July 1932, p. 22

August 1933, p. 33
Household
Cappers Publication, Inc., Topeka, KS
December 1952, p. 62

House Beautiful
Hearst Magazines Inc., New York, NY
June 1931, p. 577
November 1935, p. 13
July 1945, p. 106
October 1947, p. 169
November 1948, p. 140
May 1949, p. 76
June 1949, p. 18
October 1949, p. 159
November 1949, pp. 30, 75
March 1950, p. 83
May 1950, p. 40
April 1951, p. 74, 131
September 1951, p. 33
November 1953, pp. 52, 118
May 1954, p. 122
December 1955, p. 74

House and Garden
Conde Nast Publications, New York, NY
June 1944, p. 21
December 1947, p. 62
November 1949, p. 55
October 1950, p. 50
March 1953, pp. 60 & 74
October 1956, p. 139
November 1957, p. 154

Liberty Magazine
McFadden Publications, Inc., New York, NY
January 15, 1927, p. 37
March 3, 1928, p. 71

Pottery, Glass & Brass Salesman
The O'Gorman Publishing Company, New York, NY
November 1939, p. 29

Redbook
The McCall Company New York, NY
August 1953, p. 15
January 1955, p. 16

Saturday Evening Post
Atkinson & Alexandra, Philadelphia, PA
June 1936, p. 2

❖ Index